HOW TO PREVENT COUPS D'ÉTAT

HOW TO PREVENT COUPS D'ÉTAT

Counterbalancing and Regime Survival

Erica De Bruin

CORNELL UNIVERSITY PRESS   ITHACA AND LONDON

Cornell University Press gratefully acknowledges receipt of a grant from The Foreman Fund at Hamilton College, which aided in the publication of this book.

Copyright © 2020 by Cornell University

All rights reserved. Except for brief quotations in a review, this book, or parts thereof, must not be reproduced in any form without permission in writing from the publisher. For information, address Cornell University Press, Sage House, 512 East State Street, Ithaca, New York 14850. Visit our website at cornellpress.cornell.edu.

First published 2020 by Cornell University Press

Library of Congress Cataloging-in-Publication Data

Names: De Bruin, Erica, 1982– author.
Title: How to prevent coups d'état : counterbalancing and regime survival / Erica De Bruin.
Description: Ithaca [New York] : Cornell University Press, 2020. | Includes bibliographical references and index.
Identifiers: LCCN 2020005767 (print) | LCCN 2020005768 (ebook) | ISBN 9781501751912 (hardcover) | ISBN 9781501751929 (epub) | ISBN 9781501751936 (pdf)
Subjects: LCSH: Coups d'état—Prevention. | Civil war—Prevention. | Balance of power. | Political leadership. | Political stability. | Military policy. | Civil-military relations. | National security.
Classification: LCC JC494 .D43 2020 (print) | LCC JC494 (ebook) | DDC 321.09—dc23
LC record available at https://lccn.loc.gov/2020005767
LC ebook record available at https://lccn.loc.gov/2020005768

For Sam

Contents

List of Tables and Figures	ix
Acknowledgments	xi
Introduction: Preventing Coups d'État	1
1. The Logic of Counterbalancing	13
2. Counterbalancing and Coup Failure	38
3. How Counterbalancing Works: Testing the Causal Mechanisms	57
4. An Effective Deterrent? Counterbalancing and Coup Attempts	79
5. Challenges to Building Coercive Institutions	93
6. How Coups d'État Escalate to Civil War	115
Conclusion: Coercive Institutions and Regime Survival	131
Appendix	141
Notes	155
Index	193

Tables and Figures

Tables

1.1. Causal mechanisms linking counterbalancing to coup failure   20

1.2. Causal mechanisms linking counterbalancing to the incidence of coup attempts   27

2.1. States included in the statistical analysis   41

2.2. Cross tabulation of coup outcomes and counterbalancing   48

2.3. Descriptive statistics for dependent and independent variables (coup outcomes)   50

2.4. Coup success: Logit results   52

2.5. Correlations: Coup success, counterbalancing, and military strength   54

3.1. Evidence on causal mechanisms during sixteen coup attempts   70

4.1. Cross tabulation of coup attempts and counterbalancing   81

4.2. Descriptive statistics for dependent and independent variables (coup attempts)   83

4.3. Coup attempts: Logit results   84

4.4. Coup attempts: Survival analysis   88

4.5. Correlations: Coup attempts, new counterweights, and military strength   91

5.1. Summary of case outcomes: New counterweights and coup attempts   94

5.2. The context of counterweight creation in Ghana, Sierra Leone, Mali, and Cuba   95

5.3. Comparing coup-proofing strategies and forms of counterbalancing   112

5.4. Coup attempts: Logit results with forms of counterbalancing disaggregated   113

6.1. Summary of case outcomes: Counterbalancing and the escalation of coups to civil war   116

A.1. Coup attempts included in the statistical analysis   141

Figures

2.1. Map of the highest number of counterweights employed, 1960–2010   45

2.2. Counterbalancing by region   46

2.3. Coups and counterbalancing over time   47

2.4. Marginal effect of selected variables on coup outcomes (from table 2.4, model 3)   53

4.1. Marginal effect of selected variables on coup attempts (from table 4.3, model 4)   86

4.2. Change in coup risk with the creation of a new counterweight   89

4.3. Counterbalancing by regime type   90

Acknowledgments

This book has benefited from the feedback and support of many people. It has its origins in my time in the Department of Political Science at Yale University. Steven Wilkinson's enthusiasm for this project got it off the ground, and I have benefited from his sound advice at every step in the process. I could not have asked for a better mentor. I was also particularly fortunate to have the opportunity to learn from Thad Dunning, Bruce Russett, and Nicholas Sambanis, who provided generous and thoughtful comments on the earliest iterations of ideas that made their way into this book. Other professors at Yale, including Alexandre Debs, Susan Hyde, Stathis Kalyvas, Adria Lawrence, Nuno Monteiro, Frances Rosenbluth, Susan Stokes, and Elisabeth Wood, were wonderful teachers and mentors. I owe tremendous thanks to my graduate school peers as well. I entered with an impressive cohort of women, including Allison Carnegie, Adi Greif, Corinna Jentzsch, Calvert Jones, Bonny Lin, Cory McCruden, and Angelika Schlanger, all of whom I learned a great deal from. Special thanks are due to Callie in particular for her willingness to talk about coups any hour of the night. Early feedback from Matthew Cebul, Julia Choucair-Vizoso, Will Nomikos, and Pia Raffler was also helpful in developing the central arguments in the book.

Peter Bergen, Anatol Lieven, Rajan Menon, and Nicholas Thompson at the New America Foundation fostered my interest in research, and taught me a great deal about their own research and writing processes. I benefited enormously from serving as a research associate to Jim Goldgeier and Lee Feinstein at the Council on Foreign Relations. Thanks are also due to Stephen Biddle, Steven Cook, and Daniel Markey at the Council for their advice and support. Robert Legvold and Scott Martin at Columbia University first encouraged me to pursue a Ph.D., and I will always be grateful.

Along the way, I benefited from feedback at a number of workshops and conferences. The ideas in this book began to take shape at the Empirical Implications of Theoretical Models Summer Institute at the Harris School at the University of Chicago, led by Scott Ashworth and Ethan Bueno de Mesquita. Both were generous with their time, and I thank them for that. Mentoring faculty in residence, including Bethany Lacina, Maggie Peters, and Daniel Berger, provided invaluable feedback and advice on navigating academia more generally. I also benefited from attending the Institute for Qualitative and Multi-Method Research at Syracuse University, as well as from feedback from participants in the Journeys in World

Politics Workshop at the University of Iowa, Conflict Consortium Virtual Workshop, Virtual Workshop on Intrastate Conflict and Violence at George Washington University, and Workshop on Intra-State Peace and Security at the University of Mannheim.

Many scholars provided feedback that improved the manuscript in concrete ways. I thank Risa Brooks for reading numerous drafts of my work and always giving thoughtful comments. I have also been fortunate to receive feedback from Holger Albrecht, Ariel Ahram, Yelena Biberman-Ocakli, Jessica Maves Braithwaite, Adam Casey, Damon Coletta, Christian Davenport, Kerstin Fisk, Hanne Fjelde, John Ishiyama, Jaclyn Johnson, Drew Kinney, Peter Krause, Patrick M. Kuhn, Yonatan Lupu, Jacqueline McAllister, Will Moore, Deborah Norden, Lindsay Reid, Lee J. M. Seymour, Paul Staniland, Harold Trinkunas, Jessica Weeks, and David Andrew Weinberg. I thank Kristen Harkness, Paul Lorenzo Johnson, Max Margulies, Theo McLauchlin, Jun Koga Sudduth, Ches Thurber, Peter B. White, and other members of the Security Force Loyalty Contact Group for their feedback on many different aspects of the arguments and data presented in this book. I have learned so much from their work and from our conversations. In building the dataset in this book, I also benefited from helpful conversations with Sabine Carey, Aila Matanock, Michaela Mattes, and Jonathan M. Powell. This book owes an intellectual debt to Caitlin Talmadge and Sheena Greitens, whose own work has indelibly influenced my own. For book advice over the years, I am grateful to Jonathan Caverley, Jeff Colgan, Danielle Lupton, and Gwyneth McClendon, among others.

I am grateful to Kelly Kadera, Ashley Leeds, and Sara Mitchell for their efforts to foster a supportive climate for women in academia. I have benefited so much from their advice and guidance. I thank Eva Bellin, Mary Gallagher, Kelly Greenhill, Courtney Hillebrecht, Vesla Weaver, and Krista Wiegand for sharing the ups and downs of their own career trajectories and their advice on publishing; hearing about their varied paths to success has motivated me more than they can know. Rebecca Barrett-Fox cultivated an online writing community that sustained me from the initial book proposal through final manuscript revisions.

At Hamilton College, I have been fortunate to work in a department full of wonderful colleagues. I thank Phil Klinkner for his friendship, and for advocating for me in ways both big and small. I am grateful to Alexsia Chan, Gbemende Johnson, Kira Jumet, Heather Sullivan, and Joel Winkelman for their camaraderie, and as well as for their feedback on different parts of the manuscript. I thank Frank Anechiarico, Alan Cafruny, Peter Cannavò, Robert W. T. Martin, Omobolaji Olarinmoye, Stephen Orvis, David Rivera, Sharon Rivera, and Gary Wyckoff for making the Government Department a supportive environment for junior faculty. Joan Kane provided crucial moral and logistical support and encouragement throughout the process. At Hamilton, I have benefited from generous support from the Dean of Faculty's office in the form of sabbatical and research funding; I thank Margaret Gentry, Suzanne Keen, Gill King, Linda Michels, Onno Oerlemans, Sam Pellman, and Patrick Reynolds for their support. Amy Lindner and Jeff Ritchie in the grant office also provided a great deal of assistance.

For financial support, I am also grateful to the International Peace Research Association Foundation, which provided a Peace Research Grant that was instrumental in helping me expand the dataset of state security forces used in this manuscript. In doing so, I received excellent research assistance from Keshav Arvind, Annika Jonas-Day, Maggie Joyce, Isaac Kirschner, Casey Kopp, Chloe Ma, Conor O'Shea, Connor Sharkey, Monique St. Jarre, and Florence Turiaf. Lora DiBlasi helped me work through thorny coding issues, and I am particularly grateful for her assistance. I am grateful to the archival staff at the U.S. National Archives (College Park, MD), The National Archives (Kew, United Kingdom), John F. Kennedy Presidential Library, and Moorland-Spingarn Research Center at Howard University for helping me navigate their archival collections. Special thanks are due to Adam Zinkin, who conducted research for me at Kew when I could not travel. I am also grateful to Jeffrey Biggs and Veronica Jones at the American Political Science Association Centennial Center for hosting me in Washington, D.C., while I conducted archival research.

Earlier versions of some of the material in this book were previously published in "Preventing Coups d'État: How Counterbalancing Works," *Journal of Conflict Resolution* 62, no. 7 (2018): 1433–1458, and "Will There Be Blood? Explaining Violence during Coups d'État," *Journal of Peace Research* 56, no. 6 (2019): 797-811. I thank the publishers of these journals for their permission to integrate this material into the book.

At Cornell University Press, I am incredibly grateful to have had Roger Haydon as an editor; his incisive questions and comments improved the manuscript at multiple stages. For their thoughtful feedback on the book, I am also very grateful to Nicolas van de Walle and two anonymous reviewers.

I would not have been able to finish this manuscript without the support of my family and friends. I thank Consuelo Amat, Suparna Chaudhry, Madhavi Devasher, Shawn Fraistat, and Celia Paris for their support, advice, and encouragement. I thank Livia Schubiger and Michael Weintraub both for their friendship and for their patience with me on the occasions that I had to set aside our joint project to finish book revisions. I am also grateful to Sarah Katz, Sarah Travis, Maria Larsen, Sameer Lalwani, Rob Blair, Tatiana Neumann, Josh Finnell, Anne Valente, Jaime Kucinskas, Alex List, Celeste Day Moore, Peter Simons, Ross Mulcare, Erin Quinn, Sudhir Muralidhar, Aditi Sen, Alex Plakias, Doug Edwards, and Will Smiley and for their friendship.

I thank my mother, Lynne De Bruin, whose twenty years of public service as a Milwaukee County Supervisor first motivated my interest in politics. More concretely, she provided childcare in crucial moments that enabled me to complete this book. The work ethic and political activism of my father and stepmother, David and Linda De Bruin, continue to be an inspiration, and I thank them for their love and support. I was fortunate to marry into a family of academics, including Fran Hoffmann, Richard Rosenfeld, Janet Lauritsen, and Jake Rosenfeld, from whom I have learned a great deal. Their advice and encouragement have been invaluable. I am also grateful to my siblings, Chris, Laura, and Natalee De Bruin, and to my sister-in-law, Erin McGaughey, for their moral support. I thank Sue Winkler, Liz Fletcher, and the rest of the staff at the Clinton Early Learning Center, as well as Ursula Castiblanco, Susan Mojave, and Paige Zupan, for the excellent childcare they provided while I worked on this book.

I thank my children, Henry and Frankie, who have been the source of so much unmitigated joy in my life. Frankie's arrival made the last few months of revising and editing the manuscript more fun than they had any right to be. Finally, this book is dedicated to Sam Rosenfeld, whose timely advice and sharp eye have improved its writing and argument in more ways than I can count. Even more important than his specific contributions to the manuscript, however, have been his confidence in me and the optimism and good humor he brings to our lives together every day. He has been the model of a publicly engaged scholar—someone I am both proud of and inspired by—and a true co-parent, without whose support this book would not have been possible. I could not be more grateful.

HOW TO PREVENT COUPS D'ÉTAT

INTRODUCTION
Preventing Coups d'État

In April 2003, when the United States invaded Iraq, Saddam Hussein's military collapsed within weeks. While the mismatch between the adversaries' capabilities left little doubt about the eventual outcome of the war, the conflict was notable for the speed with which conventional military resistance fell apart.[1] There was a reason for this. For most of his time in office, Saddam had divided the country's coercive power into multiple, overlapping security and intelligence organizations—efforts to insulate his regime from coups d'état that also sapped morale within the armed forces and undermined military effectiveness.[2] A decade later, following a multiyear, $20 billion effort to rebuild military capacity, it became clear that Prime Minister Nouri al-Maliki had hobbled the reconstituted Iraqi army in similar ways.[3] As a result, in the spring of 2014, when the Islamic State began capturing territory across northern Iraq, Maliki took much of the blame.[4]

The dilemma Iraqi rulers have faced is hardly unique. How to build a military strong enough to defend the state against the threat of war and rebellion—but not so powerful as to undermine civilian rule—is a fundamental challenge for democratic and authoritarian rulers alike. For individual leaders, the decision to prioritize coup prevention is a rational one. The threat of a coup is more immediate and unpredictable than the threat posed by civil war or international conflict. The overwhelming majority of rulers removed from power via a coup face death, exile, or jail.[5] In their efforts to prevent coups, rulers adopt a range of coup-proofing strategies that can hinder military effectiveness, reinforce ethnic and political divides, and drain financial resources. Some rulers artificially inflate defense budgets and salaries, while others take the opposite approach—keeping the size of the military small, restricting soldiers' access to arms, or rotating officers frequently to prevent them from developing their own bases of power. Elsewhere, leaders manipulate recruitment and promotion within the military to surround themselves with loyal troops.[6]

The choices that Saddam and Maliki made are particularly common ones: counterbalancing the military with republican guards, militarized police, and other paramilitary forces is often a central feature of rulers' coup-prevention strategies.[7] From the praetorian guard in ancient Rome to the secret police in Soviet Russia and national militia in contemporary Venezuela, coercive institutions outside the regular military have long been used as a bulwark against coups.[8] Yet despite the frequency with which counterbalancing is employed—and the ways in which it can weaken military capacity—we know little about whether and how it works. Is counterbalancing an effective way to prevent coups d'état?

This book demonstrates that the way rulers structure their coercive institutions can indeed have profound effects on the survival of their regimes. Drawing upon an original dataset of security forces in 110 countries, combined with careful process tracing in cases of individual coup attempts, it shows that counterbalancing the military with coercive institutions outside the regular military chain of command increases the risk that coup attempts will fail. The presence of additional security forces can make it more difficult for coup plotters to recruit among key units in advance. While a coup attempt is under way, counterbalancing creates incentives to resist the coup. Because the consequences for being on the losing side of a coup attempt can be dire, most officers remain on the sidelines until it is clear what the outcome of the coup will be.[9] When rulers organize security forces outside of military command, however, it changes the calculus, increasing the costs of inaction and creating incentives for officers in such forces to defend the incumbent regime. Counterbalancing also complicates coup plotters' efforts to monopolize information during a coup, increasing uncertainty about the outcome of the coup—and thus also the odds that at least some officers will resist. However, counterbalancing is not without risk for the leaders who adopt it. Where counterweights compete with the military for resources and recruits, resentment and fear about a decline in status among military officers can provoke new coup attempts, even as counterbalancing creates obstacles to their execution. Furthermore, the way in which counterbalancing works—by creating incentives for armed resistance—increases the risk that coup attempts will escalate to civil war.

Understanding how counterbalancing works can thus help us predict where coup attempts will occur, whether they will succeed, and how violent they are likely to be. Taken together, the arguments and evidence in this book suggest that while counterbalancing may prevent successful coups, it is a risky strategy to pursue—and one that may weaken regimes in the long term.

Why Stopping Coups Matters

Between 2000 and 2019, soldiers in thirty-one different states attempted to seize power, staging more than fifty different coup attempts altogether.[10] While coups are no longer as common as they once were, the threat of a coup thus remains a pressing one. Coups are the most common way dictatorships begin and end. They also remain common in many democracies. Newly democratizing regimes, which have not yet developed norms of civilian and democratic governance, are particularly vulnerable.[11] Knowing what works, and what does not, in stopping coups is important because their outcomes can have alarming consequences. About half of coup attempts succeed overall, and those staged against democratic regimes are more likely to succeed than those against dictatorships.[12] In the past decade alone, newly elected rulers in Egypt, Honduras, and Thailand have fallen to coups. The 2013 coup in Egypt ousted Mohamed Morsi, the country's first democratically elected leader, from power. In its aftermath, human rights organizations documented mass, arbitrary arrests; the detention of protestors and human rights workers; new restrictions on nongovernmental organizations; and a crackdown on political opposition.[13]

To be sure, some successful coups do usher in more democratic regimes.[14] In recent years, some observers have gone so far as to suggest that coups may be the most practical way to force long-entrenched dictators from power. Since the end of the Cold War, the number of so-called "good coups"—defined as those that are followed by competitive elections—has been on the rise. But more often than not, coups in authoritarian regimes still simply replace one dictator with another. Those coups that are followed by elections, moreover, typically revert to authoritarianism within a few years. In part, this is because many coup leaders receive support and protection from autocratic sponsors abroad. More generally, military intervention in politics undermines norms of civilian control that are a prerequisite for stable, democratic rule.[15]

Even failed coup attempts can have deleterious effects. Rulers who have survived a coup frequently take violent measures to prevent subsequent efforts to oust them from power, using the coup as justification for increased repression against political opponents.[16] For example, after he survived a failed coup in April 2002, Venezuelan president Hugo Chávez cracked down on the press and repressed supporters of the opposition. In the year following the failed 2016 coup attempt in Turkey, President Recep Tayyip Erdoğan led a sweeping purge of political opponents. An estimated fifty thousand people were arrested and another one hundred and fifty thousand dismissed from their jobs.[17] Finally, no matter their outcome, coup attempts themselves can also result in a significant amount of bloodshed. The 2016 coup in Turkey resulted in an estimated 265 deaths.[18] Some coup attempts even escalate to civil war. The Spanish Civil War began with a failed coup, as did more recent civil wars in Nigeria and Guinea-Bissau. All told, an estimated 22 percent of civil wars between 1946 and 2011 had their origins in coups or other mass defections from the military.[19] The analysis in this book suggests that the risk that coup attempts will escalate to civil war is higher when rulers use other coercive institutions to counterbalance the military.

Designing Coercive Institutions to Combat Coups

How rulers design their coercive institutions varies widely. Some countries, like Chile under Augusto Pinochet, centralize control over all state security forces under military command, while others, like Libya under Muammar Qaddafi, rely on a complex web of overlapping and competing coercive institutions to check and balance one another.[20] How states configure their coercive institutions is, in part, a reflection of their historical experiences and the particular combination of threats they face. More fragmented and politicized coercive institutions are thought to help rulers combat threats to their power from within their ruling coalitions, while more centralized and merit-based institutions are more effective at combating threats from other states and rebel groups.[21] Where rulers organize coercive institutions outside of military command, they have the potential to serve as counterweights to the military.

A wide range of coercive institutions may be capable of balancing the military. Some rulers have focused on strengthening presidential guards or elevating individual units within the military. In Haiti, François Duvalier split a number of units off from the regular military to form counterweights; they began to report directly to him without going through the normal military chain of command. Duvalier also raised a civilian militia commonly known as the Tonton Macoutes, which both served as a check on the military and harassed regime opponents.[22] Other leaders depend on interior troops, gendarmerie, or small, militarized units within the regular police. In the Ivory Coast, for instance, the National Gendarmerie "provide[d] a military counterweight to the army, which could not seize power without securing the unlikely consent of the Gendarmerie."[23] Elsewhere, rulers turn to secret police, like those under the Ministry for State Security (Stasi) in East Germany, or the State Security Department in North Korea.[24] What these very different types of coercive institutions—presidential guards, interior troops, civilian militia, and secret police—have in common is their independence from the regular military and access to the centers of political power that are the targets of coups.

While counterweights might help insulate rulers from successful coups, their use weakens the state in a number of ways. As Saddam Hussein and Nouri al-Maliki found in Iraq, counterbalancing and other coup-proofing measures undermine military professionalism and hinder the coordination crucial to success in conventional warfare, making states more vulnerable to external threats. Counterbalancing in particular makes it more difficult for different security forces to work together on the battlefield and execute more complex operations.[25] Counterbalancing can also help institutionalize factional and ethnic divides within the state apparatus, which affects how regimes respond to domestic threats such as revolutions and mass uprisings. The proliferation of coercive institutions can demoralize soldiers in regular army units, creating grievances against the regime and making them less likely to defend rulers in the face of widespread protest.[26] More fragmented security sectors have also been associated with higher levels of repression and violence against civilians. In a study of Taiwan, South Korea, and the Philippines, for instance, Sheena Greitens found that "a fragmented, exclusive coercive apparatus gives its agents social and material incentives to escalate rather than dampen violence, and also hampers agents from collecting the intelligence necessary to engage in targeted, discriminate, and pre-emptive repression."[27]

The costs of counterbalancing make it all the more imperative to understand whether, and how, it does what it is intended to do: stop coups. While the causes of coups have been the subject of an immense body of research in political science and sociology, important gaps remain in our understanding of coup prevention strategies.[28] An emerging literature on coup prevention, or coup-proofing, has brought new focus to the practice of counterbalancing and other strategies rulers use to insulate themselves from coups.[29] Existing studies have provided important insights, but debate remains over whether or not counterbalancing strategies actually work to prevent coups. In part, this is because central works on counterbalancing are primarily descriptive in nature; they do not develop or test arguments about how counterbalancing is supposed to work.[30] It is not obvious why police and paramilitary units would be any more reliable than the regular military. Nor is it clear how the presence of a small presidential guard force or a lightly armed civilian militia might block a larger, better-trained, and better-equipped military from seizing power. Some studies depict counterbalancing as complicating the coordination of a coup attempt, but typically do not specify *how* it might do so. Partly because of this under-theorizing, there is no consensus about whether counterbalancing is effective at preventing coups.

Identifying the mechanisms linking counterbalancing to the incidence and outcomes of coup attempts is important because doing so can help reconcile conflicting theoretical predictions about the strategy's effectiveness. Case studies of long-standing civilian regimes frequently highlight the role of counterweights in preventing military intervention in politics. For instance, in an influential study of coup-proofing practices in the Middle East, James Quinlivan empahsized the role of counterbalancing or "parallel militaries" in keeping rulers in power. Ibn Saud, the founder of Saudi Arabia, built two coercive institutions outside the regular army: a Royal Guard made of tribal retainers and the White Army (now called the National Guard). Likewise, in Indonesia, Robert Bruce argues that counterbalancing was responsible for delaying for several years the coup attempt that eventually ousted Sukarno, Indonesia's first president, from power.[31] Yet there are reasons to be skeptical of counterbalancing: as the case of Indonesia highlights, coup attempts still regularly occur in states that counterbalance. Indeed, coup plotters frequently cite efforts to establish counterweights among their motives for seizing power.[32] Statistical evidence on whether counterbalancing is effective is also mixed.[33]

Part of the reason for the lack of consensus stems from limitations in the empirical approaches used in existing studies. Some restrict their focus to long-serving civilian regimes. This method of case selection makes it difficult to know whether it is counterbalancing or some other factor underpinning regime stability.[34] Efforts to test theories of coup prevention more systematically have been hindered by poor quality data. Existing analyses depend almost exclusively on the *Military Balance*, an annual defense review published by the International Institute for Strategic Studies (IISS). However, a number of studies have documented biases, inconsistencies, and errors in IISS data that limit its utility in mapping the use of counterweights.[35] In more recent editions, the IISS itself explicitly cautions against using its data to capture changes over time in how states organize their security sectors.[36] As a result, scholars and policymakers do not yet know what works to prevent coups.

The Argument: Counterbalancing and Regime Survival

This book shows that the way rulers organize their coercive institutions affects the survival of their regimes. In particular, counterbalancing the military with security forces outside the military chain of command increases the likelihood that efforts to oust rulers from power through a coup will fail. To see why this is the case, it is important to understand how coup attempts unfold. Coup attempts can be understood as illegal and overt actions intended to seize executive authority in a state. In contrast to insurgencies or rebellions, coups originate from *within* the regime in power at the outset of the coup.[37] While many coups are bloodless, the threat of violence underlies all coup attempts. It is what distinguishes coups from voluntary transfers of power. The perpetrators of most coup attempts are therefore those within the state apparatus best positioned to threaten violence: members of the state's military and security forces. Nonmilitary elites can also instigate coup attempts, but must depend on armed actors if the threat of violence is to be carried out.[38]

Coup plotters begin their efforts to seize power by recruiting potential supporters. Those at the top of the military hierarchy have the most resources at their disposal to do this. Where coup plotters can coordinate extensively in advance, the coup can be accomplished without visible movements of troops at all. Instead, coup plotters simply announce that they have taken power. In most cases, however, such coordination is too risky and the number of conspirators is kept to a minimum to prevent the plot from being exposed. This means that when the coup begins, most officers are not yet committed to one side or the other. Whether the coup succeeds or fails depends crucially on how they respond.[39] Where no officers move to resist the coup, it can succeed bloodlessly. Where some resist, there is some probability that the coup will succeed and some probability that it will fail. Each outcome entails a combination of costs and benefits for all involved. The question then becomes how the relevant actors—officers in military and security forces in a position to intercept the coup attempt—perceive these costs and benefits.

I argue that three factors are particularly important for officers weighing whether or not to resist: the likelihood the coup will succeed, the costs of it doing so, and the costs of using violence to stop it. The estimate of whether the coup will succeed is important because the consequences of backing the wrong side can be severe. Those on the losing side of a coup may be executed, dismissed from their posts, or otherwise punished. If the coup fails, the military as a whole may face a loss of prestige, cohesion, discipline, resources, and political standing.[40] In consequence, the vast majority of soldiers during any coup attempt adopt a "wait and see" approach, only committing to a side when it is clear what the outcome will be. Actors also weigh the costs involved in using violence to resist the coup. These costs include the loss of life and damage to property and infrastructure. Where coup attempts pit members of the military against one another, using violence to resist the coup may also undermine military cohesion and morale.[41] The costs of using violence mean that coup plotters frequently choose to return to the barracks rather than engage in a bloody and protracted fight for power against other members of the armed forces. According to Naunihal Singh, army officers in Ghana weighing whether or not to join a coup attempt expressed a firm desire to avoid "unnecessary violence."[42] Such caution helps explain why almost half of failed coup attempts end without a single fatality.[43]

I argue that counterbalancing the military with republican guards, secret police, and other security forces outside the regular military chain of command increases the likelihood that a coup attempt will face resistance—and with it, the odds that the coup will fail. The presence of multiple armed actors makes it more difficult for coup plotters to coordinate in advance of the coup attempt and to control the flow of information once it is under way. Counterbalancing also affects actors' estimates about the costs of defeat and violence. For officers and soldiers in counterbalancing forces, the costs of the coup succeeding are likely to appear higher than they would to those in the regular army. This is because, over time, presidential guards, secret police, civilian militia, and other security forces develop their own organizational interests, distinct from those of the military. Rulers can deliberately hasten this process by staffing or paying security forces differently than the military. They may also find that personnel changes are easier to make in new security forces than they are in the regular military, where existing positions are already filled. This enables them to stack counterweights with co-ethnics or party loyalists.[44] Rulers can also facilitate diverging interests by compensating different forces for different tasks—paying the army to defend the country from rival states, for instance, and the police to monitor the army.[45] As a consequence, officers in counterbalancing forces may be less likely to view a coup from within the regular military as serving their interests.

Furthermore, military coup plotters cannot credibly commit to refrain from dissolving other security forces or incorporating them into the military if the coup succeeds. The creation of coercive institutions outside of the military challenges the latter's core interest in holding a monopoly on the state's use of force.[46] Coup-installed regimes frequently disband competing coercive institutions. In Indonesia, for example, a mobile police brigade that had been built up as a counterweight to the army was placed under military command after the 1957 coup attempt. As a result, "Police officials found themselves taking orders from army personnel as low in rank as corporal; they found this humiliating and resented it."[47] The inability of coup plotters from within the military to commit to maintaining the existence and status of other coercive institutions if the coup succeeds creates powerful incentives for officers in counterbalancing forces to get off the sidelines when a coup is under way and defend the regime in power.

Finally, where a coup attempt pits military officers against those in other coercive institutions, the costs of using violence to shape the coup's outcome are likely to appear lower. Firing on other security forces does not threaten to undermine military cohesion or require soldiers to overcome normative prohibitions on violence against those with whom they have lived, worked, and trained in the same way that firing on members of the same force would. More broadly, violence is likely to be seen as less detrimental in an already divided and politicized security sector. For these reasons, counterbalancing the military with republican guards and other security forces should increase the likelihood that attempts to oust rulers through a coup d'état will fail. This is not to say that counterweights themselves never participate in coup attempts. The 1975 coup in Peru, for instance, had the support of the Civil Guard, which had initially been built up as a counterweight to the army, but was deliberately marginalized under the regime of Juan Velasco in the years leading up to the coup. And in Ethiopia, the commander of Haile Selassie's Imperial Guard, created as a counterweight to the army, staged a failed coup attempt in 1960. For the most part, however, counterweights refrain from staging coups.[48] And it is their resistance that makes coup attempts staged in states with more fragmented coercive institutions less likely to succeed.

Yet counterbalancing is not without risk for the rulers who use it. Even as it makes coups more difficult to carry out successfully, counterbalancing frequently triggers fears about a decline in status within the regular military that can provoke coup attempts. In Ghana, for instance, the 1966 coup was staged by officers aggravated by Kwame Nkrumah's efforts to elevate his presidential guard, the President's Own Guard Regiment (POGR), into a formidable counterweight.[49] As one participant in the coup explained, "All the emphasis was on the POGR, while the rest of the forces suffered." Another argued: "In all this plan to build a second Army [out of the POGR] one thing stood out prominently: and that was a plan gradually to strangle the Regular Army to death."[50]

The resentment among regular military officers that counterbalancing generates can provoke new coup attempts, even as it simultaneously creates obstacles to their execution. These grievances are likely to be most deeply felt in the immediate aftermath of creating a new force. In Nigeria, for instance, the military intervened to disband President Ibrahim Babangida's new National Guard force in 1993, less than a year after it was created.[51] The 1977 coup in Pakistan was also staged in large part to disband President Zulfiqar Ali Bhutto's recently established Federal Security Force, which the military viewed as "a potential rival institution—a threat to their autonomy and monopoly of coercive power."[52] Establishing new coercive institutions to counterbalance the military thus increases the risk of a coup in the short term.

The mechanisms through which counterbalancing works also mean that coup attempts against regimes that counterbalance are more likely to escalate to civil war. This is for two reasons. First, because coup-installed regimes cannot credibly commit to refrain from disbanding counterweights or impinging on their autonomy, officers in these forces have incentives not only to resist the coup attempt but to "fight to the death," increasing the odds that conflict between coup plotters and regime loyalists will escalate to higher levels of violence. Second, where coup plotters gain the upper hand in their initial effort to seize power, counterweights can serve as a pre-organized source of armed resistance—helping ousted rulers quickly circumvent the challenges of recruiting, training, and equipping an armed group to challenge the new regime. As a result, coups in states that use counterbalancing are at greater risk of escalating to civil war than those in states that do not.

The Plan of the Book

The chapters that follow trace how leaders choose to structure their security forces and what the consequences of those choices are for individual leaders, the soldiers under their command, and the citizens under their rule. Does counterbalancing affect the incidence or outcomes of coup attempts? If so, how? And under what conditions does counterbalancing best achieve those effects? What are the risks of using this strategy? Finally, what recommendations can be made regarding how leaders in democratizing states can best prevent coups? This book combines theory, statistical analysis, and historical case studies to answer these questions.

The first chapter presents the core of the argument. It begins by spelling out how coups d'état progress, from the initial plot to the consolidation of power by a new regime. It then describes how the presence of coercive institutions outside the military might affect the incentives facing relevant actors during each stage of a coup. In addition to considering the constraints facing officers in the regular military, I consider the preferences of those in other coercive state institutions. The discussion generates testable hypotheses about how counterbalancing affects the incidence and outcome of coup attempts, as well as the risk that coups will escalate to civil war. I also describe and address potential alternative arguments that focus on the strength of the military or the extent of coup risk faced by the incumbent regime. The chapter closes by discussing the strategies the book will use for testing the theory's predictions empirically, explaining the criteria used to select cases for closer analysis.

Chapters 2 and 4 assess the predictions of the theory using a new dataset that tracks how rulers organize and use the presidential guards, police, and other coercive institutions under their command. The dataset includes 110 countries between 1960 and 2010. Because it includes fine-grained information on features of individual security forces, including the chain of command through which each force reports to the regime and where it is deployed, the dataset allows me to develop more precise measures of counterbalancing than previously possible. Chapter 2 first presents descriptive data on the frequency with which rulers counterbalance and how the use of counterbalancing varies across countries and over time. It then tests statistically the argument that counterbalancing is associated with coup failure. In order to test arguments about the determinants of coup failure, I also compile new data on the identity of coup plotters in four hundred coup attempts. The chapter considers competing explanations for the negative association between counterbalancing and coup success, which posit that some other factor might explain both counterweights and coup outcomes, but shows that available evidence is inconsistent with them. The finding that counterbalancing makes coups less likely to succeed helps explain why some leaders have successfully prevented military coups, while others have not.

While chapter 2 presents statistical evidence consistent with the argument that counterbalancing decreases the likelihood that a coup attempt will succeed, it provides little information on the causal factors at work. I thus turn, in chapter 3, to a close examination of the role of counterbalancing during individual coup attempts. I examine in detail coups staged to unseat Daniel Arap Moi in Kenya, King Hassan II in Morocco, and Manuel Noriega in Panama. In each case, counterbalancing affected the outcome of the coup attempt: while soldiers within the regular military were hesitant to take a side, presidential guards, Ministry of Interior units, and militia built up as counterweights to the military defended incumbent rulers. In contrast to most existing accounts, which suggest that counterbalancing works primarily by creating obstacles to coordination between different security forces, the evidence in these cases suggests that counterbalancing creates incentives to resist the coup.

Chapter 4 examines whether counterbalancing can deter soldiers from attempting to seize power in the first place. I conduct an array of analyses of patterns of coup attempts, which show that organizing security forces outside of military command is not associated with a reduction in coup attempts. In fact, establishing a new counterweight *increases* the risk of a coup attempt in the following year. These results challenge the widespread assumption that counterbalancing deters coup attempts, and help to explain why counterbalancing is not even more widespread than it is. Yet the results in this chapter also raise another question: What explains why some rulers are able to establish counterweights without provoking a backlash from the military, while others are not? To address this question, chapter 5 compares Kwame Nkrumah's failed effort to counterbalance with efforts by leaders in similar political and economic circumstances: Saskia Stevens in Sierra Leone, Fidel Castro in Cuba, and Modibo Keita in Mali. The comparison provides support for the proposed causal mechanism linking counterweight creation to coup attempts: in each case, the creation of a new counterweight generated resentment and fear about a decline in status within the regular armed forces. The comparison also helps refine the arguments developed in chapter 1, suggesting new hypotheses about the conditions under which this resentment will result in a coup attempt. It emphasizes the other strategies of coup prevention that rulers adopt in conjunction with counterbalancing, as well as the type of security force used to counterbalance the military. The findings suggest limits to the conditions under which counterbalancing is feasible, as well as concrete steps that rulers might take to mitigate some of the risks associated with counterbalancing.

Chapter 6 identifies an additional and previously unknown risk of counterbalancing: it can increase the risk that coup attempts escalate to civil war. The chapter compares two coup attempts in the Dominican Republic: the bloodless coup in 1963, which removed the country's first democratically elected president, and the 1965 coup, which sought to return him to power, and which escalated to a civil war resulting in over two thousand fatalities. In doing so, it leverages variation over time in one country, which enables me to hold constant several of the historical and contextual factors thought to affect the onset of civil war. The comparison shows that a crucial difference between the two coups was the presence, in 1965, of a new counterweight to the military. Chapter 6 then briefly compares the 1965 Dominican coup to one in a very different context that also escalated to civil war: the 1962 coup in Yemen. The comparison illustrates how very different types of counterweights employed in very different settings can affect the process of violent escalation in similar ways, and suggests that the dynamics in these cases might hold more broadly.

The conclusion explains the book's implications for theory and policy. After briefly summarizing the book's findings, it describes their implications for our understanding of democratization, civil-military relations, and civil war. Exploring patterns in how states organize and use their security forces can shed light on when and where coup attempts will occur, and what their outcomes are likely to be. The results of this study emphasize that while counterbalancing can help rulers stay in power, it also carries important risks. While no simple policy solutions follow from the arguments and evidence in this book, its findings can offer some guidance to policymakers interested in shoring up civilian control over the military.

1
THE LOGIC OF COUNTERBALANCING

Counterweights are meant to prevent military coups. But how exactly do they do so? Do they complicate coordination and recruitment prior to the coup attempt? Make it more difficult for coup plotters to seize their targets? In theory, a large, militarized counterbalancing force might be able to outgun military coup plotters. But more often than not, rulers employ comparatively small or lightly armed counterweights. How could a small presidential guard force prevent a powerful standing army from seizing power? How could a lightly armed civilian militia stop professional soldiers? Why would these security forces be any more reliable than regular military? And if counterbalancing does impede the execution of coups, does it also deter potential coup plotters from staging them in the first place? In other words, what causal mechanisms link counterbalancing to regime survival?

This chapter spells out multiple mechanisms through which counterbalancing might affect the incidence and outcomes of coup attempts. Doing so is important because it can help resolve conflicting theoretical expectations about whether and how counterbalancing works, and because different mechanisms have different implications for the risk that coup attempts will escalate from an intra-regime struggle into more widespread political violence. In what follows, I first describe what staging a coup involves. I argue that whether a coup attempt succeeds or fails depends crucially on how members of military and security forces that were uncommitted at the outset of the coup choose to respond to it. Each potential outcome to a coup attempt entails a combination of costs and benefits for these officers. I argue that particularly important in shaping their responses are perceptions about the likelihood the coup will succeed, the costs of it doing so, and the costs associated with using violence to resist.

I then explain how counterbalancing can affect these perceptions, distinguishing between two potential causal logics or sets of causal mechanisms—statements about how the independent variable, counterbalancing, exerts an effect on the dependent variable, coup failure. The first emphasize *coordination*: they posit that counterbalancing works by impeding recruitment prior to the coup, or complicating the seizure of targets during it, in a way that makes it more difficult for coup plotters to shape expectations about the coup's likely outcome and enable officers to coordinate around it. The second emphasize the incentives counterbalancing creates for armed *resistance* to the coup attempt: under this logic, counterbalancing creates security forces with institutional interests that are distinct from those of the regular armed forces, and links their fates more closely to that of the incumbent regime in a way that makes the costs of the coup succeeding appear higher. The costs associated with using violence to resist a coup are also likely to appear lower in a security sector already divided by counterbalancing.

After spelling out these two potential causal logics and the multiple mechanisms that might operate under each, I then turn to the question of how counterbalancing affects the incidence of coup attempts rulers will face. I argue that counterbalancing has two countervailing effects on the likelihood of a coup attempt. Because counterbalancing makes coup failure more likely, the presence of counterweights should deter potential coup plotters from attempting to seize power. At the same time, because police and other paramilitary forces frequently compete with the regular military for funds and recruits, counterbalancing also generates grievances and triggers fears about a decline in status that can prompt new coup attempts. As a result, I argue, counterbalancing will not necessarily decrease the overall incidence of coup attempts rulers face. Furthermore, because the grievances created by new counterweights are likely to be highest when counterweights are first created, establishing a new force is likely to *increase* the risk of a coup in the short term. The next section of this chapter spells out the implications of these arguments for the likelihood that a coup attempt will escalate to civil war. I argue that the risk that successful coup plotters will disband counterbalancing forces or bring them under military command creates incentives for protracted resistance to a coup that can prevent a coup-installed regime from consolidating its control of the state. Counterbalancing may also aid ousted rulers in overcoming the challenges required to organize a rebellion against the new regime. The chapter concludes by discussing in more detail the strategy the book uses to test each argument.

How Coup Attempts Unfold

The aim of a coup d'état is to seize executive authority within a state. While violence need not be present in a coup attempt, the threat of it must be. The perpetrators of most coup attempts are thus those within the state apparatus best positioned to threaten violence: members of the state's military and security services. Nonmilitary elites can also instigate coup attempts but must depend on the military if the threat of violence is to be carried out.[1] The dynamics of coups closely resemble "coordination games," in which each actor bases his or her decisions on beliefs about what others are going to do, and the outcome is determined when the beliefs of relevant actors converge.[2] The relevant actors in the context of a coup are almost entirely within the state's military and security forces. Success depends on the ability of coup plotters to quickly convince other officers that victory has in fact already occurred and that resistance to the new regime will be punished—a process Naunihal Singh memorably calls "making a fact."[3]

Classic how-to manuals for coups map out three stages involved in seizing power: the planning stage, the attack stage, and the consolidation stage.[4] In the planning stage, coup plotters must recruit participants without being found out. Coup plotters from within the military have different techniques available for them to stage a coup. Those at the top of the military hierarchy may be able to seize power without the visible movement of troops or use of force at all. In some cases, they may be able to use face-to-face meetings to propose a coup attempt, and use the meeting itself—where officers' responses to the proposal become common knowledge—to create self-fulfilling expectations about its likely success. Where such a meeting is too difficult to organize, senior officers may instead simply announce that they have seized power on behalf of the armed forces, and hope that their announcement is not challenged.[5] These coup attempts can begin and end with an announcement. The 2011 coup in Egypt illustrates this type of coup attempt. It occurred without the use of violence or the movement of troops. Instead, the country's vice president and intelligence chief, Omar Suleiman, simply announced that President Hosni Mubarak had been removed from power and that a council of military leaders had taken power.[6]

In many cases, however, such consultation and coordination ahead of time are too risky for coup plotters, even those from within the higher ranks of the military. As Ed Luttwak describes in *Coups d'État: A Practical Handbook*, "The danger of denunciation will also increase as more and more people become aware that a coup is being planned."[7] For this reason, conspirators are typically kept to a minimum. When the coup begins, the majority of military officers are not yet committed to one side or another. Coup plotters attempt to make the coup a fact through a use of force. In doing so, conspirators aim to take advantage of the "machine-like" functioning of the military chain of command, in which orders that come from the appropriate source are followed without question, and focus their recruitment efforts on the leaders of units in and around the capital, which could block the attempt.[8]

In the attack phase, coup plotters attempt to seize control of symbolic centers of political power, such as the presidential palace or the legislature, along with radio or other broadcast facilities that they can use to publicize their actions. In seizing these targets, tactical considerations, such as location, timing, speed, and coordination, are key. Coup plotters must neutralize any troops stationed near coup targets that were not recruited in advance. In the successful 2017 coup in Zimbabwe, for instance, which ousted Robert Mugabe, coup plotters placed Mugabe under house arrest and seized control of the state-run broadcasting company. To deter Mugabe's supporters from resisting, tanks were "stationed around strategic government buildings and intersections in the capital."[9] Because the targets of coups are typically small in number and concentrated in the capital, successful coups do not require a large military force. In Gabon, for instance, only 150 soldiers participated in the 1963 coup that overthrew President Léon M'Ba, while in Dahomey, President Christophe Soglo was ousted by sixty troops in 1967.[10] The 1981 coup in Ghana is a particularly extreme example: it was successfully executed by only ten soldiers.[11] Where coup plotters fail to capture their targets, the coup fails quickly.

If coup leaders are able to seize their initial targets, their final task is to consolidate power. Political opposition from outside the armed forces is likely to subside when coup plotters demonstrate control of the security forces and state bureaucracy.[12] Particularly important are officers in the vicinity of coup targets, who could contest control of them or issue their own counter-broadcasts, challenging the coup plotters' narrative. In choosing how to respond, Barbara Geddes contends, "the most important concern for many officers deciding whether to join a coup conspiracy is their assessment of how many others will join."[13] Military officers are typically portrayed as wanting to act in concert with other officers because of their shared interest in protecting the corporate or institutional interests of the military.[14] The military is frequently described as the quintessential "total institution," able to inculcate in its members a common culture, mission, and sense of brotherhood.[15] Central among the corporate interests of the military are the unity and cohesion of the armed forces.[16] Indeed, there is "a consensus in the literature that most professional soldiers place a higher value on the survival and efficacy of the military itself than on anything else."[17] Yet acting in concert with other officers—and thus being on the winning side of the coup attempt—is best for officers' individual fates as well. Those on the losing side of a coup attempt may be dismissed from their posts, executed, or otherwise punished.[18]

Whether the coup succeeds or fails depends crucially on how members of the military and security forces in the vicinity of coup targets choose to respond. Where no resistance forms, the coup attempt succeeds. Where some segment of the military or security forces resists, there is some probability that the coup will fail and some probability that it will succeed. Each potential outcome of the coup entails a combination of costs and benefits to officers. As Luttwak notes, "If we go up to an army officer and ask him to join in a projected coup, he will be faced—unless he is a total loyalist—with a set of options, offering both dangers and opportunities." The question is then how these officers perceive the dangers and opportunities associated with the choices before them.[19]

The Preferences and Perceptions of Military Officers

I argue that there are three preferences and perceptions central to understanding the dynamics of coup attempts. First, each actor estimates some *likelihood the coup will succeed*. This calculation is by no means straightforward. The large literature on bargaining, information, and conflict suggests that because war is costly, if parties in dispute could agree about its likely outcome, they would be able to reach an agreement that would avoid it.[20] Where they cannot, fighting helps reveal information about the capabilities and resolve of combatants. In the context of a coup attempt, information problems are likely to be even more acute. The need to plot in secret makes it difficult for incumbent rulers, coup plotters, and officers uncommitted at the outset of the coup attempt to estimate the depth of support for the coup within the military and security forces before it begins. It is also difficult for coup plotters to credibly convey their strength to other actors while the coup is under way. They have incentives to exaggerate their support in order to convince potential opponents to remain on the sidelines.[21] Take the case of coup plotters in the 1973 coup in Laos. As one account of the coup explains, "their plan was to create the impression of mass support for the coup by a series of air and ground attacks on the capital." In the initial hours of the coup, this plan succeeded: "With the identity of the coup leaders a mystery and its chances for success unknown, the military leadership was not about to expose itself to retribution from a new government by attempting to suppress the insurgents."[22] Estimating the likelihood the coup will succeed is also difficult due to the prevalence of side switching that occurs during coup attempts. Soldiers who initially move to defend the regime, or who remain on the sidelines, are likely to defect if the coup appears to be succeeding—and vice versa, if the coup appears to be failing. For instance, in the case of the "April Fool's coup" in Thailand in 1981, a number of senior officers first "joined the coup before defecting to the government side."[23] The difficulty in estimating in advance whether a coup will succeed keeps the vast majority of military officers on the sidelines while a coup is under way.

The actions that coup plotters take prior to the coup attempt and while it is under way are intended to credibly convey their strength and to convince officers who could block the attempt that the likelihood it will succeed is high. Because officers would prefer to act in concert with one another, information plays a crucial role in the dynamics and outcome of a coup. The more decisively coup plotters can monopolize information during a coup attempt, the more effectively they can deter resistance.[24] This helps explain why radio and television stations are primary targets of coups.[25] Where coup plotters are unable to control the flow of information to other officers, resistance is much more likely. The January 1971 coup in Bolivia, for example, failed because "while the opinion within the military was largely favorable to the movement, too few senior officers had formally committed themselves" ahead of time; as a result, other soldiers were reluctant to join.[26]

Second, actors consider the *costs of defeat*. Ousted leaders lose office, and frequently see additional punishment in the form of exile, imprisonment, or death.[27] Within the military and other security forces, those on the losing side of the coup may also be dismissed, executed, or otherwise punished. For instance, analyzing the failed August 1991 coup in the Soviet Union, Brian Taylor concludes that "the belief that a coup attempt would fail and that the instigators of a military putsch would be punished" was the central determinant of soldiers' behavior.[28] Even officers with strong preferences in favor of the coup or against it may feel responsible for protecting those troops under their command. Singh emphasizes how the military officers he interviewed in Ghana "felt it was wrong to use their troops, possibly endangering their lives, to support the side they preferred if it was likely to lose."[29] In addition to the cost to individual participants, in the wake of a failed coup, the military as a whole may face a loss of prestige, cohesion, discipline, resources, and political standing.[30]

Finally, there are *costs to using violence* during a coup, no matter what its outcome is. Material costs may include the loss of life and damage to property and infrastructure. Where the violence that occurs pits members of the military against one another, it can undermine the cohesion and morale of the armed forces. The use of violence during a coup attempt may also be counterproductive if it undermines support for the coup within the military.[31] In planning for the 1965 coup in Indonesia, for instance, plotters expressed concern that "the battle for power could claim many victims."[32] During the April 1989 coup in Haiti, coup plotters seeking to overthrow Prosper Avril "emphasized they wanted to avoid such a clash at all costs, maintaining, 'Lt. Gen. Avril isn't worth it.'"[33] The ideal coup, then, from the perspective of coup plotters, is one that involves no violence at all.

This is why coup plotters aim to capture their targets quickly, putting themselves in a defensive position—and putting the onus on regime loyalists to either accept the new status quo or take responsibility for the violence that resistance entails. For example, Eric Nordlinger recounts how during the 1961 coup in South Korea, "once the capital had been taken, the unpalatable responsibility for dividing the army and the country lay with the loyalists"; when they refused, the coup succeeded.[34]

This discussion provides a framework for understanding the outcomes of coup attempts. In particular, it suggests that where coup plotters are better able to coordinate in advance of the coup, or monopolize information flows during it, they will be more likely to deter resistance that could undermine their efforts. In contrast, where information about the capabilities and resolve of coup plotters is more opaque, the likelihood they will face armed resistance increases. This discussion also suggests that actors are likely to balance the costs of defeat against the cost of using violence to attempt to alter its course. Where their post-coup fate appears more dire, officers should be more willing to use force to combat the coup; officers with less concern about how they will fare under a coup-installed regime may be more willing to let the coup succeed without a protracted fight. Finally, where the costs of using violence to resist the coup appear lower, officers who oppose the coup may be more willing to step off the sidelines to combat it. In the next section, I describe the mechanisms through which counterbalancing could affect officers' perceptions about the likelihood of success, the cost of defeat, and the cost of violence—and with them, the outcome of the coup.

How Counterbalancing Affects Coup Outcomes

The first set of causal mechanisms that link counterbalancing and coup outcomes posit that counterbalancing impedes *coordination* between potential coup plotters, preventing them from making the coup's success appear inevitable. Most accounts of counterbalancing assert that it impedes coordination in some way, but are vague about how exactly it might do so. In what follows, I identify a number of different causal mechanisms that might operate through the logic of coordination. In the planning stage, counterbalancing may impede the ability of coup plotters to recruit and coordinate with troops in the vicinity of coup targets. In the attack and consolidation phases of a coup, counterbalancing might make it more difficult for coup plotters to seize their targets and shape expectations about the outcome of a coup attempt. The second set of causal mechanisms posit that counterbalancing works by changing perceptions about the costs of the coup

CHAPTER 1

TABLE 1.1 Causal mechanisms linking counterbalancing to coup failure

LOGIC	CAUSAL MECHANISM		OUTCOME
PRIOR TO THE COUP			
Coordination	Fewer face-to-face meetings restricts recruitment	→	Coup failure
Coordination	Better monitoring restricts recruitment	→	Coup failure
DURING THE COUP			
Coordination	Better monitoring impedes seizure of targets	→	Coup failure
Coordination	Tactical challenges impede seizure of targets	→	Coup failure
Resistance	Decline in post-coup status encourages resistance	→	Coup failure
Resistance	Lower cost to violence encourages resistance	→	Coup failure

succeeding and the cost of using violence to prevent it, generating incentives for resistance to the coup once it has gotten off the ground. Because coup-installed regimes frequently disband or downgrade the status of other security forces, counterweights have incentives to resist coups. In an already divided security sector, the costs of using violence to resist a coup might also appear lower to all officers. Table 1.1 summarizes these causal mechanisms linking counterbalancing to the outcomes of coup attempts. Each causal mechanism identified suggests that counterbalancing will be associated with failed coups, but makes a different claim about the reasons for the association.

Causal Mechanisms: Coordination

Prior to the coup attempt, counterbalancing might make it more difficult for high-ranking officers to meet face-to-face, impeding recruitment and forcing them to use less effective tactics to seize power. In Singh's words, "Such meetings are powerful because they create public information quickly and effectively in a stage-managed environment, allowing the challengers to most effectively make a fact around their success."[35] In more unified security sectors, regular meetings between high-ranking officers can be used to feel out potential supporters before the coup begins or to create common knowledge once it has begun.[36] Holger Albrecht and Ferdinand Eibl describe the example of Egypt in the run-up to military coups in 2011 and 2013, where "in the absence of independently operating paramilitary forces, elite officers' communication for the intervention in politics is facilitated by the presence of a unified military command."[37] The Supreme Council of the Armed Forces (SCAF), which includes representatives from each branch of the armed forces, would meet regularly to discuss military matters. Even in the best of circumstances, using face-to-face meetings to create common knowledge during a coup is rare: they are logistically difficult to arrange and entail more risks for all involved.[38] But in more divided security sectors, meetings between commanders of the relevant units are not a regular occurrence, and might immediately draw suspicion. These might prevent some coup plotters from staging a coup attempt—a possibility I return to below. Where high-ranking coup plotters do go forward with the coup, they may be forced to adopt other tactics to seize power, such as issuing a proclamation claiming to have the support of other forces they have not actually coordinated with or using force to capture coup targets. Both are less credible signals of their strength than face-to-face meetings, which make it more difficult for them to shape expectations about the likely outcome of the coup, and thereby increase the risk that the coup attempt collapses.

Counterbalancing may also force potential coup plotters of all ranks to restrict their recruitment efforts where counterweights are tasked with monitoring other security forces. Security forces outside the military are frequently tasked with just this function. In Cameroon, for example, former president Ahmadou Ahidjos used the paramilitary Brigades Mixtes Mobiles as "institutions of surveillance and intimidation" against the military.[39] Monitoring does not require a particularly large force or one with heavy weaponry. In Haiti under Jean-Claude Duvalier, for example, the comparatively small Presidential Guard force based at the presidential residence was tasked with "monitoring the activities of all the other security forces."[40] Such monitoring could result in fewer coup plots progressing to the attack stage. As Barbara Geddes, Joseph Wright, and Erica Frantz argue, in the context of dictatorships, personal "control of security forces can make talking about ousting a dictator so dangerous that party executive committees with the formal power to replace dictators never discuss doing so and plots are never developed."[41] Where coup plots do go forward, the need to restrict recruitment in advance means that more depends on their actions during it.

During a coup attempt, counterbalancing might impede the seizure of coup targets in one of two ways. First, effective monitoring may alert rulers to suspicious troop movements and allow them to evade capture or intercept coup plotters before they secure their targets. In Malawi, for example, Samuel Decalo describes how Hastings Banda used the Young Pioneers, the paramilitary wing of the Malawi Congress Party, to keep watch on any "unusual traffic."[42] Second, counterbalancing might create obstacles to cross-unit coordination that impede the seizure of coup targets.[43] This argument, which is stressed in many accounts of counterbalancing, builds on a growing body of literature on conflict that emphasizes how coup-proofing measures, including counterbalancing, undermine military effectiveness.[44] Where rulers divide their coercive power into multiple, overlapping security forces, which report to the regime through different chains of command, it is thought to impede the communication and coordination between forces required to execute complex operations. This was the case in Syria, for instance, where, as Risa Brooks describes, "the air force, Special Forces, Republican Guard, Struggle Companies and many of the army's other select units operate outside the formal chain of command, answering directly to [Hafez al-] Assad," complicating coordination between forces.[45]

The same problems may arise in efforts to capture coup targets. According to Luttwak, "The active phase of a coup is like a military operation—only more so," because it occurs in such a compressed time frame.[46] In order to succeed, coup plotters must quickly neutralize any forces that could block their access to key targets. The more armed groups that are present, the more difficult this task may be. As Jonathan Powell argues, counterbalancing "undermines the fighting capacity of a military by creating coordination challenges. This is as true for waging battle as it is for attempting a coup."[47] The difficulty of coordinating between multiple forces is exacerbated by the fact that security forces outside the military are typically trained and equipped in different ways, making it harder for them to work together. Where tactical challenges prevent coup plotters from capturing their targets, they will have more trouble controlling the flow of information during a coup attempt and creating expectations that it will succeed.

Causal Mechanisms: Resistance

The second set of mechanisms linking counterbalancing to coup failure focus on the incentives officers face to resist the coup. Under this logic, counterbalancing changes officers' perceptions about the costs of the coup succeeding or the costs of using violence to stop it. In particular, officers in coercive institutions outside of military command are likely to perceive the costs of the coup succeeding to be higher than those in the regular military, while both those in counterweights and the regular military may perceive the costs of violence to be lower.

It is reasonable to wonder why the preferences of military and security forces might differ at all. After all, both are agents of the state. Over time, however, security forces outside the military can develop their own organizational interests distinct from those of the armed forces. Leaders may deliberately foster diverging interests by staffing or paying security forces differently than the military. Since personnel changes are easier to make in new forces than in the army, where existing positions are already filled, filling counterweights with co-ethnics or party loyalists is common.[48] As a result, "loyalist paramilitary officers stand or fall with the dictator."[49] Counterbalancing forces are also frequently paid at higher rates than the regular army, which fosters hostility between the forces. The Jatiyo Rakkhi Bahini in Bangladesh, for example, received "preferential budgetary allocations," which deepened its rivalry with the military.[50] Rulers can also facilitate diverging interests by compensating different forces for different tasks—paying the army to defend the capital from rival states, for instance, and the police to monitor the army.[51] These efforts encourage officers in counterbalancing forces to view their interests as distinct from those of the military.

In part because different security forces develop distinct institutional interests, coup plotters from within the military cannot credibly commit to refrain from dissolving other security forces or incorporating them into the military if the coup succeeds. Even where police and paramilitary forces do not oppose the coup, their continued presence outside the military chain of command can be perceived as an affront to the military's core interest in preserving a monopoly on the state's use of force.[52] Donald Horowitz explains, "What is attractive about such units to political leaders is exactly what is provocative about them to military forces": in a number of cases, "the creation of separate units, outside the chain of command, infuriated regular military officers."[53] Military coups thus frequently result in the subordination of other security forces to the military chain of command. This was the case following the 1975 coup in Argentina, for instance, after which the military assumed command of the gendarmerie, as well as after the 1944 coup in Ecuador. This raises perceptions about the costs associated with the coup succeeding, and creates powerful incentives for officers in counterbalancing forces to actively defend the regime—incentives regular military officers do not have. As Bruce Farcau describes, "The great fear of the police is that their command will be taken over by a military officer."[54]

Finally, where the coup pits military coup plotters against presidential guards or other independent security forces charged with defending the regime, all parties may perceive that the costs of using violence are lower, and take less care to avoid it. Firing on members of an independent presidential guard or the president's personal militia, for instance, does not threaten to undermine military cohesion nor require officers to overcome normative prohibitions on violence against fellow military officers with whom they have worked, trained, and lived. More broadly, violence is likely to be seen as less detrimental in an already divided and politicized security sector. Thus, where rulers counterbalance, officers in both military and security forces who oppose the coup may be less hesitant to use force to stop it.

Where counterweights choose to resist, they can do so by physically interposing themselves between coup plotters and their targets or launching counterattacks to recover targets captured by coup forces. Theoretically, a large counterbalancing force may be able to defeat an attack by the military. For instance, in the 1982 Kenyan coup attempt against Daniel Arap Moi, it was the paramilitary General Services Unit that led a counterassault on rebelling forces, resulting in the deaths of some 145 people.[55] Similarly, in the 1990 coup in Afghanistan, military police and secret police units defended then-president Mohammed

Najibullah's regime, dragging the fighting out for days.[56] But because the targets are few in number and typically well concentrated, the presence of even a small counterbalancing force can raise the costs of a coup simply by being in the way. For instance, in Fiji, the Tactical Response Unit (TRU), which was established in 2003 to "counter the influence of the military," remained small in size compared to the army.[57] While the TRU might not have been able to beat the army in direct combat, the idea was that "it would have made the process difficult, and potentially caused bloodshed," which would raise the costs of a coup.[58] In addition to confronting coup forces, counterweights can also resist a coup by using radio or television broadcasts to offer a counternarrative to that being provided by coup plotters, undermining their efforts to convince other officers that the coup has already succeeded and encouraging further resistance.

Take the case of the 2002 coup in Venezuela, which attempted to unseat President Hugo Chávez. The coup attempt occurred after months of tension and protest over the management of Venezuela's national oil company. On April 11, Chávez dismissed the company's executives, sparking demonstrations in which pro- and anti-regime protestors clashed violently in front of the Miraflores Presidential Palace in Caracas. Chávez ordered the military to step in, but it refused, instead placing him under arrest and announcing his resignation. Officers organizing the coup appointed Pedro Carmona, president of the national business federation, to lead a transitional government. Carmona and his advisers moved into Miraflores the same day. Shortly thereafter members of Chávez's presidential guard declared their continued loyalty to Chávez and retook the palace, arresting Carmona's government. With the coup government unseated, Chávez was able to successfully reassert his authority, and the officers detaining him granted his release. He was back in power less than three days after the attempted coup began.[59]

Even small presidential guards or lightly armed civilian militia might be able to impede the execution of a coup by leading violent protests or launching counterattacks that force coup leaders to engage in protracted battles. Farcau argues: "While a militia is generally less well armed than the professional military, the small arms it possesses and its rudimentary military organization and training pose the problem of a massive guerrilla army which the military might have to suppress. This complicates the problem of simply taking over and certainly weighs heavily in the minds of any officers considering the possibility of mounting a coup."[60] For instance, in Madagascar, members of President Philibert Tsiranana's bodyguard, who had been dismissed after his ouster in 1972, assassinated one of his successors, instigating fighting that nearly dragged the country into a civil war.[61]

This discussion suggests the following hypothesis about counterbalancing and coup outcomes:

Hypothesis 1: Coups are more likely to succeed against regimes that do not counterbalance than coups against those that do.

It also generates two different hypotheses about *how* counterbalancing impedes successful coups—about the causal logic linking counterbalancing to coup failure:

Hypothesis 1a (coordination): Counterbalancing decreases the probability a coup will succeed by impeding coordination between coup plotters.
Hypothesis 1b (resistance): Counterbalancing decreases the probability a coup will succeed by creating incentives to resist to the coup.

Alternative Arguments: Coup Outcomes

These hypotheses are not trivial ones. Where counterweights are present, coup plotters might anticipate the obstacles they create to successful coups, and compensate by putting more effort into pre-coup planning. If that were the case, we would see no association between the presence of counterweights and the success rate of coups. Albrecht and Eibl, for instance, argue that for combat officers that stage coups, counterbalancing should have no effect on the outcome of the attempt. In particular, they argue, combat officer coups will "have to overcome the threat of resistance from the armed forces irrespective of the presence of unified or fragmented military command structures. Whether the presidential palace is guarded by a special force or regular troops, their typically substantial resistance is likely going to be taken into account."[62] It is also plausible that even where officers in counterbalancing forces see their interests as distinct from those of the regular military, the desire to remain on the winning side of the coup overrides their preferences about which side wins. For example, Farcau describes how, in interviewing Ecuadoran police officers, one commented that "during a coup, he was very much opposed to the military, but he not only did not defend the building he was guarding, but smiled politely as he held the door open for the soldiers as they came storming in, not wishing to commit suicide."[63] If these alternative arguments are correct, we would expect to see no association between the use of counterbalancing and the outcomes of coup attempts.[64]

It could also be that while counterbalancing is associated with coup failure, this association is driven by some other factor—and that counterbalancing itself has no independent effect on the likelihood a coup succeeds. One plausible candidate is the strength of the military: it may be that counterbalancing does not itself affect the outcome of coup attempts, but instead simply reflects the preexisting strength of the military. According to this logic, where the military has leverage over civilian authorities, it may be able to prevent rulers from counterbalancing. The military's strength compared to civilian elites may also increase the odds that any coup attempts it stages will succeed. There are reasons to be skeptical of this argument, however. What we know about the dynamics of coup attempts suggests that the relative strength or weakness of the military as an institution is unlikely to shape the outcome.[65] While perceptions about the government's legitimacy or the popularity of the military might influence the decision to stage a coup, once the attempt is underway, whether it succeeds or fails depends more on the actions of other officers. Furthermore, since military officers prioritize acting in concert with one other, a smaller, more unified military may actually be more effective than a larger but less cohesive one at successfully seizing power.

If military strength accounts for the relationship between counterbalancing and coup failure, we would expect to see measures of military strength—such as the resources and manpower it controls or the extent of policymaking power that it has—negatively associated with the use of counterweights and positively associated with successful coup outcomes. Yet, as I document in chapter 2, stronger militaries are no more likely to succeed in their efforts to seize power than those that are weak. The correlations between indicators of military strength and the use of counterweights are also weak and inconsistent. This suggests that it is unlikely that military strength can account for the association between counterbalancing and coup failure.

How Counterbalancing Affects Coup Attempts

If counterbalancing makes coup attempts less likely to succeed, does it also deter soldiers from staging them in the first place? In order to answer this question, we need to understand the causes of coup attempts. Theories about the causes of coups may be categorized into three approaches: those that emphasize *norms* against intervention, those that emphasize *opportunities* for intervention, and those that emphasize the military's disposition or *motives* to intervene.[66] Norms against intervention can explain why the most powerful militaries in the world, such as those in the United States or the United Kingdom, are also the least inclined to intervene in politics, at least in the form of a coup d'état. In *The Soldier and the State*, Samuel Huntington argues that a professional ethos shared by the military's officer corps is what prevents military grievances from translating into coups.[67] Others point to a "norm of civilian control" or a "cult of obedience" found in long-standing, consolidated democracies.[68] Outside of consolidated democracies, norms against intervention may vary considerably. For example, militaries in countries with a prior history of coups, or that are situated in coup-prone regions, may face fewer normative prohibitions against coups than those in other countries.[69] In these cases, rulers turn to what Huntington called strategies of "subjective" control—those that subordinate the military to a particular ruler, political party, or segment of the population, rather than "objective" civilian control—that aim to restrict opportunities for intervention, or resolve sources of tension between military and civilian leaders that might motivate coup attempts.

Theories that emphasize opportunities for intervention describe both long-standing, structural features of governments and societies that leave states more vulnerable to coups as well as more short-term factors that increase civilian dependence on the military, such as an economic crisis or a war.[70] The efforts rulers undertake to establish barriers to seizing power, such as deploying security forces away from centers of political power and restricting access to arms, can also affect the military's ability or opportunity to intervene. Theories that focus on motive primarily emphasize the corporate interests of the military as an institution. Such interests may include preserving the unity of the armed forces, the authority of officers over enlisted men, the autonomy of rank and seniority systems from political interference, the monopoly of armed force by the traditional military services, historic levels of funding, good relations with the civilian population, and the military's reputation as a competent fighting force.[71] These approaches need not be seen as alternative or competing explanations. Indeed, taken in isolation, motives are too ubiquitous to explain where coups will occur; opportunity theories have difficulty explaining why challenges to the regime are likely to take the form of a military coup rather than protest or insurgency.

In what follows I explain how counterbalance affects both opportunities for a coup and soldiers' motives for intervention. I begin with the intuition that counterbalancing, like other strategies of coup prevention, has multiple, potentially-contradictory effects on the incentives of soldiers to intervene in politics. Table 1.2 summarizes four distinct mechanisms that link counterbalancing to the incidence of coup attempts. Three suggest that counterbalancing will result in fewer coup attempts, while the fourth suggests it will result in more.

TABLE 1.2 Causal mechanisms linking counterbalancing to the incidence of coup attempts

LOGIC	CAUSAL MECHANISM		OUTCOME
Opportunity	Anticipation of coup failure	→	Fewer coup attempts
Opportunity	Successful repression of political opposition	→	Fewer coup attempts
Motive	Removal of military from internal security duties	→	Fewer coup attempts
Motive	Perceived decline in military status	→	More coup attempts

Causal Mechanisms: Opportunity

There are a number of ways in which counterbalancing might restrict opportunities to stage coup attempts. As I describe above, counterbalancing might impede recruitment prior to a coup attempt because it makes face-to-face meetings between senior officers more difficult, or because it improves monitoring across the ranks. This increases the risk that any coup that is staged will fail, and might dissuade some coup plotters going forward. As Farcau describes it, "The more units which are necessary to recruit to mount a successful coup, the more difficult such a coup will be to organize."[72] Even where coup plotters believe they will eventually be victorious, the prospect that counterweights will defend the incumbent regime raises the risk that they will need to injure or kill other soldiers, increasing the costs associated with the coup.

Counterbalancing may also decrease the risk of a coup through more indirect channels. Counterweights are frequently tasked with the repression of domestic political opponents. While the majority of coup attempts originate within the armed forces, some efforts are instigated by nonmilitary elites, who recruit military officers to intervene in politics to help them undercut rivals.[73] Where rulers use counterweights to repress political opponents, it may thus limit the capacity of civilian elites to stage coups. The Tonton Macoutes in Haiti are an example of counterweights fulfilling this dual function. As Robert Fatton notes, they "not only became a counterweight to the armed forces and neutralized the traditional capacity of the military to wage a coup d'état, but they also represented a significant popular mass support for [François] Duvalier's regime," which could be mobilized to intimidate and harass regime opponents.[74] Similarly, in Togo, Gnassingbé Eyadéma employed three different intelligence networks to monitor political opposition.[75]

Causal Mechanisms: Motive

The overall effects of counterbalancing on the military's motive or disposition to intervene are more ambiguous. In some circumstances, where counterweights take over internal security duties that were a source of conflict between military and civilian leaders, their presence might alleviate grievances that would otherwise result in a coup attempt. The military may resist demands to repress political opponents or rebels if doing so will harm its reputation and standing.[76] Tasking other security forces with repression may thus help preserve the military's status and reduce incentives to stage a coup. In Malawi, for instance, President Hastings Banda was able to use Special Branch and Mobile Unit paramilitary forces for the "more onerous political duties" that would have sullied the army's popularity.⁷⁷ Similarly, in Russia in the 1990s, "The army objected to being used for internal security missions, so the other so-called power ministries had to be beefed up."⁷⁸ More generally, using counterweights to combat internal security threats might depoliticize the military and give it fewer motives for intervention.⁷⁹ States in which the military controls internal security forces have a more difficult time preventing military intervention in politics. Take the case of the Central Reserve Police Force in India. In establishing the security force, a central though largely unstated aim "was to relieve the army of having to carry out prolonged aid to the civil deployments on riot control, and the possibility that might draw the force into a larger political role."⁸⁰

In other cases, however, counterbalancing may *provoke* new coup attempts as soldiers respond to a perceived decline in their status. There are numerous examples in which counterbalancing backfired in this way. In Honduras in 1963, President Villeda Morales tasked his Civil Guard with "supervising" the conduct of an election pitting the Liberal Party successor he favored over the Nationalist Party candidate backed by the army. The military staged a coup "immediately after the Liberal Party's presidential candidate publicly proclaimed his preference for the Civil Guards."⁸¹ Likewise, the 1971 coup in Bolivia was motivated, in part, by resentment over counterbalancing. Of particular concern to the military was the regime's proposal to create "two powerful battalions of Military Police, of 1,000 men each, which would be under direct presidential command, similar to a kind of praetorian guard which the late President [René] Barrientos had instituted."⁸²

Counterbalancing conflicts with a central institutional interest of the military: a monopoly on the regime's use of force. In particular, placing security forces outside of the military chain of command creates a situation that "constitutes a grave breach of expectations regarding civil-military relations." From the military's perspective, Nordlinger describes, "the creation of functional rivals is almost as galling and threatening as civilian manipulation and penetration"—themselves common causes of coups.⁸³ Discussing motives for the 1964 coup in Bolivia, an army commander explained that the regime had created a new militia, provoking fears that it "wanted to put an end to the army."⁸⁴ It is for these reasons that Farcau calls the creation of counterweights "a very dangerous" strategy, going so far as to assert that "in every instance where a government has attempted the creation of such a rival armed force in the face of an established one, the military has eventually perceived the threat . . . and overthrown the regime before the militia could take the field."⁸⁵ Writing about coups in Sub-Saharan Africa, Decalo similarly notes, "Creating competitive armed structures can set loose destabilizing forces. The existence of better-equipped and (usually) better paid praetorian guards has triggered inter-arm jealousies that became prime motivations for coups."⁸⁶

In other words, counterbalancing can be expected to create two countervailing effects on the incidence of coup attempts. As a consequence, even though counterbalancing reduces the likelihood a coup will succeed, it may not necessarily result in any fewer coup attempts. I argue that the grievances generated by counterbalancing are likely to be sharpest in the immediate aftermath of their creation. As Farcau observes, "The problem with this system [of counterbalancing] is that it cannot be created overnight."[87] Similarly, Geddes, Wright, and Frantz observe, "It takes resources and time to build a dependable internal security force because of the need for trained and committed personnel to staff it."[88] Whether or not their perceptions are accurate, potential coup plotters may wager that new counterweights will lack confidence in their ability to confront the military directly while they are getting up and running. The institutional interests of new forces are also likely to be less firmly established—a fact that may lead potential coup plotters to assume that new counterweights have fewer incentives to engage in a protracted fight. This discussion leads to two hypotheses about counterbalancing and the incidence of coup attempts:

> Hypothesis 2: Counterbalancing does not decrease the likelihood of coup attempts.
> Hypothesis 3: The creation of a new counterweight increases the risk of a coup attempt.

I have argued that because counterbalancing generates new grievances within the military, it is unlikely to decrease the incidence of coup attempts that rulers face, even as it creates obstacles to their execution. If this argument is correct, it can help explain why counterbalancing is not a ubiquitous response to the threat of a coup. Theories that emphasize the potential deterrent effect of counterbalancing, without considering other mechanisms linking it to coup attempts, tend to predict that it will be more widespread than it is. Aaron Belkin, for instance, argues that "the possibility of a coup should almost always prompt regimes to pursue counterbalancing strategies."[89] Similarly, Steven David contends, "it requires no great feat of political evolution or development to divide" the state's coercive power.[90] Other scholars suggest that counterbalancing may not provoke grievances. Geddes, Wright, and Frantz, for instance, view counterbalancing as a less risky prospect than other forms of coup-proofing, such as ethnic stacking; they argue that "the implications of creating a new presidential guard or other paramilitary force . . . may be less initially obvious to regular officers" than the implications of other coup-proofing strategies.[91] If this argument is correct, we would expect no association between the creation of a new counterweight and the incidence of coup attempts.

Alternative Arguments: Coup Attempts

I have identified in this chapter potential causal mechanisms that link counterbalancing to the incidence of coup attempts. These mechanisms suggest that counterbalancing may not deter coup attempts, even as it makes their execution more difficult, and that the creation of a new counterweight may increase the risk of a coup. However, rather than provoking coup attempts, the creation of a new counterweight may simply indicate that a ruler perceives the risk of a coup to be high. Indeed, the idea that rulers create counterweights when the risk of a coup is high is an intuitive one. If this argument is correct, then the creation of a new counterweight itself may have no effect on the likelihood of a coup attempt, even if a positive association between them is found. Yet the available evidence suggests that the relationship between coup risk and counterweight creation is not this simple. As I discuss in more depth in chapter 4, recent research on coup risk suggests that rulers become *less* likely to counterbalance as the risk of a coup increases, for precisely the reasons I outline above: rulers fear that their efforts will provoke military intervention. Indeed, some scholars suggest that counterweight creation is so dangerous that it might be advisable only during brief windows of opportunity in which the military itself is being remade from scratch—following violent struggles for national independence, in the midst of successful revolutions, or during other situations in which the traditional military has been incapacitated or destroyed and the risk of a coup is thus low.[92]

Another possibility is that military weakness can explain both counterbalancing and coup attempts. This argument is the inverse of the one made about military strength and coup outcomes, which suggested that strong militaries can deter rulers from creating counterweights and successfully carry out coup attempts. Some scholars contend that it is not strong militaries that stage coups, but weak and divided ones.[93] As with coup outcomes, however, explanations for coup attempts grounded in military strength or weakness compared to civilian authorities leave much to be desired. As Samuel Finer describes, the military has a number of advantages over civilian authorities in terms of its organization, symbolic status as defender of the nation, and access to arms, yet military regimes remain relatively rare.[94] Civilian regimes perceived as illegitimate are more likely to experience coup attempts, no matter the characteristics of the military itself. As Aaron Belkin and Evan Schofer conclude in their review of the causes of coups, the theoretical links between military strength and coup attempts are "not compelling."[95]

The empirical evidence in support of this view is also weak. If military weakness explains both the creation of new counterweights and the incidence of coup attempts, we would expect to see negative associations between indicators of military strength, counterbalancing, and coup attempts. Yet it does not appear to be the case that weaker militaries stage more coup attempts or that stronger militaries are less likely than weaker ones to be counterbalanced. As chapter 4 shows, the correlations between indicators of military strength, coup attempts, and counterweight creation are weak to nonexistent. These findings suggest that it is unlikely that military weakness drives both the creation of counterweights and the incidence of coup attempts.

Implications for the Escalation of Coups to Civil War

The arguments made here have important implications for the violence associated with a coup attempt, and in particular, for the risk that a coup attempt escalates to civil war. Civil wars are commonly understood as a form of large-scale violence that pits an incumbent regime against one or more armed challengers.[96] Many civil wars originate in armed rebellion, in which regime opponents must overcome a series of organizational and logical hurdles in order to build armed groups capable of challenging the state. Others, however, escalate from coups and other splits in the armed forces.[97] Despite the potential for coups to escalate to civil wars, scholars of civil-military relations have focused primarily on the causes and outcomes of coup attempts rather than the violence associated with them. This is the case even though many early theorists of coups identified their connections to other forms of political violence. Writing in 1962, for instance, Donald Goodspeed notes: "Lenin's seizure of power was followed by more than three years of civil conflict and by Stalin's proscriptions. The Italian peninsula was fought over mile by mile between 1943 and 1945. Political murder, far from being a final solution, often appears to touch off a chain reaction of violence that continues until it exhausts itself."[98] Most scholars emphasize instead the efforts soldiers undertake to prevent coups from escalating to civil war. Geddes, for instance, argues that "the worst threat to the military as an institution is civil war in which one part of the armed forces fights another."[99] In these accounts, violence is portrayed primarily as a miscalculation or an unfortunate accident.

Meanwhile, theories about the causes of civil wars focus almost exclusively on the conditions that favor insurgency, a form of civil war in which small, lightly armed bands of rebels challenge the state from mostly rural bases. For instance, James Fearon and David Laitin focus on the structural conditions that facilitate the formation of rebel organizations without government interference, including state weakness and rough terrain.[100] Paul Collier and Anke Hoeffler similarly focus on factors such as natural resources that make rebellion feasible.[101] In these studies, and in much of the vast literature that followed them, civil war is treated as synonymous with insurgency. They do not spell out how conflict between military and civilian leaders might escalate. One exception is Fearon's article on civil war duration, which acknowledges these different types of civil wars and explicitly aims to develop a theoretical account that explains both coups and insurgencies as resulting from the same commitment problem.[102] Efforts to disaggregate different forms of civil war have largely emphasized that ethnic wars may have different causal pathways than other types of civil wars.[103] However, as Nicholas Sambanis notes, "It is accepted practice in the literature to pool events of civil war without exploring whether, in fact, they all result from the same causal process."[104] As a result, we know little about the conditions under which coups escalate to civil war.

More recently, research on coup-proofing suggests that some strategies leaders employ to deter military intervention in politics may increase the risk of insurgency or mass protests that are not connected to coup attempts. Sheena Greitens finds that coup-proofing strategies, including counterbalancing the military with other security forces, weaken leaders' ability to defend against popular unrest in authoritarian regimes.[105] Philip Roessler argues that a strategy of ethnic exclusion, in which leaders exclude their rivals from positions of political power, increases the risk that the excluded parties will turn to insurgency to seize power over the state.[106] Almost uniquely among work on the causes of civil war, this argument connects strategies of coup prevention to insurgency, but it does not explain the process by which a coup, once staged, might escalate into civil war.

In developing and testing arguments about how coups escalate to civil war, it is important to be clear about the distinctions between these different forms of political violence. Recall that coups involve illegal, overt efforts by the military or other elites within the state apparatus to seize executive power. Civil wars can be defined as "armed combat taking place within the boundaries of a recognized sovereign entity between parties subject to a common authority at the outset of the hostilities."[107] There are three key distinctions. First, while the goal of a coup is presumed to be seizing power, the goals and motivations of combatants in civil wars may be more varied. Second, while coups are staged by elites within the state apparatus, the combatants in a civil war need only be subject to a common authority at the outset of the war. In the context of coups that escalate to civil war, coup plotters who are part of the state apparatus at the start of the coup might recruit and arm civilian supporters, or defect from the state apparatus themselves. Third, while coup attempts do not need to include bloodshed, the "armed combat" inherent in civil war implies violence of some magnitude. A challenge to the regime that begins as a coup attempt can thus be understood to escalate into a civil war where it broadens from an intra-regime conflict to include nonstate actors and results in a substantial amount of violence.[108]

I argue that there are at least two mechanisms through which counterbalancing can facilitate the escalation of a coup to civil war. First, in order to escalate to civil war, resistance to the coup from some segment of the state's security forces is necessary. For the reasons noted above, the presence of counterweights makes armed resistance to a coup attempt more likely. Counterbalancing also increases the likelihood that such resistance will involve armed combat that is sustained enough to generate fatalities sufficient to meet common numerical thresholds for civil war. Because coup-installed regimes cannot credibly commit to refrain from disbanding counterweights or impinging on their autonomy, officers in these forces have incentives not only to resist the coup attempt, but to "fight to the death," increasing the likelihood of a substantial number of combat fatalities.

Second, where coup attempts succeed in ousting rulers from power, counterbalancing can help them to overcome organizational challenges in mounting a rebellion against the coup-installed regime. In most civil wars, potential rebels have a long list of tasks to accomplish before they can begin to challenge the state. As Jeremy Weinstein summarizes, "potential rebels must raise capital to finance the logistics of a military campaign, recruit foot soldiers willing to risk their lives in battle against a stronger government force, and generate support from civilians who can supply food, information about the location and strategies of government forces, and valuable labor in support of the movement."[109] In comparison, rebel forces in civil wars that escalate from coups do not face the same challenges. Instead, the core of rebel forces comes from those who have defected from state security forces. This means that rebels are usually already within striking distance of major centers of political power. Their soldiers are already trained and equipped. Furthermore, as Theodore McLauchlin points out, they have also "presumably accepted some risk that they will actually have to fight."[110] In other words, many of the logistical and organizational challenges that typically face rebel groups are not present in the case of civil wars that originate in coup attempts. For an ousted leader determined to hold on to power, counterbalancing forces can serve as a "ready-made" rebel army available to challenge a coup-installed regime. This discussion suggests the following hypothesis:

> Hypothesis 4: Coup attempts are more likely to escalate to civil war when they are staged against regimes that counterbalance than when they are staged against regimes that do not.

Testing the Arguments

The above discussion produced a series of hypotheses about the conditions under which soldiers stage coups, the outcomes of coup attempts, and the risk that coups will escalate to civil war. I argue that creating coercive institutions outside of military command does not reduce the incidence of coup attempts leaders face; in fact, efforts to create counterweights risk *provoking* coups. This risk is highest in the immediate aftermath of their creation, when grievances are freshest and military coup plotters may judge counterweights too weak to effectively stop the coup. Once established, however, counterbalancing should reduce the likelihood coup attempts will succeed. This could be for two different reasons. First, it might be that counterbalancing impedes recruitment prior to the coup, or the ability of coup plotters to seize their targets while the attempt is under way, which prevents coup plotters from making the coup's success appear inevitable. Second, it might be that, for officers in security forces outside of military control, the costs of a coup succeeding appear higher, while the costs of using violence to stop it appear lower, creating incentives for them to resist. If this is the case, counterbalancing should also increase the risk that coup attempts will escalate to civil war.

To evaluate these hypotheses, I use a nested analysis, which combines the statistical analysis of a large sample of coup attempts (chapters 2 and 4) with in-depth investigation of several cases contained within the larger sample (chapters 3, 5, and 6).[111] The goal of the statistical analysis, in chapters 2 and 4, is to identify whether the incidence and outcomes of coup attempts vary with the use of counterweights. Chapter 2 tests whether coup attempts against regimes that counterbalance are less likely to succeed than those against regimes that do not (hypothesis 1), while chapter 4 evaluates whether counterbalancing is associated with changes to the risk that coup attempts will be staged (hypotheses 2 and 3). The advantage of the approach in these chapters lies in being able to simultaneously estimate and control for the effects of other potential explanations for coup attempts and outcomes, estimate the magnitude of the effect that counterbalancing has, and evaluate the generalizability the findings. The statistical analysis makes use of new data on state security forces in 110 states between 1960 and 2010, which allows me to track the use of counterweights with more precision than was possible with previous datasets; in particular, it allows me to identify security forces that are independent from military command and deployed in the capital—two central characteristics of security forces capable of counterbalancing the military. The case studies, in contrast, provide insight into the causal mechanisms at work and help refine the theoretical arguments developed here; they draw upon a broad array of archival sources, newspaper reporting, memoirs of coup participants and rulers, and academic accounts of civil-military relations in each state.

Of course, selecting a small number of cases for study involves important trade-offs, and I take different approaches in different chapters. In chapter 3, which tests hypotheses 1a and 1b, about the causal mechanisms through which counterbalancing prevents successful coups, my approach is based on a "most likely" research design, in which the cases selected are ones in which the hypothesized causal mechanisms are deemed most likely to be found.[112] It is important to note that not all of the causal mechanisms thought to impede coordination or encourage resistance described here can be confirmed or disconfirmed in the case studies examined in chapter 3. In particular, recruitment prior to the coup is too difficult to observe in individual cases of coup attempts: it occurs in secret and is restricted as much as possible so as to avoid detection before the coup plot gets off the ground. Furthermore, the universe of potential coup plots is likely unknowable; coup plots are both too common and too poorly documented to identify systematically. Examining coup attempts that have progressed past the planning stage for evidence of failures to recruit prior to the coup would also likely bias the study toward finding no effect of coordination—after all, coup attempts are those plots that have gone forward, and thus represent cases in which coup plotters deemed the extent of recruitment sufficient to risk the attempt. In testing hypotheses 1a and 1b, I thus focus in chapter 3 on causal mechanisms that operate *during* the coup attempt.

In this chapter, I evaluate evidence in support of each potential mechanism linking counterbalancing to coup outcomes in sixteen coup attempts: twelve in which the coup failed, as predicted, and four in which the coup succeeded, despite the use of counterbalancing. The cases were chosen to ensure regional and temporal variation representative of the larger universe of cases, as well as variation in the identity of coup plotters, but without prior knowledge of which, if either, of the proposed causal logics was at work. In cases that fit the patterns anticipated by the theory well—cases in which coup attempts against rulers that counterbalanced their militaries failed—I report which of the observable implications of each mechanism are present. Three cases are presented in particular detail: the 1982 coup in Kenya, the 1971 coup in Morocco, and the 1989 coup in Panama; others are summarized more briefly in the main text or the appendix. I use atypical or deviant cases, the 1975 coups in Bangladesh and Peru, which are not well predicted by the theory, to suggest potential refinements and scope conditions for the argument.

The book then turns to the question of how counterbalancing affects the incidence of coup attempts. While the statistical analysis in chapter 4 documents that the risk of a coup attempt increases immediately following a coup attempt, it cannot shed light on the causal mechanism at work or explain why some rulers succeed in creating new counterweights, while others do not. In chapter 5, I compare Kwame Nkrumah's experience transforming the President's Own Guard Regiment from a ceremonial unit within the army to a formidable independent counterweight—which provoked the 1966 coup attempt that ousted him from power—to three other cases of counterweight creation: those undertaken by Modibo Keita in Mali, which similarly failed, and those undertaken by Siaka Stevens in Sierra Leone and Fidel Castro in Cuba, which succeeded. My approach in this chapter is to compare cases with different values on the dependent variable, whether or not there was a coup attempt, but similar values on as many independent variables as possible, including wealth, economic performance, regime type, and political instability. This "most similar" case selection strategy has the advantage of allowing me to hold constant several of the structural factors thought to cause coup attempts, and focus on the strategic choices available to rulers establishing counterweights.[113] These cases are intended as "heuristic" or hypothesis-generating case studies in which the aim is to both explain the differing experiences Nkrumah, Stevens, Keita, and Castro had in establishing counterweights, and to inductively develop new hypotheses about the conditions under which establishing new counterweights is feasible for leaders. The comparison highlights the role of other coup-proofing strategies that rulers chose to adopt alongside counterbalancing, as well as the type of counterweights established, as important determinants of whether the creation of a new counterweight will provoke a coup attempt.

Finally, chapter 6 examines whether coup attempts are more likely to escalate to civil war when they are staged against regimes that counterbalance than when they are staged against regimes that do not (hypothesis 4). It uses qualitative evidence from three coups to probe the plausibility of the proposed causal mechanisms. I first leverage over time variation within a single country. Two coup attempts in the Dominican Republic, in 1963 and 1965, occurred in similar political, cultural, and economic contexts, but resulted in different levels of violence: the 1963 coup was bloodless, while the 1965 coup escalated to a civil war that killed over two thousand people. This comparison highlights the role of counterbalancing in explaining the differing consequences of the coups. I then compare the 1965 Dominican coup to the 1962 coup in Yemen—a comparison that illustrates how very different types of counterweights, used in very different circumstances, similarly facilitated the escalation of coups to civil war.

2

COUNTERBALANCING AND COUP FAILURE

In the aftermath of Iraq's defeat in the Gulf War, it appeared to be only a matter of time until Iraqi president Saddam Hussein would be ousted from power by his own military. In May 1991, the George H. W. Bush administration authorized covert action against Saddam. As Judith Miller describes, "Both the Bush Administration and its Arab coalition allies continue[d] to hope for a palace coup in which, as one official said, 'a nice Sunni general will finally get fed up and remove Saddam.'"[1] Saddam's generals tried their best: coup attempts occurred in September and December of that year. But neither succeeded in toppling his regime.[2] What explains why some coup attempts succeed and others fail? The previous chapter argued that the answer lies, in part, in how rulers organize and use their coercive institutions. In particular, those rulers who counterbalance the military with security forces independent from military control are better positioned to defeat coup attempts that threaten to remove them from power.

This chapter tests the hypothesis that coups are more likely to fail where rulers counterbalance than where they do not by analyzing patterns in the outcomes of coup attempts between 1960 and 2010. In doing so, it draws upon a new cross-national time-series dataset of state security forces, as well as new data on the identity of coup plotters in each coup attempt during this same period.[3] After describing the data, the chapter presents some descriptive trends that illustrate variation in the use of counterweights. While counterbalancing is widespread, it is not a ubiquitous response to the risk of coups. The subsequent statistical analysis shows that counterbalancing is associated with coup failure—a finding that is robust to a number of different estimation methods and the inclusion of potential confounders. The association between counterbalancing and coup failure also does not appear to be driven by another factor, like the strength of the military. The analysis thus provides support for the book's first hypothesis: coup attempts are less likely to succeed where rulers counterbalance the military with other security forces.

Measuring Counterbalancing

Testing hypotheses about whether counterbalancing works requires detailed data on how states command and deploy their coercive institutions. Existing efforts to test arguments about coup-proofing depend almost exclusively on *The Military Balance*, an annual defense review published by the International Institute for Strategic Studies (IISS) in London each year since 1959.[4] The central focus of *The Military Balance* is on regular military forces, but it also includes other security forces "whose training, organization, equipment and control suggest they may be used to support or replace regular military forces."[5] The initial aim of the review was to track the balance of power between NATO and Warsaw Pact members. Commonly used indicators of counterbalancing, which draw upon *The Military Balance*, include ratios of the total number of paramilitary to military personnel and indices that combine this ratio with the number of different military branches and paramilitary forces that a state employs.[6]

However, a number of studies have documented biases, inconsistencies, and errors in IISS data that limit its utility for testing theories about counterbalancing.[7] Coverage of most developing states is particularly poor before the 1990s, given the review's focus on Cold War alliance systems.[8] Some errors are random, but others display systematic bias. A review in 1982, for instance, concluded that the IISS's figures "nearly uniformly *under*state the capabilities of the United States and of the West, and *over*state those of the Soviet Union" and its allies.[9] These problems are more pronounced for security forces outside of the regular military. While *The Military Balance* has broadened its geographic scope and made its methodology more transparent over time, prior editions of the review are not updated when new information becomes available. For this reason, the IISS itself explicitly warns users against using its data to track changes over time within countries.[10]

In order to test theories about the ways in which counterbalancing works, I thus compiled a new dataset that tracks how states organize and use their coercive institutions. The dataset includes a number of features of state security forces, including the chain of command through which each force reports to the regime and where it is deployed—features that capture its potential to counterbalance the military. Since coding the internal structure of security forces over time is time intensive, I selected states for inclusion in the dataset through random sampling. In doing so, the aim was to ensure that differences between the sample and the broader population were unrelated to characteristics of the countries excluded. The dataset includes 110 countries, which together account for 93 percent of the world's population. The countries included are listed in table 2.1. They are similar to the broader population of states in the international system in terms of their wealth, population, regime type, and geographic distribution.[11]

For each state in the dataset, I identified security forces that were in operation at any point between 1960 and 2010. Security forces are defined as armed groups, beyond the army, navy, air force, and coast guard that comprise a traditional military, which are under the control of a recognized state in the international system. This definition emphasizes three features of state security forces. First, state security forces are armed groups: organizations with an identifiable name and leader, whose members carry weapons. This excludes agricultural and other workforces that might bear the name "army" but that are unarmed. It also excludes intelligence services whose agents are unarmed. For instance, Romania's Communist era secret police force, the Securitate, is included, but its successor, the Romanian Intelligence Service, which was deprived of arms and law enforcement powers, is not.[12]

Second, security forces are under the control of a recognized state in the international system. This distinguishes state security forces from private military companies and militia that may be pro-government, but which lack status as part of the state's official security sector.[13] It also distinguishes state security forces from those organized at a subnational level, such as local and municipal police.[14] In this context, control refers to administrative control—the ability to organize, recruit, train, equip, and fund a security force—rather than operational control, or the ability to initiate and terminate operations and specify permissible repertoires of violence. I focus on administrative control because operational control can vary extensively by region and over time within countries even for regular military forces.[15] Finally, I define state security forces as those forces established beyond the army, navy, air force, and coast guard of the traditional military. The types of security forces in the dataset include presidential guards, republican guards, interior troops, militarized police and gendarmerie forces, border guards, and state-run militia. While these security forces are used for a variety of purposes, they are distinguished from the regular military in that they do not serve as the state's primary line of defense against external threats.[16]

From this list of security forces, I identify as a "counterweight" any security force that fulfills the following criteria: (1) it is independent from military command; instead, control rests with the executive, interior ministry, or other government

TABLE 2.1 States included in the statistical analysis

Afghanistan	Fiji	New Zealand
Algeria	France	Nicaragua
Angola	Georgia	Niger
Argentina	German Democratic Republic	Nigeria
Australia	German Federal Republic	Norway
Austria	Germany	Pakistan
Azerbaijan	Ghana	Panama
Bahrain	Greece	Peru
Bangladesh	Guatemala	Philippines
Belarus	Haiti	Poland
Belgium	Honduras	Portugal
Benin	Hungary	Romania
Bolivia	Iceland	Russia (Soviet Union)
Botswana	India	Rwanda
Brazil	Indonesia	Saudi Arabia
Bulgaria	Iran	Serbia (Yugoslavia)
Burundi	Iraq	Sierra Leone
Cambodia	Israel	Singapore
Cameroon	Italy	Slovakia
Canada	Japan	South Africa
Cape Verde	Jordan	Spain
Central African Republic	Kazakhstan	Sri Lanka
Chad	Korea, Republic of	Sudan
Chile	Korea, People's Republic of	Swaziland
China	Latvia	Sweden
Colombia	Lebanon	Syria
Cote d'Ivoire	Liberia	Taiwan
Cuba	Libya	Tajikistan
Czech Republic	Malaysia	Tanzania
Czechoslovakia	Mali	Tunisia
Djibouti	Mauritius	Turkey
Dominican Republic	Mexico	Uganda
East Timor	Mongolia	Ukraine
Ecuador	Morocco	United States
Egypt	Mozambique	Venezuela
El Salvador	Myanmar (Burma)	Yemen (Yemen Arab Republic)
Ethiopia	Nepal	

body besides the ministry that controls the military; and (2) the force is deployed within sixty miles of the capital, a distance that suggests it has at least the possibility of being able to intercept a coup while it is in progress. These criteria exclude border guards, rural militia, and other forces deployed outside the capital from the indicator of counterbalancing.

Independence from the military and access to the capital are two dimensions of counterweights central to classical conceptions of counterbalancing. As Donald Horowitz emphasizes, independence from the military is a crucial component of counterbalancing: "To be completely reliable," he argues, "they must be placed outside the normal chain of command."[17] James Quinlivan similarly states that a parallel military used to counterbalance "should report to the regime leader through some chain other than the regular defense ministry." Both emphasize access as well. In particular, Quinlivan notes that the force must be "deployed so that it can engage and perhaps defeat any disloyal forces in the immediate vicinity of the critical points of the regime."[18] I do not incorporate the size of a counterweight as a dimension of counterbalancing because the dynamics of coups are such that they can be staged—and stopped—by very small numbers of troops.[19] As Morris Janowitz argues, "The size of paramilitary units does not in itself determine their actual and potential function and influence . . . it is the structure of these organizations and the functions they perform that are important."[20] In practice, rulers frequently depend on very small security forces such as presidential guards to serve as counterweights.

The variable *number of counterweights (log)* is a logged count of the number of counterweights in each state in each year. I log the number of counterweights because I do not expect that the addition of a new counterweight to an already very divided security sector would have the same effect as it would where the military has a monopoly on the use of force. I also create a dichotomous indicator for *counterbalancing*, equal to 1 where the regime employs one or more counterweights.

Data Sources and Coding Process

There are several challenges inherent in collecting data on state security forces. Rulers have strategic incentives to misrepresent features of their security forces: they may seek to inflate the size or strength of their coercive institutions so as to deter domestic or international challengers; they may also try to distance themselves from forces employing repressive tactics. The extent of coverage security forces receive in news sources and policy reports is also likely to vary over time as a function of technological changes that have made travel and the dissemination of information less costly and geopolitical changes since the end of the Cold War that have increased international attention to human rights and domestic uses of force involving state security forces. These trends could result in the artificial absence of data in earlier decades that may introduce temporal bias in the data. Furthermore, no matter the time period, more information is readily available in English and in translation for countries of strategic interest to the United States, the United Kingdom, and their allies and countries that have been involved in international conflict.

To limit gaps and reporting bias that may be present in any one type of source, I drew upon as wide an array of source material as possible as a form of triangulation. To code each security force in the dataset, over 2,200 unique sources were used. I began with academic accounts of the political history and civil-military relations in each country; historical dictionaries; Library of Congress Country Studies; encyclopedias of policing and law enforcement; and annual defense assessments, including *The Military Balance*, *Statesman's Yearbook*, and regional military balance reports. I used these sources to generate an initial list of security forces that I then searched for additional information on in national defense legislation, government websites, and other primary source documents available in translation; historical news sources as collected and translated by LexisNexis, the Federal Broadcast Information Service, World News Connection, and Keesing's World News Archive; and reports from nongovernmental organizations, such as Human Rights Watch, Amnesty International, International Crisis Group, and Small Arms Survey.

For sources available electronically, I used search terms including "security force" and "paramilitary," as well as specific types of security forces such as "presidential guard," "police," "militia," "secret police," "intelligence agency," "border guard," and variants thereof. I also searched for references to individual leaders' use of "counterweights" or efforts to "counterbalance" or "coup-proof." Country-specific academic sources and historical dictionaries frequently provided much more detailed information on the composition of state security forces in the 1960s and 1970s than annual defense reviews from the period, while reports from nongovernmental organizations filled in information missing in official government sources. All observations in the dataset were hand-coded by the author, and coding decisions are documented in standardized coding notes.[21]

Patterns in Counterbalancing

The new data compiled reveals substantial variation in the ways in which rulers organize their coercive institutions. There are important variations across states, and within them over time, in the extent of counterbalancing. Documenting this variation is an important starting point for understanding how the choices rulers make in organizing their security sectors might affect the incidence and outcome of coup attempts.

Frequency and Forms of Counterbalancing

The number of counterweights that rulers in the dataset employed ranged from zero to nine. In 65 percent of the observations in the dataset, rulers employed at least one security force with the potential to counterbalance the military. Of rulers that counterbalanced their militaries, 47 percent used one counterweight, 34 percent used two counterweights, 14 percent had three, and the remaining 5 percent had four or more counterweights. On average, rulers employed 1.2 counterweights per year between 1960 and 2010. The most common types of counterweights used were militarized police (45 percent) and Ministry of Interior troops (23 percent). Presidential guards accounted for 13 percent of the counterweights in the dataset; 11 percent of counterweights took the form of intelligence agencies or secret police. While militias were common in the dataset, most were usually deployed in rural areas away from the capital. As a result, militias were the least frequent type of counterweight used (6 percent).

Variation by Country/Region

Figure 2.1 maps the highest number of counterweights in simultaneous operation for each country in the dataset at any point between 1960 and 2010. It highlights the high rate of counterbalancing in countries such as Syria, Sudan, the Philippines, and North Korea, whose coup-proofing efforts have been well documented. But it also suggests that counterbalancing has been used extensively in less well-studied cases, including Portugal, Russia, Ukraine, India, and Yemen. In India, for instance, following the assassination of Prime Minister Indira Gandhi, a security review suggested the creation of a new, independent security force, the Special Protection Group, specifically for the protection of the prime minister. Throughout the 1960s and 1970s, security sector fragmentation was employed as a deliberate hedge against the power of the military. A central purpose of the Central Reserve Police Force, which was expanded rapidly in the 1960s, was also "to play an explicit coup-proofing role."[22] The dataset also identifies a number of countries that have maintained more consolidated security sectors. Eighteen countries have not employed any security forces independent from the regular military since 1960. These include not only countries at low risk of a coup, such as Canada and Japan, but also several in which coup attempts have occurred, including Cambodia, Colombia, Myanmar, and South Korea. Argentina, Bolivia,

FIGURE 2.1. Map of the highest number of counterweights employed, 1960–2010

Chile, and Honduras maintained only one counterweight throughout the fifty-year period covered by the dataset. On the whole, the data suggests that there is a great deal of variation in the extent to which rulers counterbalance—and that this variation is not simply a result of variation in the risk of a coup.

While there are countries that counterbalance across the globe, there are also some regional patterns of note. Figure 2.2 illustrates this variation. Countries are classified into regions based on geographic proximity and political connectedness as identified by area specialists.[23] For each region, the dashed line identifies the mean number of counterweights established by countries in the region across all years in the sample. The top of the box indicates the upper quartile of the data, while the bottom of the box indicates the lower quartile. The circles indicate outliers. Not surprisingly, counterbalancing is rare in North America and Western Europe. However, there are also relatively low rates of counterbalancing in East Asia, Southeast Asia, and Latin America. In contrast, counterbalancing is most common in Eastern Europe and the Middle East and North Africa. As figure 2.2 illustrates, a number of states in Eastern Europe are outliers, with 7, 8, or 9 counterweights in operation at one time. One example is Russia. In the early 1990s, after the collapse of the Soviet Union and end of the Cold War, Russia extensively reorganized its security sector. A number of new ministries, directorates, and services controlling troops were established.[24] Over the course of the decade, the number of different government bodies outside of the military supervising troops fluctuated between six and nine.[25] Of these moves, arguably the most important

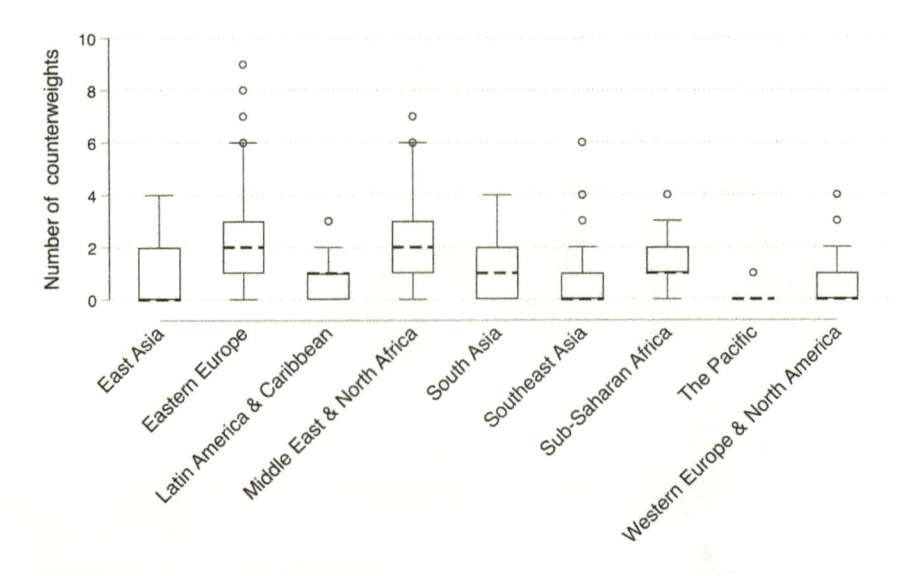

FIGURE 2.2. Counterbalancing by region

was the shift of troops responsible for the protection of top government officials from the KGB directly to presidential control. The changes were, in part, a response to increasing domestic unrest and the conflict in Chechnya. Interviewing Russian military officers, however, Anatol Lieven found that many "believe[d], with good evidence, that they also reflected a strategy of 'divide and rule' on Yeltsin's part, designed to set the different security forces against each other and reduce the possibility of any threat to his rule from this quarter."[26]

Variation over Time

The data also show that states have increasingly fragmented their security sectors over time, even as the risk of a coup declined (see figure 2.3). In the figure, the bars show the number of coup attempts and successful coups in each year, while the dashed line shows the average number of counterweights employed per country. The data on coups comes from the Center for Systemic Peace (CSP).[27] In this dataset, a coup d'état is defined as a forceful seizure of executive power by a faction within the country's ruling or political elites. In order to be successful, the new executive must exercise effective authority for at least one month. As figure 2.3 shows, the average number of counterweights per country increased from around 0.9 in 1960 to 1.3 in 2010. The use of counterweights increased

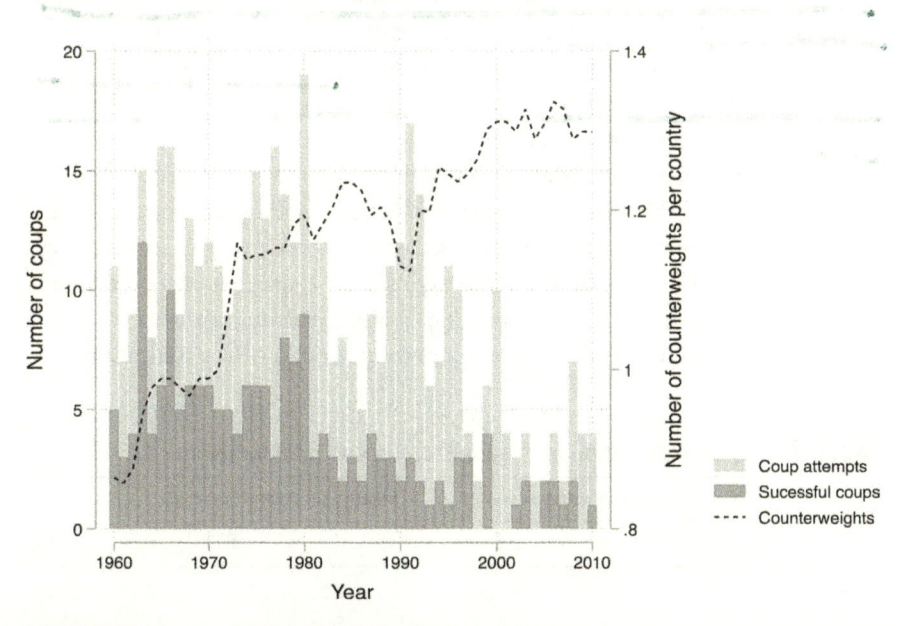

FIGURE 2.3. Coups and counterbalancing over time

Note: Data on coups comes from the Center for Systemic Peace. Successful coups are those in which the new executive has exercised authority for at least one month.

particularly rapidly in the 1960s and 1970s. This shift was driven in large part by decolonization in Africa and Asia, where rulers in newly independent states quickly confronted the problem of how to prevent domestic challenges to their rule. A common way in which these rulers responded was by establishing new coercive institutions as counterweights.[28] Yet the relationship between counterbalancing and coups is not straightforward: rulers continued to counterbalance at high rate even after the risk of a coup declined starting in the early 1980s. In part, this may reflect increases in the resources states had available to invest in their coercive institutions. In the Middle East and North Africa, an influx of military assistance and rising oil rents during this period facilitated investments in counterweights.[29] The average number of counterweights per country dipped briefly at the end of the Cold War, as states in Eastern and Central Europe reorganized their security forces, and then continued to rise again through the 1990s.[30]

Description of the Dependent and Control Variables

The Dependent Variable: Coup Success

Coup success is a dichotomous indicator that is equal to 1 where coup leaders held power for at least one month. Table 2.2 presents a cross tabulation of coup outcomes broken down by the use of counterbalancing. It shows that as the number of counterweights a regime employs increases, the likelihood a coup will succeed declines. Where regimes do not counterbalance, coups succeed some 51 percent of the time. In contrast, where rulers employ at least one counterweight, coups succeed only 37 percent of the time. This difference is statistically significant in a t-test ($p < 0.05$). The likelihood of success decreases as more counterweights are employed. Where rulers use three or more counterweights, only 28 percent of coup attempts succeed—a decline of 45 percent from no counterbalancing. In what follows, I show that these patterns hold up under more complex statistical investigation.

TABLE 2.2 Cross tabulation of coup outcomes and counterbalancing

	COUNTERBALANCING		NUMBER OF COUNTERWEIGHTS				
	NO	YES	0	1	2	3+	TOTAL
Total coup attempts	86	180	86	83	68	29	266
Failed	42	113	42	52	40	21	155
Successful	44	67	44	31	28	8	111
% Attempts successful	51%	37%	51%	37%	41%	28%	42%

Controlling for Confounding Factors

I control for several additional factors likely to influence the outcome of coup attempts. Coups succeed where leaders are able to capture their targets and consolidate power by convincing other soldiers that victory is imminent. The rank of the coup leader is particularly important in signaling the likelihood of success. As Naunihal Singh argues, while all coup makers are trying to "make a fact," the resources they have for doing so vary with their position within the military hierarchy.[31] He identifies coups from the top (those carried out by generals and above) as most likely to succeed, followed by those from middle-ranking officers such as majors and colonels. I coded the rank of coup plotters from the CSP data, which identifies the leaders of each coup attempt, in conjunction with other supplemental sources.[32] I follow Singh in dividing the military into three strata that reflect "a fundamental functional division of the armed forces."[33] The variable *coup leader: general* is a dichotomous indicator equal to 1 where the coup leadership involves one or more military officers with the rank of general or above, and 0 otherwise. *Coup leader: major, colonel* indicates coups led by majors and colonels, who are in control of the fighting units of the military. Coups staged by captains, lieutenants, officer cadets, noncommissioned officers, and enlisted men, as well as coups staged from outside the military and security forces, are coded as 0 on both variables. I use the highest-ranked coup plotter publicly associated with the coup.[34]

Regime type is also likely to affect the outcome of a coup. If democratic governments are perceived as more legitimate than nondemocratic ones, coup plotters may have a harder time convincing other soldiers that the coup attempt will succeed. At the same time, however, less repressive political systems may make plotting relatively safe, and enable more consultation and coordination before the coup is under way, which would suggest that coups against democratic states may be more likely to succeed rather than less. Democratically constrained rulers may also be less likely to repress political opponents; as a result, when a coup attempt does occur, it may remain uncontested.[35] Because military regimes prioritize maintaining the unity of the armed forces, they may be more likely to resign in the face of a coup than other types of regimes. The indicators for regime types come from Barbara Geddes, Joseph Wright, and Erica Frantz.[36] They capture the de facto regime in power, rather than the de jure constraints on the executive.

Coups staged in poorer states, with weaker political institutions, may be more likely to succeed than those staged in wealthier ones.[37] Economic downturns may also spark popular dissatisfaction with the regime that increases confidence that the coup will find public support.[38] To capture these dynamics, I include controls for the annual change in GDP per capita as well as a log of GDP per capita.[39] The

TABLE 2.3 Descriptive statistics for dependent and independent variables (coup outcomes)

VARIABLE	N	MEAN	STANDARD DEVIATION	MIN	MAX
Coup success	433	0.430	0.496	0	1
Counterbalancing	5,047	0.648	0.478	0	1
Number of counterweights	5,047	1.168	1.184	0	9
Number of counterweights (log)	5,047	0.634	0.530	0	2.303
Coup leader: General	400	0.370	0.483	0	1
Coup leader: Colonel, major	400	0.295	0.457	0	1
Military regime	4,804	0.094	0.292	0	1
Democracy	5,043	0.386	0.487	0	1
GDP/capita (log)	5,041	8.285	1.184	4.889	11.637
Change in GDP/capita	5,005	0.017	0.099	−1.130	2.007
Recent successful coup	5,259	0.090	0.286	0	1
Recent revolution	4,401	0.033	0.178	0	1
Cold War	5,259	0.606	0.489	0	1

recent past may also affect soldiers' estimations of the coup's likely outcome. Recent successful coups are likely to raise expectations about the prospects of future coups. I thus include an indicator that is equal to 1 if there was a successful coup in the past three years. I also control for recent revolutions because they typically involve a reorganization and weakening of the armed forces that is thought to make coups more difficult to carry out.[40] Recent revolution is an indicator equal to 1 if in the past three years the government of a state transformed the existing social, political, or economic relationships of the state.[41] Finally, I include a control for the Cold War equal to 1 in the years 1960–1991. During this period, the United States and former colonial powers in Europe frequently intervened in coup attempts, sometimes helping them along and sometimes thwarting them.[42] Since the end of the Cold War, however, international opposition to coups may undermine the ability of coup leaders to successfully consolidate their power.[43] Table 2.3 presents summary statistics for the variables used in the analysis.

Statistical Analyses and Results

To determine whether counterbalancing is associated with coup outcomes, I use regression analysis to estimate the effect of counterbalancing while controlling for potentially confounding variables. I estimate logit models on the set of all coup attempts between 1960 and 2010. Logit models are used to estimate the probability of a binary response—in this case, whether or not the coup succeeds. I lag all of the independent variables, with the exception of those capturing the rank of coup leaders, by one year. This ensures that the annual measures of counterbalancing and control variables are not a consequence of a coup attempt that occurred earlier in the calendar year. To account for the fact that countries were randomly selected for inclusion in the counterbalancing data—and thus that there are clusters in the population of states that we do not see in the sample—standard errors are corrected for clustering at country level.[44] Table 2.4 shows the results using both the dichotomous measure of counterbalancing (models 1–3) and the logged count of the number of counterweights a regime employs (models 4–6). For each set of models, I first estimate the bivariate relationship between counterbalancing and coup success. I then estimate models that include controls for the rank of coup leader, and finally those that include the full set of control variables.

The analysis provides strong support for the hypothesis that counterbalancing is negatively associated with coup success. The estimated coefficient on counterbalancing is negative and statistically significant in all models. The likelihood a coup succeeds also decreases as the extent of divisions in the state's security sector increases. This result holds when controlling for a number of other factors likely to affect both counterbalancing and the outcomes of military coups, including the rank of coup plotters, different political and economic contexts, and the precedent set by recent coups. In this analysis, several other variables are significant predictors of whether or not a coup will succeed. While the coefficients on control variables should be interpreted with caution, most operate as anticipated.[45] In these regressions, coups staged from higher ranks within the military are more likely to succeed than those mounted from lower ranks. The controls for GDP per capita are negative and statistically significant, while there is a positive, statistically significant association between democracy and coup success. Coups staged in the wake of recent successful coups or revolutions are also associated with higher rates of coup failure than those staged in other times and places.

The relationship between counterbalancing and coup outcomes is also substantively large. Figure 2.4 shows how the predicted probability a coup succeeds changes with changes in selected independent and control variables while holding all others at their medians (from table 2.4, model 3). The use of counterbalancing has a substantively large effect on the likelihood a coup will succeed: the probability of a successful coup is 12 percentage points lower where rulers have at least one counterweight than where they do not. These findings provide support for the book's first hypothesis, which predicted a negative association between counterbalancing and coup success.

TABLE 2.4 Coup success: Logit results

	MODEL 1	MODEL 2	MODEL 3	MODEL 4	MODEL 5	MODEL 6
Counterbalancing	−0.569**	−0.685**	−0.612*			
	(0.285)	(0.278)	(0.333)			
Number of counterweights (log)				−0.545**	−0.612**	−0.559*
				(0.260)	(0.259)	(0.315)
Coup leader: General		1.848***	2.066***		1.826***	2.054***
		(0.416)	(0.473)		(0.414)	(0.471)
Coup leader: Colonel, major		0.793*	0.711		0.774*	0.697
		(0.439)	(0.508)		(0.441)	(0.510)
Military regime			0.242			0.190
			(0.384)			(0.382)
Democracy			0.597*			0.557*
			(0.338)			(0.341)
GDP/capita (log)			−0.444**			−0.435**
			(0.175)			(0.175)
Change in GDP/capita			−0.772			−0.869
			(1.749)			(1.751)
Recent successful coup			−0.672**			−0.669**
			(0.321)			(0.318)
Recent revolution			−1.465*			−1.476*
			(0.782)			(0.763)
Cold War			0.685			0.694*
			(0.430)			(0.420)
Constant	0.047	−0.753*	1.979	0.016	−0.807**	1.880
	(0.200)	(0.400)	(1.256)	(0.176)	(0.386)	(1.254)
Log likelihood	−178.410	−150.685	−129.677	−178.280	−150.939	−129.844
Pseudo R-squared	0.013	0.115	0.177	0.014	0.114	0.176
Observations	266	248	229	266	248	229

Notes: Robust standard errors clustered by country in parentheses. *** p<0.01, ** p<0.05, * p<0.1.

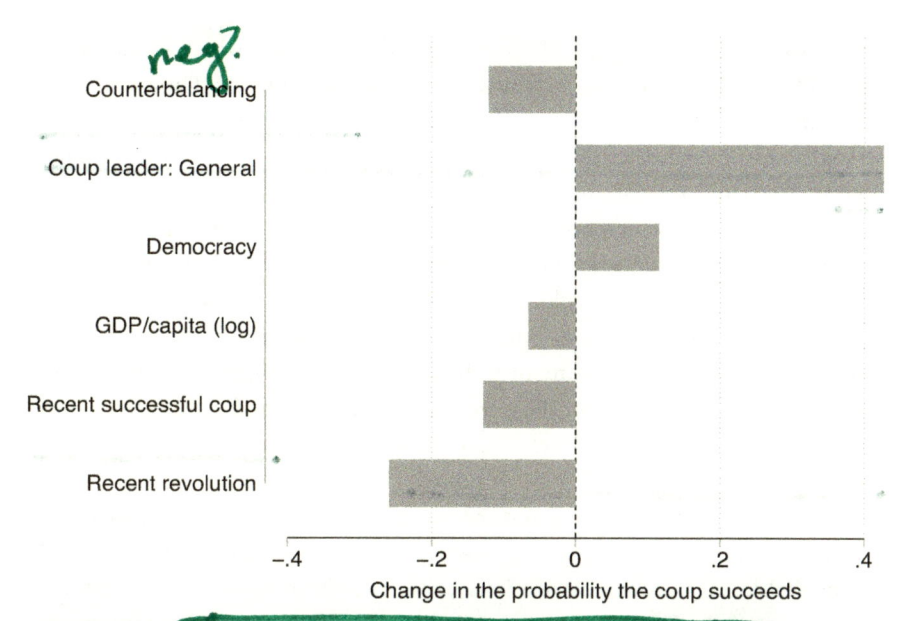

FIGURE 2.4. Marginal effect of selected variables on coup outcomes (from table 2.4, model 3)

Note: For discrete variables, the marginal effect of a change from 0 to 1 is shown. For continuous variables, a change of one standard deviation is shown.

Alternative Arguments and Robustness Checks

I have outlined a number of causal mechanisms that might account for the association between counterbalancing and coup failure, including those that focus on coordination challenges created by counterweights and those that emphasize incentives for resistance for counterbalancing forces. However, the statistical association presented here could also be consistent with no causal relationship between the two variables. One plausible alternate interpretation of the findings in this chapter is that leaders are only able to create counterweights where the military is too weak to object—and that it is this weakness that also accounts for the increased likelihood that coups will fail when rulers counterbalance. In chapter 1, I argued that this alternative argument assumes that coup attempts are more likely to succeed where the military's political clout is stronger—an assumption not borne out by existing studies of the dynamics of coups.

In this chapter, I bring additional data to bear on this question. If military strength can explain both the creation of counterweights and the outcomes of coup attempts, it should be positively correlated with coup success and negatively correlated with counterbalancing. While military strength cannot be measured directly, there are several proxies for it that are commonly used. The most straightforward are indicators of military spending and size, which should reflect the military's ability to extract resources from the government. These indicators are taken from the Correlates of War dataset. Another indicator for military strength captures whether the military governs directly, in the form of a military regime.[46] To capture more subtle forms of military influence in politics, I use an index of militarism, which takes into account whether the ruler is or was a high-ranking military officer, whether officers hold cabinet positions other than minister of defense, whether the military high command is consulted about political matters in addition to security ones, whether most cabinet members are civilians, and whether the government to be "military" or "military-civilian."[47] Finally, I also consider data on the percentage of cabinet and state council-level positions held by military officers.[48] For each measure, higher values indicate a stronger influence of the military in politics. If military strength could explain both the use of counterweights and the outcome of coup attempts, it should be positively correlated with coup success and negatively correlated with counterbalancing. Table 2.5 presents correlations between indicators of military strength, coup outcomes, and counterbalancing. It suggests that military strength cannot explain the relationship between counterbalancing and coup outcomes: the correlations between indicators of military strength, coup success, and counterbalancing are weak or nonexistent, and they are not consistent across indicators.

I also test this alternative argument more systematically, finding that the relationship between counterbalancing and coup success is robust to the inclusion of controls for each indicator of military strength described above (results not shown). Another, related, possibility is that the relationship between counterbalancing and coup success is driven by military dictatorships, in which the unusually strong position of the military simultaneously reduces counterbalancing and increases the likelihood of successful coups. To test for this possibly, I exclude military regimes from the analysis, but find that the negative association between counterbalancing and coup success remains (results not shown). In other words, there is no evidence that military strength is driving the association between counterbalancing and coup failure.

TABLE 2.5 Correlations: Coup success, counterbalancing, and military strength

	COUP SUCCESS	COUNTERBALANCING
Military expenditures (log)	−0.09	0.08
Military personnel (log)	0.01	0.10
Military regime	0.06	−0.12
Militarism index	−0.05	−0.06
Proportion of government active military	−0.03	−0.03

I next examine whether selection effects explain the association. If potential coup plotters from within the military take the likelihood of success into account when deciding whether to intervene, then it may be that the only coups staged in the presence of counterweights would be those in which coup plotters had some other reason to expect victory. If the selection process into a coup attempt alters the estimation of the effect of counterbalancing, and if the parameter then estimates that the correlation in the error terms between the selection and outcome equations is significant, that would raise concerns about selection bias. To explore this possibility, I model selection effects explicitly using a two-stage model of coup attempts and outcomes. I use the "probit-probit" variation on the Heckman model suggested by Wynand Van de Ven and Bernard Van Praag.[49] This approach has the advantage of explicitly modeling the selection problem, but may also result in biased estimates if the selection and outcome equations include a similar set of variables. Because regressors in the second stage must be a strict subset of those in the first, I exclude the rank of coup leaders and replace indicators for recent coups with the years since last coup attempt and associated cubic splines. The findings suggest no relationship between counterbalancing and the incidence of coup attempts—a finding explored in detail in the following chapter. The negative association between counterbalancing and coup success, however, remains robust to the use of a two-stage selection model. Furthermore, the correlation of errors between the selection and outcome equation is not significant in a Wald test, indicating that selection bias does not account for the relationship between counterbalancing and coup outcomes (results not shown).

In order to ensure that the results are not simply the artifact of including particular combinations of control variables, I re-estimate the models after removing each control variable. The central results on counterbalancing do not change (results not shown). Finally, I examine whether the results hold when the coup attempts in the analysis are restricted to those that appear in both the Center for Systemic Peace's coup dataset and that compiled by Jonathan Powell and Clayton Thyne.[50] While the two datasets cover similar time periods and geographic scope, there are a number of coup attempts in the Center for Systemic Peace dataset that do not appear in Powell and Thyne, and vice versa. Powell and Thyne also use a less restrictive coding rule for whether or not a coup attempt succeeds; in the CSP data, perpetrators must hold power for one month for the coup attempt to count as a success, while Powell and Thyne require only one week. The results remain unchanged when this alternate source of coup data is used (results not shown).

The statistical analysis in this chapter provided strong support for one of the central arguments in this book. I find a consistent and significant negative association

CHAPTER 2

between counterbalancing and coup success. This result is robust to the inclusion of a number of potentially confounding variables. Counterbalancing the military can reduce the likelihood of a successful coup by 12 percentage points—a large effect for something that rulers themselves can control. The analysis also demonstrates that military strength or weakness cannot explain the relationship between counterbalancing and coup outcomes. Yet while these analyses show a strong association between counterbalancing and coup failure—and address one potential selection effect—the statistical analysis is limited in what it can tell us about the mechanisms through which counterbalancing might affect the outcomes of coup attempts. In the next chapter, I examine in depth a number of cases of counterbalancing to test the causal mechanisms at work.

3
HOW COUNTERBALANCING WORKS
Testing the Causal Mechanisms

The previous chapter showed that the success rate of coups varies with the structure of states' coercive institutions: coups in states with more fragmented security sectors tend to fail more often. There are a number of potential explanations for this association. It could be that counterbalancing impedes coordination, creating tactical challenges that prevent coup plotters from seizing their targets and effectively shaping expectations about the coup's outcome. Alternatively, it could be that counterbalancing is associated with coup failure because it changes how officers view the potential costs associated with a successful attempt, or with using violence to stop it, in a way that creates incentives for armed resistance. Finally, it may be that the association between counterbalancing and coup failure documented in chapter 2 is spurious—that some other factor accounts for both counterbalancing and coup failure, while counterbalancing itself exerts no causal effect.

This chapter draws on qualitative evidence from sixteen coup attempts to test the mechanisms linking counterbalancing to coup failure. The cases examined in this chapter were chosen to maximize the chances of observing causal mechanisms at work: all are cases in which leaders counterbalanced their militaries at the time of the coup. They were also chosen to ensure regional and temporal variation representative of the larger universe of cases, but without prior knowledge of which, if any, of the proposed causal mechanisms was at work. I include twelve coup attempts that failed, as predicted, and four that succeeded despite counterbalancing. I examined more cases of failed coups than successful ones because the aim is to identify which, if either, of the potential mechanisms linking counterbalancing and coup failure operated, and I expect the mechanisms to be easier to observe in failed coups. Nonetheless, I also include four successful coups to see whether there is any evidence that the counterweights resisted but were unable to stop the coup, or whether coup plotters faced coordination problems but overcame them.[1] I examine in detail three typical cases—those that fit well within the broader patterns in the data. These include failed attempts against Daniel Arap Moi in Kenya, King Hassan II in Morocco, and Manuel Noriega in Panama. I summarize the findings in the remaining cases more briefly either in the text of the chapter or in the appendix. The cases draw on a wide range of source material, including archival materials, academic accounts, contemporaneous newspaper reports, and the memoirs of coup participants.

Because these cases were selected on the logic of "most-likely" research design, I should be able to tell a compelling narrative that links counterbalancing to the outcomes of the coups. That said, in examining these cases, we should not necessarily expect rulers or coup plotters to identify the incentives and constraints shaping their behavior. Whether the coup succeeds or fails is likely to shape actors' recollections of it, as well as whose accounts are heard. Leaders who have overcome a coup attempt are likely to emphasize how poorly planned and executed it was to discredit coup plotters and cast doubt on the depth of the coup's support. Failed coup participants may claim to have been misled about the aims of the coup, or not to even have been aware that it was a coup attempt they were participating in. Those who have been successful are likely to highlight motives grounded in the national interest, rather than concerns about a decline in their own status. At the same time, successful coup plotters are much more likely to have had an opportunity to explain themselves in the form of interviews and memoirs than those who have failed.

Instead, my approach has been to look for evidence of the effects of counterbalancing on the ability of coup plotters to shape expectations during a coup. The two causal logics theorized here have different observable implications for the dynamics of coup attempts. If counterbalancing works because it impedes coordination between coup plotters, making it more difficult for them to make their success appear inevitable, we should see coup plotters being intercepted prior to capturing their targets, making tactical errors, or encountering difficulties timing attacks concurrently or coordinating across units from different security forces. If counterbalancing works because it creates incentives for resistance the coup, we should see counterweights use force to defend or recapture coup targets or serve as a source of organized resistance to a coup-installed regime. In each coup examined, I construct a play-by-play of the coup attempt, with the goal of identifying whether one or more of the proposed causal mechanisms linking counterbalancing and coup outcomes is present. Did counterweights defend the incumbent regimes from coup plotters? Did their presence hinder coordination between coup plotters? Or were their actions largely incidental to the outcome of the coup?

It is important to emphasize here that these cases are all case of coup *attempts*—instances in which the plan to oust the executive has moved from the planning stage into an overt, visible attempt to claim power, whether that takes the form of a declaration or a movement of troops. Coup plots and rumors are both too common and too difficult to verify to be tracked systematically. As a result, the case studies examined here cannot speak to what effect, if any, counterbalancing has on the initial development of coup plots or the likelihood that a coup plot will turn into an overt attempt. Instead, they test the mechanisms linking counterbalancing to failure *during* coup attempts.

The evidence presented in these cases is more consistent with the logic of resistance than that of coordination. The coups that failed did not do so because they faced coordination problems. In most cases, coup plotters were able to broadcast their actions and capture symbolic seats of political power with ease. Instead, the coups that failed did so primarily because officers in counterbalancing forces chose to violently resist, engaging in pitched battles with coup forces and staging counterattacks to recapture targets coup plotters had already taken. In Kenya, it was President Daniel Arap Moi's General Services Unit, which was built up as a counterweight to the military, that stopped the 1982 attempt to oust him from power. In Morocco, King Hassan II was unable to rally the regular army to his defense. Instead, it was Interior Ministry troops that crushed the 1971 coup. And in Panama, it was Manuel Noriega's paramilitary Dignity Battalions and other special military units under his command that resisted the 1989 coup staged by members of the Panamanian army. The patterns across the other cases examined are similar: counterweights resisted in nine of the twelve successful coups, and in two of the failed coup attempts as well. In contrast, there was little evidence that counterbalancing hindered coordination. These findings suggest that the mechanisms through which counterbalancing works will result in more-violent coups—an implication explored in depth in chapter 6.

Resistance to the 1982 Air Force Coup in Kenya

The 1982 coup attempt in Kenya failed, in large part, because of resistance mounted by counterbalancing forces. Early on the morning of August 1, noncommissioned officers in Kenya's air force seized control of the Voice of Kenya radio station in Nairobi and announced that they had ousted President Daniel Arap Moi from power. In their radio address, coup plotters blamed Moi for the country's economic and political woes, arguing that "rampant corruption and nepotism have made life almost intolerable in our society. The economy is in shambles, and the people cannot afford food, housing, or transport."[2] The radio address also criticized Moi for the creation of a one-party state.[3]

Moi had assumed the presidency four years earlier, following the death of Jomo Kenyatta, Kenya's first president. Even though Moi had served as Kenyatta's vice president and was—according to the country's constitution—the next in line to rule, many of Kenyatta's supporters did not approve of Moi assuming power. While Kenyatta had come from Kenya's largest ethnic group, the Kikuyu (which made up about 22 percent of Kenya's population), Moi was a member of a smaller tribe, the Kalenjin (which made up around 12 percent).[4] Moi also lacked the charisma that had made Kenyatta popular outside his own ethnic group. To help legitimize his regime, Moi took a number of steps to signal that he intended to follow in Kenyatta's footsteps. He developed stronger ties to prominent Kikuyu politicians, promised to end political factionalism and corruption, and traveled around the country to build support for his rule. Moi also enacted a series of more populist economic reforms. But rising oil costs, declining export prices, and a run of poor weather, which damaged corn and wheat production, resulted in deteriorating economic conditions.[5]

As public criticism of the government's response to the economic crisis grew, Moi began a political clampdown. He expelled some of the most vocal critics from within his own political party, the Kenya African National Union (KANU), and pushed constitutional amendments through the National Assembly that prevented the formation of opposition parties, effectively turning Kenya into a one-party state. At the same time, Moi began a campaign of harassment against academics, students, and public intellectuals.[6]

Meanwhile, tensions between Moi and the Kenyan military grew. The military that Moi had inherited from Kenyatta was disproportionately filled with Kikuyu officers. Upon coming to power, Moi worked quickly to reduce Kikuyu dominance within the officer corps of the military, replacing Kikuyu officers, wherever possible, with Kalenjin ones. These efforts generated substantial resentment among the remaining non-Kalenjin members of the armed forces.[7] Moi also slashed the military's budget, even as he expanded its ranks. Morale, particularly within the lower ranks, plummeted. Soldiers' complaints were numerous and included "the conditions of service, the lack of housing and uniforms, the poor food, and relations with senior officers."[8] By the summer of 1982, multiple coup plots were brewing within the armed forces.[9]

The August 1 coup attempt began around 2:00 a.m., when soldiers from the ground air defense units from the Nanyuki, Embakasi, and Eastleight air bases, located on the outskirts of Nairobi, marched into the capital. In addition to the economic complaints coup plotters cited in their broadcast, halting demographic changes in the military also appears to have been a motive. The coup was spearheaded by Kikuyu, Luo, and other non-Kalenjin junior officers.[10] One of the coup's leaders, James Dianga, later described in his memoirs the blocking of Luo officers' promotions as a contributing factor to the coup.[11] Over the course of the next three hours, coup plotters seized the post office, the international airport, the Central Bank of Kenya, the Voice of Kenya radio station, and other telecommunications stations. On their march into town, rebelling soldiers stopped at Kenyatta University College, waking up students and urging them to join the coup.[12] The coup plotters initially proceeded unopposed. The coup attempt was planned for a date on which most of the army units normally stationed in Nairobi would be away on exercises near the Ugandan border. While the coup leaders did not appear to have widespread support within the army, most army units were outside the capital when the coup began and thus not well positioned to intervene. For four hours after the radio announcement was made, none of the army units that remained in Nairobi moved to oppose the coup.[13]

Coup leaders believed the coup had succeeded. They left a small number of men to guard key posts and began raucous celebrations in the capital. Student leaders broadcast their support and demonstrated in the streets in support of the coup.[14] In the wake of the coup's apparent success, looting began in the capital. As one contemporary account described, "Scenes of wild disorder began in the capital. Road blocks were thrown up by the rebels, cars seized, and drivers robbed."[15] Some rebelling soldiers handed out light weapons to civilian supporters; others commandeered cars to drive around in, waving banners and shouting support for the coup.[16]

At the time of the coup, Moi employed three separate counterweights to the military. The most prominent was the General Services Unit (GSU), a mobile paramilitary unit within the Kenyan police. Established during the Mau Mau rebellion in the 1950s, the GSU was not originally conceived as a counterweight to the military. It came to play this role during Kenyatta's tenure, however, slowly turning into "a political force, the regime's coercive arm against its internal enemies."[17] Kenyatta staffed the GSU predominantly with Kikuyu soldiers and used it to guard his private residence. It was strengthened following a failed coup attempt in 1964. Over time, it became a formidable rival to the military. When he came to power, Moi expanded its ranks and "Kalenjinized" the force. He also ensured that senior commanders within the GSU and other counterbalancing forces, unlike those within the regular military, remained well compensated.[18] In the years leading up to the 1982 coup attempt, Moi increasingly used the unit to repress domestic opposition. It became well known for extrajudicial killings and torture of political prisoners.[19]

In addition to the GSU, Kenya also had a secret police force, the Special Branch, established during the Mau Mau rebellion. Kenyatta shifted the Special Branch under his direct control in 1969. He also posted Special Branch officers to army barracks to monitor and deter the development of coup plots. In the wake of Kenyatta's death, the head of the Special Branch, James Kanyotu, helped ensure Moi's succession, heading off a challenge from within KANU.[20] Moi increased its budget as domestic opposition to his rule grew and continued to use it to monitor other security forces. Finally, Moi encouraged rivalries between different branches of the armed forces and between different units within the army. In 1980, he created a new infantry battalion, nicknamed the "Moi Battalion," and separated it from the regular military chain of command, putting the force under his direct control. It was used for his personal protection.[21]

There is evidence that coup plotters sought to coordinate with the heads of at least some of the counterbalancing units in advance. Ben Gethi, the chief of police, which supervised the GSU, admitted after the coup that he had been contacted by coup plotters and knew that the coup attempt was going to take place. The Special Branch also appears to have known about the coup plot in advance.[22] Neither the police nor the Special Branch alerted Moi ahead of time.

Once the coup attempt began, however, it was the GSU, together with the Moi Battalion and a small number of army units within the capital, whose actions ultimately undermined the rebellion. Based near the presidential estate at Gatundu, the GSU was close to central coup targets; it marched quickly on the airport as well as the air force base at Embakasi, where the revolt had begun.[23] When the GSU moved toward the radio station, rebel troops initially believed that the force was joining the revolt; they "raised their hands with victory sign and were promptly met with fusillade of fire."[24] Instead, the police remained loyal. The GSU established and manned roadblocks that prevented more students from Kenyatta University College from joining the coup.[25]

After several hours of firing, in which some three hundred officers were killed and the GSU base was bombed, the majority of coup plotters surrendered. Moi, who had been at his country home when the coup began, returned to the capital that evening and was able to reassert control, making a radio broadcast proclaiming that he was back in power. Two of the coup plotters escaped to Dar es Salaam on a transport plane they commandeered. Fighting continued for several days at the Nanyuki air base near Mount Kenya, but eventually, there too, coup plotters surrendered. The final death toll was estimated between 600 and 1,800.[26] As Jendayi Frazer concluded in her analysis of the coup, "Civilian control was preserved through armed counterbalancing."[27]

Specifically, counterbalancing worked because counterweights resisted the coup. The presence of counterweights did not result in early warning about the coup attempt or create tactical challenges that prevented coup plotters from seizing the broadcasting facilities and using them to attempt to create common knowledge about the coup. Instead, the coup failed because officers in the GSU and the Moi Battalion in particular decided to side with the regime and launched successful counterattacks to retake coup targets. The way in which the 1982 coup in Kenya unfolded is thus more consistent with the logic of resistance than that of coordination.

Resistance to the 1971 Cadets' Coup in Morocco

Although the circumstances of the Moroccan coup attempt on July 10, 1971, differed from those of the Kenyan coup in many respects, armed resistance from counterweights was similarly central to its failure. The Moroccan coup began at the royal palace in Skhirat during a lavish party for King Hassan II's forty-second birthday. Fourteen hundred armed cadets from the Ahermoumou cadet training school, led by Colonel Mohamed Ababou, commander of the cadet school, and General Mohammed Medbouh, head of the royal household, stormed the gates of the summer palace, hurling grenades and opening fire on the diplomats, cabinet ministers, and military officers in attendance.[28]

There were a number of factors that motivated the coup attempt. King Hassan had come to power a decade earlier upon the death of his father, Mohammed V. During his rule, Hassan built up a system of royal patronage that senior officers benefited from. As John Waterbury describes, "Many of the officers were already wealthy men, but as European *colons* and businessmen sold off their interests after 1956—often illegally—many farms and enterprises found their way into the hands of the officers with the active connivance of the Palace."[29] Over time, however, some officers resented that the status and salaries accorded to them lagged behind those of politicians, civil servants, and even some junior officers.[30] In the years leading up to the coup, Hassan had bowed to pressure from junior officers, who were primarily of middle-class Arab origin, to create more avenues for promotion to higher ranks traditionally dominated by Berber nobility. As the military and security forces were progressively mechanized, the more recent training of junior officers, both at the Royal Military Academy and in specialized courses abroad, better qualified them to command new mechanized units, which received new equipment and more resources, creating resentment among senior officers. At the same time, Hassan frequently rotated senior officers through different posts and kept them under surveillance in a way that made it difficult for them to amass their own bases of power.[31]

Coup plotters also voiced political concerns. In the decade since King Hassan had come to power, he had overseen the adoption of Morocco's first constitution, which established the country as a multiparty state, but which also granted the monarchy sweeping powers. Hassan invested heavily in infrastructure development and agricultural modernization, boosting economic growth, but the benefits were concentrated among a small elite. In 1965, in response to student agitation and rioting in Casablanca, Hassan declared a state of emergency, dissolved the national parliament, and called on the Moroccan armed forces to violently repress the protesters.[32] The army's operations resulted in the arrest of a number of prominent opposition figures.[33] A new constitution, adopted in 1970, restored the parliament, but with diminished authority. The result was a monarchy with "virtually unlimited powers."[34] Some senior officers were vocal in their criticism of Hassan's efforts to centralize power, and chafed at being asked to repress student protesters. Others were critical of Hassan's failure to crack down on political corruption. In April 1971, three cabinet ministers were implicated in a sweeping corruption scandal. When Hassan indicated that he did not intend to bring criminal charges against them, this appears to have been a turning point for some of the coup plotters.[35]

The attack on the summer palace was a violent one. One witness described the scene at the palace, during the cadets' initial attack, as "an orgy of apparently indiscriminate shooting."[36] As head of the royal household, General Medbouh was able to limit the ammunition available to the palace guard on the night of the coup, and it was quickly overpowered. When it was clear that the palace had been secured, rebels read out a list of names of attendees; those who came forward, including a number of army generals and colonels, as well as members of the king's personal staff, were executed.[37] All told, over one hundred people were killed in the attack. While the cadets secured the palace, other rebelling soldiers captured the Ministry of Interior headquarters and the radio station in Rabat, broadcasting that an "army of the people" had taken power but offering few other details about the coup plotters' aims.[38]

It was sheer luck that Hassan survived the attack on the palace. The king hid in the bathroom with his bodyguard but was soon captured. However, General Medbouh was among those killed in the attack on the palace. His death left coup plotters to debate their next steps. As Frank Braun describes, Medbouh's position was key to planning: "When he was killed at an early stage, the putsch leaders were unable to agree on either objectives or the tactics to reach them."[39] While the remaining coup plotters debated their next steps, Hassan was able to convince the cadets guarding him to let him go. At that point, Hassan tried to rally loyal troops to his defense. However, the majority of the army remained on the sidelines as the coup progressed, taking "a wait and see attitude throughout the day."[40]

At the time of the coup attempt, Hassan employed several counterweights. By the late 1960s, the threat of a coup had become "the primary source of anxiety for the king."[41] He responded by dividing the state's coercive power into a series of new paramilitary units and specialized military forces under the Ministry of Interior that were used to check the power of the military. These included the Gendarmerie, National Security Police (Sûreté Nationale), Mobile Intervention Force, and Light Security Brigade; together, there were some forty thousand troops under the Ministry of Interior, compared to sixty thousand in the regular armed forces as a whole.[42] The Minister of the Interior, General Mohammad Oufkir, wielded enormous influence. Soldiers in the regular military were bitter. As one observer described, "The special relations between the king and these officers [commanding counterweights] were greatly resented by the rest of the senior officer corps. In particular, General Oufkir's National Security Police represented an ever-present threat to all senior officers."[43] The gendarmerie was also perceived as receiving better treatment than the regular military, in part due to Oufkir's personal prominence and perceptions of his close relationship with the king. The result was a developing rivalry between the gendarmerie and military.[44]

In contrast to the coup attempt in Kenya, coup plotters in Morocco did not attempt to reach out to officers in other security forces in advance of their attack. They did anticipate resistance from counterweights. To preempt it, coup plotters attacked the Interior Ministry headquarters in addition to the summer palace and the radio station. The hope appears to have been that General Oufkir would sit the coup out. But officers in counterbalancing forces were concerned that Interior Ministry troops would be disbanded if the coup plotters took power. Waterbury also argues that had the coup succeeded, Oufkir himself would most likely have been executed.[45] These concerns created incentives to oppose the coup.

Oufkir's decision to defend Hassan's regime was decisive for the coup's outcome. He used Ministry of Interior troops, including the Sûreté Nationale and the Light Security Brigade, to bring the coup plotters' efforts to a halt. He led an attack to retake the radio station; this proved to be "an arduous affair," in which "an untold number [of cadets] were summarily executed," but was ultimately successful.[46] Tanks drove through the streets of the capital, and skirmishes between coup forces and Ministry of Interior troops continued through the next day. When one of the coup plotters attempted to rally cadets from another military school, Oufkir's troops cut them off. By Sunday evening, rebelling soldiers in the capital had been captured. Another 158 people had died in the fighting. It was later described as a "savage internecine army bloodbath."[47] When it was clear that the coup attempt had failed, Oufkir was given temporary control of the Ministry of Defense, in addition to the Ministry of Interior, in order to pursue potential supporters of the coup; the U.S. embassy noted at the time that "for all practical purposes, [he] is the man actually running the country at the moment."[48]

In short, the 1971 coup in Morocco failed because Hassan's counterweights resisted. The way the coup unfolded does not suggest that counterbalancing created coordination problems that impeded coup plotters from seizing their targets. Coup plotters anticipated resistance from counterweights in the Ministry of Interior and took steps to head it off. But as Hassan himself noted in a radio address the day after the coup attempt, "Rebels had taken over the Ministry of Interior but had forgotten the Sûreté Nationale."[49] The lesson that Hassan took from the coup attempt was that counterbalancing works. In the wake of the coup, he sought "even more than in the past to play against one another various army units as well as the security police, gendarmerie, and auxiliary forces."[50]

Resistance to the 1989 Coup in Panama

Like counterweights in Kenya and Morocco, those in Panama also resisted the 1989 coup attempt against President Manuel Antonio Noriega. On the morning of October 3, Major Moisés Giroldi Vega, along with several other senior officers in the Panamanian Defense Forces (PDF), moved to oust Noriega from power. Noriega had been the chief of staff of the Panamanian military and the de facto ruler of Panama since 1983. In the years since, with aid from the United States, Noriega tripled the size of the military and allowed its entry into a range of illicit economic activities.[51]

By the late 1980s, however, Noriega's relationship with both the United States and much of his own military had deteriorated. The United States imposed a series of economic sanctions that resulted in record unemployment and drastic cuts to social spending and the military budget. The torture and murder of Hugo Spadafora, a longtime critic of Noriega's regime, also increased opposition within Panama. In 1987, Noriega forced the military chief of staff, Roberto Díaz Herrera, to retire. In response, Díaz took to the radio to accuse Noriega of electoral fraud and the assassination both of Spadafora and of Omar Torrijos, who had been commander of the Panamanian National Guard and de facto ruler of Panama prior to his death in an airplane crash in 1981.[52]

Washington soon began pressuring the PDF to replace Noriega. James A. Baker III, secretary of state at the time, recalled in his memoir: "In truth, we were doing our best to foment a coup. The policy we were pursuing was steadily increasing pressure across the board. The message to be conveyed at every level was simple: either the Panamanian defense forces took Noriega out, or we might."[53] At the same time, Noriega began using the military more frequently for internal repression—a task that many officers chafed at being asked to perform. Following a failed coup attempt in March 1988, Noriega also purged nearly one-quarter of the officer corps of the PDF. Those officers that remained feared more purges were to come.[54]

At the same time, Noriega lavished resources on counterbalancing forces. He maintained independent chains of command to a number of elite units within the PDF. These included the presidential guard; Battalion 2000, an elite unit originally formed to guard the Panama Canal but subsequently used for regime protection; and the Machos del Monte, "a well-armed special operations force trained only for one purpose: to protect and, if necessary, rescue Noriega."[55] Anti-riot police units, nicknamed the "Dobermans," served as Noriega's own "army-within-the-army," and "compensated for Noriega's lack of appeal by putting on public displays of political repression."[56] Finally, Noriega established paramilitary militias, called Dignity Battalions, which were administered by the army but reported directly to Noriega for operations, for the dual purpose of deterring U.S. intervention and subduing internal opponents. Eleven battalions were raised, five of which were in Panama City at the time of the coup. They were perceived as "fiercely loyal to Noriega" and in particular "more loyal to Noriega than the PDF."[57]

In the context of rapid economic deterioration, and in response to growing criticism, Noriega held presidential elections. Electoral fraud was widespread. As Arthur Davis, U.S. ambassador to Panama at the time, recalled: "Noriega had set up the books. He had controlled the books so people could go there and would not find their name on the list. He had put on 150,000 new eighteen-year-old voters. They passed a law that the members of the Panama Defense Forces and certain government people could vote wherever they happened to be. Which meant that they could go in and vote all over the country or go to any polling place." In rural areas the soldiers would tell potential voters, "I don't want to see you going to the polls."[58] In spite of these efforts, Noriega lost the election to opposition candidate Guillermo Endara, but he refused to relinquish power, instead ordering the Dignity Battalions to attack Endara and his supporters.

At that point, Giroldi, the commander of the PDF battalion in Panama City, recruited other disgruntled officers to stage a coup and approached the United States for logistical support. Giroldi told American officials that he had the support of three PDF units and that the commander of Battalion 2000 at Fort Cimarron had agreed not to get involved. The plan was to seize PDF headquarters in Panama City, rally anti-Noriega PDF units to Giroldi's side, and pressure Noriega to resign.[59] Giroldi assured U.S. representatives that it would be "less a coup than an abrupt change of command ceremony"—one with no violence, if possible.[60] Although they wanted Noriega out of power, American officials were suspicious of Giroldi's motives and concerned about his ability to carry out the plot. After all, Giroldi had helped Noriega suppress the 1988 coup attempt, and there was the possibility that his approach was a setup.[61] Colin Powell, who had been appointed head of the Joint Chiefs of Staff a few days before the 1989 coup attempt, advised President George H. W. Bush not to support Giroldi, arguing that "to get rid of Noriega had to be something that would be done through an American plan, not a half-baked coup with a half-baked leader."[62] Despite these concerns, the United States did agree to establish roadblocks on two key roads leading to military headquarters to preempt a counterattack by forces loyal to Noriega.[63]

The coup attempt went forward on October 3. It was early morning when coup plotters intercepted Noriega as he entered military headquarters for the start of the workday and placed him under arrest. Noriega's presidential guard put up some resistance, and several soldiers were killed, but Noriega was successfully apprehended. PDF units in the vicinity of the capital largely sat out the early hours of the coup. As Don Podesta explains, their inaction was "either out of confusion or because they were waiting to see which way the wind was blowing."[64] U.S. intelligence cables during the coup described Giroldi's "main asset" during the coup attempt as "the reluctance of the bulk of Noriega's forces to come to his aid."[65] Coup plotters debated what to do with Noriega—whether to kill him, turn him over to the United States, or force him to retire—as well as whether the rest of the general staff of the army should be asked to step down.[66]

Although Giroldi claimed to have secured support from the heads of both Battalion 2000 and the Doberman riot police, neither declared their support in front of other officers in advance of the coup. Other coup plotters were concerned that they would not come through. Captain Javier Licona, who commanded a cavalry company that participated in the coup, said that he went on his own to feel out the position of the commander of Battalion 2000, Major Federico Olechea, just prior to the coup, but Olechea told him, "Battalion 2000 would defend Noriega against any coup attempt."[67] It could be that Giroldi was bluffing about having the battalion's support or that Olechea did not trust Licona enough to tell him. Either way, support from counterbalancing forces was not common knowledge among military officers. However, these forces also declined to provide Noriega with the intelligence needed to head off the coup plot. Giroldi's pre-coup planning also seems to indicate that he remained concerned about resistance. Frederick Kempe describes how, after securing Noriega, Giroldi's forces "fanned out into the poor neighborhood surrounding the complex to head off what they considered their only threat: the infiltration of special forces loyal to Noriega."[68]

As it turns out, fears that at least some of Noriega's counterweights would defend his regime were well founded. In the first hours after Noriega's capture, Battalion 2000 did not make a move. But Noriega reached Olechea by phone and rallied the battalion to his defense. At that point, Olechea publicly declared the battalion's loyalty.[69] As Lawrence Yates describes, "Units from Battalion 2000, realizing that their noncommittal stance would lead to reprisals if Noriega triumphed, decided to join the countercoup."[70] The Dignity Battalions were also instrumental in opposing the coup. Their commander, Benjamin Colamarco, was with Noriega when the October 3 attack began. Colamarco was able to elude capture and directed the Dignity Battalions to oppose the coup. They were "out in force on Noriega's behalf immediately."[71] Together the Dignity Battalions and Battalion 2000 led a "bloody counterattack" on military headquarters, which circumvented the U.S. roadblock, and which "crushed the revolt within three hours."[72] The Machos del Monte also defended Noriega. In Kempe's words, "When he [Noriega] saw their black T-shirts and beards, he knew he had won."[73] Noriega himself began pressuring Giroldi to surrender. As Yates describes it, "As units loyal to Noriega mounted their counterattack, the general taunted Giroldi, yelling at the major either to shoot him or to kill him. Giroldi did neither. At that point, according to some sources, Noriega took a pistol and shot an officer standing next to Giroldi in the head. The coup attempt collapsed soon thereafter."[74]

In the weeks following the coup, Noriega drew on counterbalancing forces to stamp out remaining supporters of the coup; the Dignity Battalions and Doberman riot police "freely beat anyone considered to be even remotely dissident."[75] After the failed coup, Noriega moved swiftly to consolidate power. The Assembly of Representatives granted him additional powers. Noriega went forward with a purge of the military, arresting and jailing officers he suspected of disloyalt.y[76]

In the end, Noriega's efforts to counterbalance the military served him well: the counterweights he created resisted the coup, defending his regime against coup plotters from within the PDF. In contrast, the case provides little support for the coordination mechanisms. Coup plotters communicated with leaders of at least two of Noriega's counterweights before launching the coup attempt, but neither reported it to him, nor did their advance knowledge of the attempt enable them to intercept coup targets. There is also no evidence in this case that counterbalancing created barriers to coordination between security forces that prevented coup plotters from seizing their targets. In short, counterbalancing worked in Panama in much the same way it worked in Kenya and Morocco—counterweights resisted.

Patterns across Other Coup Attempts

In Kenya, Morocco, and Panama, counterbalancing had a causal effect on the outcome of the coup. While soldiers in the regular army largely sat on the sidelines, security forces used as counterweights to the military rallied to the defense of incumbent regimes, using force to retake coup targets or to pursue rebelling forces. In contrast, there was little evidence that counterbalancing impeded coordination between coup plotters that prevented them from seizing their targets. Do the patterns in these three cases hold more broadly? To answer this question, I briefly examine the evidence in an additional thirteen coup attempts. Table 3.1 summarizes the findings about the causal mechanisms observed. Like the coups Moi, Hassan, and Noriega faced, those in these additional cases were chosen to maximize the likelihood of observing causal mechanisms at work. Each coup is described in depth either in the main text or in the appendix.

The evidence in these cases suggests that counterbalancing contributed to the defeat of coup plotters in nine of the twelve failed coups. In these cases, however, there was little evidence that it hindered coordination between forces during the coup. In at least four cases, counterweights knew of coup plots in advance but did not report them to the regime. These include the coup attempts in Peru, Haiti, and Russia—where the counterweights participated in the coup attempts—as well as in Panama, where counterweights had advance warning of the coup plot but declined to report it to the regime. In no case did early warnings from counterweights about the coup attempt enable the regime to intercept coup plotters before they were able to capture broadcasting stations or other targets.

There was also little evidence that counterbalancing created tactical challenges to coordinating across distinct military and security forces in a way that prevented

TABLE 3.1 Evidence on causal mechanisms during sixteen coup attempts

FAILED COUP ATTEMPTS	RESISTANCE	COORDINATION
Afghanistan, 3/7/1990	Yes	No
Chad, 4/13/2006	No	No
Dominican Republic, 4/25/1965	Yes	No
Haiti, 4/2/1989	Yes	No
Iraq, 6/14/1995	Yes	No
Kenya, 8/1/1982	Yes	No
Libya, 10/11/1993	Yes	Unknown
Morocco, 7/10/1971	Yes	No
Panama, 10/3/1989	Yes	No
Russia, 8/19/1991	No	Yes?
Sudan, 7/2/1976	Yes	No
Thailand, 4/1/1981*	N/A	N/A
SUCCESSFUL COUP ATTEMPTS		
Bangladesh 8/15/1975	No	No
Ghana, 2/24/1966	Yes	No
Peru, 8/29/1975	No	No
Yemen, 9/26/1962	No†	No

Notes: *Internal counterbalancing only. †In Yemen, counterweights did not resist during the coup, but resisted the new coup-installed regime after the coup succeeded.

coup plotters from seizing their targets. In most cases, coup plotters within the military excluded counterweights from their conspiracies. Where they were included, they do not appear to have hindered coordination. In Haiti, colonels from two elite battalions, the Leopards and the Dessalines, which served as counterweights, jointly staged a coup attempt when President Prosper Avril dismissed the head of the Leopards battalion on drug trafficking charges. The coup plotters from these two different forces coordinated a successful attack on the presidential residence, as well as on television and radio stations, which they used to broadcast their actions. The coup did not fail due to tactical challenges in coordination, but because soldiers in Avril's presidential guard eventually came to his aid.[77] In Peru, extensive coordination between the commanders of the country's five military regions and between the military and the Civil Guard, which had long served in a counterbalancing role, ensured that the 1975 coup that overthrew President Juan Velasco Alvarado proceeded smoothly. The coup was accomplished by proclamation: on the morning of August 29, the coup plotters intercepted Velasco at his office and issued a joint declaration announcing the coup.[78]

The coup attempt in Russia is the only one in which the inclusion of multiple security forces in the coup plot may have created tactical challenges in coordinating across units that doomed the attempt. It is thus worth describing in more detail. On August 19, 1991, a group of hard-liners within the Soviet elite, including top-ranking officers in the military, Interior Ministry (MVD), and KGB, staged a coup to remove Mikhail Gorbachev from power.[79] The coup occurred in the run-up to the signing of a new Union Treaty, which coup plotters believed would result in a breakup the Soviet Union.[80] For decades, the military had served as a senior partner in the Communist regime, albeit one the party leadership was wary of. A number of different security forces were built up during the Soviet period, including the troops of the MVD and the KGB, at least in part to serve as counterweights to the military, although a provision remained in place for their control to revert to the military in times of war. This provision was scrapped in 1989, formally separating the Internal Troops, Border Troops, and Railway Troops from the rest of the armed forces.[81]

Several of these security forces participated in the August coup. At the outset of the coup attempt, coup plotters jointly declared a state of emergency, moved troops into Moscow, and placed Gorbachev under house arrest. Coup plotters do not appear to have developed a list of targets to seize in Moscow until the coup itself was under way. At that point, a joint army-MVD-KGB operation to storm the Russian parliament was planned for the next night.[82] Some assessments blame the failure of the coup attempt, in part, on counterbalancing. William Odom argues that one of the reasons "for disorganization is that the coup attempt involved three different military forces—the KGB, the interior ministry, and the regular armed forces—which added an extra level of complexity to the planning." When the military did produce a plan, it was "a poorly developed one with virtually no coordinating arrangements."[83]

Yet the coup did not fail because of tactical failures that prevented coup plotters from seizing their targets. As Naunihal Singh concludes in his analysis of the coup, "From a tactical perspective, there was no reason for this coup attempt to have failed."[84] Instead, it seems to have failed because of the actions taken by Boris Yeltsin, then president of the Russian Republic, who quickly denounced the coup and called for a general strike in response. In the wake of Yeltsin's denunciation, the military was "shaken by sporadic mutinies... with individual servicemen and some entire units defecting" from the coup.[85] Soon, the military units ordered to protect the coup leaders defected and arrested the coup participants.[86]

For one additional case, the 1993 Libyan coup, there was insufficiently detailed coverage of the coup to be able to rule out the presence of coordination problems. This raises concern about a possible selection effect: coups that face armed resistance may result in both higher levels of violence and more press coverage, which makes it easier to construct a case narrative. Although this possibility cannot be entirely eliminated, the fact that I encountered difficulty in only one of the sixteen cases researched suggests that it is unlikely to be biasing the findings more broadly.

Overall, the evidence in this broader sample of coup attempts echoes the findings in Kenya, Morocco, and Panama: where coup attempts failed, they did so in large part because counterweights used force to resist. In the March 7, 1990, coup in Afghanistan, it was the military police and secret police, built up as counterweights to the military, that successfully blocked rebels from seizing the presidential palace and eventually pushed them out of the capital.[87] Similarly, during the April 25, 1965, coup in the Dominican Republic, it was the National Police that retook Radio Santo Domingo headquarters and gave a radio address denying that the regime had been overthrown. Their intervention prevented coup plotters from securing a rapid victory, encouraging opponents of the coup within the military to intervene.[88] In Iraq, Saddam Hussein's Special Republican Guard led the initial response to the 1995 coup attempt; their rapid intervention deterred the participation of units that had planned to provide air support to the coup plotters. Meanwhile, the Fedayeen Saddam, a civilian paramilitary force under the command of Saddam's son, rounded up suspected participants for punishment.[89] And in Libya, it was Muammar Qaddafi's Revolutionary Guards that suppressed the 1993 coup attempt.[90]

Counterweights also sometimes resisted in coup attempts that ultimately succeeded. In Ghana, Kwame Nkrumah's President's Own Guard Regiment was eventually overpowered during the February 24, 1966, coup attempt, but only after exchanging fire with coup forces.[91] In the 1962 coup in Yemen, Imam Muhammad al-Badr used tribal militias as counterweights to the regular army. Stationed just outside the capital, they fled when coup forces took the presidential palace. The Imam survived the initial attack, however, and rallied tribal militias to form the core of the rebel army he used to challenge the new coup-appointed government. While counterweights did not resist during the coup attempt, they thus helped prevent the new regime from effectively consolidating power.[92]

Because the cases examined in this chapter are all cases that progressed from coup plots into coup attempts, these cases cannot be used to test whether counterbalancing impedes coordination *prior* to the start of a coup. It may be the case that high-ranking coup plotters were forced to adopt less effective tactics in staging the coups, or that coup plotters from all ranks had to restrict recruitment more than would have been ideal in order to prevent counterweights from revealing the coup plot.[93] What these cases can shed light on, however, is the causal mechanisms linking counterbalancing to coup failure *during* coup attempts. On the whole, the cases provide scant evidence of coordination problems during coup attempts and suggest that there may be important limitations to the conditions under which this causal mechanism operates. Instead, where counterbalancing worked, it did so primarily because counterweights resisted the coup.

Explaining Cases without Resistance

While the evidence in these cases provides support for the resistance mechanism underpinning counterbalancing, counterweights do not always resist coup attempts. The preceding discussion highlighted three coup attempts that included counterweights as coconspirators: the 1975 coup in Peru, the 1989 coup in Haiti, and the 1991 coup in Russia. While counterweights did not join the coups attempts in Thailand in 1981 or in Chad in 2006, they also did not resist them. And in Bangladesh, Mujibur Rahman's counterweight quickly stood down in the face of coup plotters in the 1975 coup that ousted him from power. The arguments developed in this book are probabilistic ones: we should not expect the presence of counterweights to result in coup failure in all instances, merely to make it more likely than in cases where rulers do not counterbalance. Nonetheless, it is useful to examine cases that are poorly predicted by the theory in order to assess whether they are idiosyncratic ones—in that some set of circumstances unique to the case can explain its outcome, or that it was misclassified in some way—or whether the case can suggest potential refinements or scope conditions to the theory. Two of the cases are in the former category. The 2006 coup in Chad differs from most coups in that it was led by rebel forces; as such, Idriss Déby was able to use the regular military to suppress it (see the appendix for more details on this coup attempt). And while a number of qualitative accounts describe Thailand in 1981 as heavily coup-proofed, analysis of the case suggests that it was misclassified: the primary form of coup-proofing used at the time involved exploiting divisions *within* the regular military rather than outside of it. In what follows, I examine in more detail two of the cases whose outcomes cannot be explained by such idiosyncratic features, Bangladesh and Peru, and which thus might suggest ways to refine the theory.

When Counterweights Are Blocked: The 1975 Coup in Bangladesh

On August 15, 1975, young officers in the Bangladeshi army began firing at the home of President Sheikh Mujibur Rahman and his family.[94] While Mujibur, who was referred to as Mujib, had counterbalanced the military, coup plotters carefully planned their attack to head off potential resistance from them. Tensions between Mujib's regime and segments of the former East Bengal Regiment (EBR) officers that formed the core of Bangladesh's new army arose in the years following Bangladesh's independence. As part of the conflict, EBR officers, concerned that they could not defend the region on their own, began training civilians for guerrilla warfare. In doing so, they were able to build on an existing but largely unarmed village-based civilian auxiliary established by the British called the Ansars Bahini. Self-defense groups and party militia formed a third strand of resistance. These included the Communist Party's East Bengal forces, led by Abdul Matin, and a number of private self-defense groups, like those of Kader Siddiqui.[95] The term Mukti Bahini or "Liberation Army" came to refer to all of the armed groups that fought for independence. The conflict ended after India intervened in early December 1971.

Many of the soldiers who fought for independence had supported Mujib's political party, the Awami League, in the years leading up to the war, but were dismayed with what they considered to be an insufficient allocation of funds to expand the regular military, reconstruct training centers and military bases destroyed during the conflict, and issue back pay to soldiers who had gone without for the duration of the conflict.[96] Mujib, however, was concerned that allocating too many resources to the military, which enjoyed a great deal of public support for its role in the secession, might enable it to interfere in politics. The example of Pakistan, where the military had become the dominant political force, loomed large.[97]

In Mujib's estimation, the new state faced few external security threats: its close ties to India in the years following the war of independence deterred any resurgent claims from Pakistan.[98] The sheer population differential between Bangladesh and its neighbors (both India and Pakistan) also meant that it was doubtful that even a military double or triple the existing size "could fight a conventional war for more than a few days without massive assistance from a foreign power."[99] Attempting to equip the military to do so thus seemed misguided. Instead, Mujib pursued a policy of conciliation with Bangladesh's neighbors.

By mid-1972, as conflict with the military increased, Mujib came to doubt the commitment of the military to his regime and began diverting defense resources to form a new paramilitary force: the Jatiyo Rakkhi Bahini (JRB), or National Defense Force. The order establishing the JRB specified that it report directly to Mujib rather than through the regular military chain of command.[100] This move was widely interpreted as an effort to hedge the power of the military. As Z. R. Khan describes it, "Mujib sought to raise a division of security forces which would have unquestioned loyalty to the new regime."[101] The Rakkhi Bahini quickly came to be known as the "personal security force and political enforcement body of the Awami League" and Mujib's "private army."[102] The force consisted of some sixteen thousand members by 1975. It was used to confiscate arms remaining in the hands of former freedom fighters, combat smuggling, maintain general law and order, and "carry out operations of a political nature which it was felt the police were incapable of handling," such as suppressing opposition rallies.[103] The military resented the diversion of resources and potential military recruits to the new force, and complained bitterly about what they considered to be preferential budgetary treatment for the Rakkhi Bahini. Dina Siddiqi explains that "the military saw its identity as protector of national interests undermined as well as its corporate interests threatened by the creation of the JRB."[104] At the same time, Mujib took steps to solidify the Awami League's position. In February 1975, Mujib told U.S. officials that he intended to establish a one-party state.[105]

These frustrations came to a head in an August 15, 1975, coup led by several young majors, including Farook Rahman and Khandaker Abdur Rashid. James Heitzman and Robert Worden argue that, "in a wider sense, the disaffected officers and the several hundred troops they led represented the grievances of the professionals in the military over their subordination to the Jatiyo Rakkhi Bahini and Mujib's indifference to gross corruption by his political subordinates and family members."[106] As the coup got under way, the majors launched simultaneous attacks on the airport, the radio station, and the barracks of both the JRB and the Bangladesh Rifles.

The coup plotters anticipated resistance from the JRB. They planned the coup for a time when the JRB commander, Brigadier General A. N. M Nuruzzaman, was out of town. As a consequence, Anthony Mascarenhas explains, "Mujib's elite storm troopers were not geared, as they normally were, for instant action."[107] The coup plotters also deployed the few tanks at their disposal to the JRB barracks, anticipating resistance. A tense standoff ensued, but neither side fired. As a result, despite their preferential treatment and close ties to Mujib, the JRB offered no resistance to the coup. Meanwhile, coup forces were able to get past the few bodyguards at Mujib's home.

Surrounding JRB headquarters isolated the unit in a way that enabled coup plotters to shape their expectations about the outcome of the coup. While the siege of the palace was under way, Mujib reportedly telephoned JRB headquarters in an attempt to rally the force to his defense, but could not get through to a senior officer. The coup plotters announced via the radio that the JRB had a new acting commander, Abdul Hasan Khan, and that they had his support.[108] No matter their personal preferences, there was little to gain from resisting a coup that had already ended. Sheikh Mujib was killed, along with several members of his family, within the first few hours of the coup. While sporadic fighting between coup forces and those loyal to Mujib continued for the next few days, it petered out as larger-scale resistance failed to materialize. In the wake of the coup, the JRB was absorbed into the army.[109]

As this discussion suggests, counterweights—even those with good reason to fear a decline in status following a military coup—are unlikely to resist where coup plotters anticipate their resistance and take steps to neutralize them. In this case, the coup attempt was timed to coincide with the absence of the JRB's commander, and coup plotters deployed the few tanks at their disposal to JRB headquarters. As a result, they were able to successfully shape expectations about the coups likely outcome. There was little to gain from resistance. In other cases in which coup plotters are able to cut off the access counterbalancing forces have to outside information, they may be able to similarly head off resistance.

When Counterweights Themselves Rebel: The 1975 Coup in Peru

While Mujib's counterweight failed to resist the 1975 coup that removed him from power, in Peru, the counterweight joined the coup attempt. On August 29, 1975, President Juan Velasco Alvarado, who had led a leftist military government in Peru for seven years, was ousted by the country's premier, General Francisco Morales Bermúdez, in a bloodless coup. The paramilitary Civil Guard, which had been built up as a counterweight to the military, participated in the coup because it had been increasingly marginalized under Velasco's regime. Velasco had come to power in a 1968 coup that overthrew Fernando Belaunde Terry. Under Velasco's rule, the military took on a key role in the country's internal development.[110] Over time, however, worsening economic conditions and high foreign debt, along with the increasing personalization of Velasco's regime, turned many officers against him. By 1975, annual inflation had reached 20 percent. New land reform initiatives and collectivization of ownership of industrial plants, undertaken by Velasco's regime, had failed to raise the living standards of most rural Peruvians. Velasco also was in deteriorating health. Coup plotters initially considered pressuring him to retire voluntarily, but Morales overruled that option in favor of an overt coup. The coup involved considerable coordination between the military and police beforehand. At 9:00 a.m. on the morning of August 29, when Velasco arrived at his office, the commander of the Lima military region telephoned and ordered him to step down. At the same time, the commanders of all five of Peru's military districts and the Civil Guard issued a joint public declaration of the coup. The declaration was issued from Tacna, a city in southern Peru, where Morales had been inspecting troops.[111]

The inclusion of the Civil Guard was surprising. The force, which was organized under the Ministry of Interior, had a historic role as a "counterforce" to the military, and as such was "grant[ed] the same prerogatives, privileges, favors, and even the same uniforms as those used by army officers."[112] It was about twenty-five thousand men strong, and based in Lima. Another militarized police force, the Republican Guard, was charged with guarding important regime buildings, prisons, and national borders. The relationship between the forces was confrontational—the tension between them was "open and explicit, and ended in spectacular shootings."[113] Frequently, the Republican Guard sided with the army against the Civil Guard. Both the Civil Guard and the Republican Guard competed with the army "over roles, responsibilities, coordination, and support."[114]

Under the military government, however, which had come to power in 1968, the Civil Guard had been neglected. Earlier in the year, members in Lima went on strike for better pay, and army tanks assaulted their headquarters. Those on strike insisted that they had no political aims: "There are no political issues involved. We support the Government."[115] Yet there were signs of growing tensions between the police and the military regime. While the central focus on the strikers' demands was on increasing pay, they also demanded that General Enrique Ibañez, head of the army garrison at the presidential palace, be reprimanded and demoted. In December of the year prior, Ibañez was reported to have hit a police officer during a disagreement. Demonstrations and rioting in Lima in support of the police were violently suppressed. Civil Guard members on strike were forcibly evicted from their barracks. Thirty police officers and seventy civilians were killed.[116] The unity displayed by coup forces was effective. When confronted the morning of the coup, Velasco deliberated briefly in his office, but decided to step down without a fight. As a result, the coup "came without the deployment of tanks and without any visible violence."[117] Velasco and his family left the presidential residence peacefully. Four hours later, Velasco took to the radio to encourage the public to support the new government. After Velasco resigned, the coup faced no other military or civilian opposition.[118]

This case suggests that where counterweights that are marginalized, they have fewer incentives to resist a coup attempt, and may have much to gain from cooperation with other military and security forces. While the Civil Guard had been deliberately built up as a counterweight, it was marginalized under Velasco's regime. This changes the calculation for soldiers within counterbalancing forces: no longer is their fate tied to that of the individual leader or the regime in power. Poor treatment may be more common under military regimes, like Velasco's, than under democratic ones or civilian dictatorships, since military rulers may be more inclined to view counterweights as competitors. In short, poorly paid counterweights are likely to be less effective at stopping coups.

This chapter tested the mechanisms that link counterbalancing to coup failure during coup attempts. Drawing on qualitative evidence from sixteen different coup attempts, it demonstrated that where counterbalancing works, it does so primarily by creating incentives for counterweights to use force to resist. There was little evidence that counterbalancing created coordination problems once the coups were under way: counterweights neither provided early warning that enabled rulers to intercept coup plotters before they captured their targets, nor, where they joined coup plots, did their presence create tactical obstacles. Instead, the evidence in these cases fits better with the logic of resistance. In Kenya, the General Services Unit recaptured the Voice of Kenya radio station from coup forces and backed Moi's return to the capital to reassert control. In Morocco, it was Ministry of Interior forces, including the Sûreté Nationale and Light Security Brigade, that rallied to the defense of King Hassan. And in Panama, Noriega's Battalion 2000, riot police, and paramilitary Dignity Battalions formed the core of armed resistance to the coup. The patterns in other cases are similar. Although counterbalancing is associated with failed coup outcomes, and the qualitative evidence brought to bear in this chapter suggests that this association is a causal one, investigation of cases that were poorly predicted by the theory suggests counterweights may be less effective where coup plotters are able to cut off outside communication, or where counterbalancing forces come to be neglected. In the next chapter, I turn to the question of whether counterbalancing can deter soldiers from staging coup attempts in the first place.

4

AN EFFECTIVE DETERRENT?
Counterbalancing and Coup Attempts

In the early 1960s, Indonesian president Sukarno found himself increasingly under fire from military leaders and domestic opposition groups for his support of the Indonesian Communist Party (PKI). Rumors of an impending coup d'état spread in 1961 and 1962. Military officers came to view the PKI as a threat to their political power and profits from state-owned businesses.[1] In an effort to secure his position, Sukarno created a new presidential guard force, the Tjakrabirawa Special Regiment, which he deployed around the capital. The regiment reported directly to him rather than through the regular military chain of command.[2] In 1964, Sukarno also transferred a mobile police brigade from the Ministry of Defense to the Ministry of Interior to serve as an additional counterweight to the military.[3] The hope was that these new counterbalancing units would deter officers from staging a coup. Harold Crouch concludes that "the reluctance of the army leadership to force a final showdown with the president was due primarily to their concern to avoid an outbreak of fighting between rival military units. The army's superiority in numbers and armaments seemed to guarantee that it would win a conflict in the end, but the costs could have been enormous."[4]

Yet the creation of counterweights was followed by two coup attempts, in 1965 and 1966. Many officers resented the resources and status Sukarno bestowed on these new forces and worried about what their creation meant for the future of the regular military.[5] Counterbalancing also did not resolve the underlying sources of tension between Sukarno and his armed forces. On October 1, 1965, a small group of officers staged a coup attempt in which they kidnapped and executed the army chief and five other high-ranking generals. Although the details of the

79

coup attempt are somewhat murky, the participants in the attack claimed that the aim was to protect Sukarno from an impending coup by right-wing generals.[6] After a violent standoff, the perpetrators were captured and executed. In the weeks and months that followed, Major General Suharto used the failed coup as a pretext to orchestrate a brutal political purge that eventually resulted in the deaths of an estimated half a million soldiers, politicians, and civilians. In 1966, Suharto himself successfully removed Sukarno from power.[7]

This chapter examines how common Sukarno's experience is. Does counterbalancing deter soldiers from staging coup attempts? Does it prevent or delay them? To address these questions, I examine patterns of coup attempts between 1960 and 2010. The analysis provides support for the book's second and third hypotheses, demonstrating that not only does counterbalancing not deter coup attempts, but that creating a new counterweight *increases* the risk of a coup in the following year. In other words, Sukarno's experience is more common than we might expect. This finding highlights one of the central risks of counterbalancing and helps to explain why counterbalancing is not more widespread.

The Dependent Variable: Coup Attempts

The dependent variable in this analysis is a coup attempt. The data on coup attempts comes from the Center for Systemic Peace (CSP).[8] In this dataset, coups are defined as forceful seizures of executive power by a faction within the country's ruling or political elite. Coup attempt is a dichotomous indicator equal to 1 in any year in which one or more coup attempts occurred. Both failed and successful coup attempts are included. I focus on the first coup attempt that occurs in each country in each year. Although this entails the loss of some data, most of the independent variables are measured on a yearly basis, and I cannot be sure that their values have not changed after the first coup attempt in a year.

Table 4.1 presents the incidence of coup attempts by the use of counterbalancing. If counterbalancing deterred coup attempts, we would expect to see that the percentage of country years with coup attempts is lower where rulers counterbalance than where they do not. Yet this does not appear to be the case. Where rulers counterbalance, there is approximately a 6 percent risk of a coup attempt in any given year; where they do not, this risk is 5 percent. This difference is not statistically significant. Yet the data in table 4.1 does show an association between coup attempts and the creation of a new counterweight. In the year following the creation of a new counterweight, the risk of a coup attempt increases from 5 percent to 14 percent—an increase of 180 percent—which is statistically significant ($p<0.01$). This data is consistent with the argument that counterbalanc-

TABLE 4.1 Cross tabulation of coup attempts and counterbalancing

	COUNTERBALANCING		NEW COUNTERWEIGHT		
	NO	YES	NO	YES	TOTAL
Total observations	1,776	3,271	4,918	129	5,047
No coup attempt	1,690	3,091	4,670	111	4,781
Coup attempt	86	180	248	18	266
% Country years with coup attempts	5%	6%	5%	14%	5%

ing does not deter coup attempts—and that the creation of new counterweights can provoke them.

Statistical Analyses of Counterbalancing and Coup Attempts

These cross-national patterns provide preliminary support to the argument that counterbalancing does not effectively deter coups, and that it can even result in new coup attempts. They do not, however, control for potentially confounding variables or test alternative explanations. To do so, I use two distinct models. I first estimate the relationship between counterbalancing and coup attempts using a logit model. This approach treats the data as binary time-series cross-sectional data. I correct standard errors for clustering at the country-level, and include fixed effects parameters in some specifications. I then use a hazard model to estimate the time to a coup attempt following the creation of a counterweight. This approach treats the data as duration data.[9]

Control variables in both models were carefully chosen to capture central theories about the causes of coups, including those that emphasize norms governing civilian rule, the military's disposition to intervene, and its ability to do so successfully. To capture normative theories of coups, which emphasize that coup attempts are likely where norms of democratic and civilian control of the military are absent, I include indicators for democratic regimes and military regimes. Political liberalization is thought to increase perceptions about the legitimacy of civilian rule and protect regimes from overthrow. Military regimes, in contrast, are thought to be particularly coup prone because of how susceptible they are to internal divisions.[10]

Several features of the military as an institution are thought to shape its opportunity and motives for intervention. Military budgets are a particularly frequent source of conflict between military and civilian leaders that may affect the disposition to intervene.[11] Elite officers can use the military budget to maintain their own patronage networks. For lower-ranking officers, larger military budgets provide benefits in the form of higher salaries, more benefits, and better equipment.[12] Low levels of military funding could also reflect a lack of training and organizational resources that might foster norms of civilian control. I control for changes in military spending from the previous year, taken from the Correlates of War capability (CINC) military expenditure component variable, as well as expenditure per soldier.[13] The size of the military may also affect the incidence of coup attempts. While some scholars have suggested that larger militaries are more likely to stage coups, others contend that military size presents an obstacle to organizing a coup attempt. An indicator for military personnel (log) is thus also included.[14]

Economic performance is thought to affect the incidence of coup attempts. Poor economic performance may decrease satisfaction with the current regime among the military and other elites. Higher levels of economic development raise the costs of coups. As a result, coup attempts are more likely in poorer states.[15] Economic crises are also expected to increase the incidence of coup attempts because they generate grievances against the regime.[16] I thus include controls for GDP/capita (log) and change in GDP.[17] Domestic political crises may also provide opportunities for coup attempts. They signal ongoing public dissatisfaction with the regime that the military or other elites may take advantage of to stage a coup. I thus include controls for domestic political instability in the form of strikes, riots, and demonstrations.[18] Other large-scale political upheavals may also provoke coups. Revolutions, which transform state institutions, threaten the status of the armed forces, which may result in more frequent coup attempts in the years immediately following. To account for this possibility, I include an indicator for recent revolutions, which captures whether the government transformed the existing social, political, or economic relations of the state within the past three years.[19]

Finally, several studies have identified a link between previous coups and subsequent ones.[20] Military seizures of power undermine norms of civilian control and open the door to subsequent coup attempts. I include a control for a country's prior history of coups (years since coup), along with associated cubic splines.[21] Table 4.2 provides descriptive statistics for each of the dependent and independent variables used in the analysis in this chapter. The independent variables are lagged one year to ensure that their values are not influenced by the coup attempt.

Table 4.3 shows the results of the logistic regression. Models 1–4 use the dichotomous indicator of counterbalancing; models 5–7 use the logged number of counterweights. The results show no clear relationship between counterbalancing and the incidence of coup attempts: the coefficients on counterbalancing and number of counterweights (log) are positive, but do not reach statistical signifi-

TABLE 4.2 Descriptive statistics for dependent and independent variables (coup attempts)

VARIABLE	N	MEAN	STANDARD DEVIATION	MIN	MAX
Coup attempt	5,259	0.082	0.275	0	1
Counterbalancing	5,047	0.648	0.478	0	1
Number of counterweights	5,047	1.168	1.184	0	9
Number of counterweights (log)	5,047	0.634	0.530	0	2.303
New counterweight	5,047	0.026	0.158	0	1
Change in military expenditure	4,535	0.082	0.354	−2.394	7.584
Military expenditure/soldier	4,601	3.676	1.785	1.189	18.343
Military personnel (log)	4,747	4.070	1.710	0	8.466
Military regime	4,804	0.094	0.292	0	1
Democracy	5,043	0.386	0.487	0	1
GDP/capita (log)	5,041	8.285	1.184	4.889	11.637
Change in GDP/capita	5,005	0.017	0.099	−1.130	2.007
Recent revolution	4,401	0.033	0.178	0	1
Instability	4,937	0.340	0.474	0	1
Years since last coup	5,259	14.718	13.650	0	59

cance at conventional levels. In contrast, the results on the dummy variable for the creation of a new counterweight indicate a positive and statistically significant relationship with coup attempts. These general patterns hold in the models with the main independent variables and no controls, as well as the models with a full set of control variables.

These findings are consistent with the argument that counterbalancing does not deter coup attempts. However, they do suggest that the creation of a new counterweight is associated with an increased risk of a coup attempt in the following year. The associations between control variables and coup attempts are largely as anticipated. In these regressions, larger militaries are associated with fewer coup attempts, while military regimes and ongoing instability are associated with more frequent coup attempts. Wealth, economic growth, and time since a previous coup are all negatively associated with coup attempts. The substantive effects of counterweight creation are large. Figure 4.1 shows how the predicted probability of a coup attempt changes with changes in selected independent and control variables while holding all others at their mean (from table 4.3, model 4). The likelihood of a coup attempt is nearly 6 percentage points higher where rulers create a new counterweight than where they do not. Since the average probability of a coup attempt in any given country-year is 5 percent, a change of 6 percentage points is large.

TABLE 4.3 Coup attempts: Logit results

	MODEL 1	MODEL 2	MODEL 3	MODEL 4	MODEL 5	MODEL 6	MODEL 7
Counterbalancing	0.135			0.060			
	(0.243)			(0.178)			
Number of counterweights (log)			0.066		0.075	-0.005	0.084
			(0.244)		(0.214)	(0.215)	(0.179)
New counterweight		1.116***	1.093***	0.850***		1.119***	0.833***
		(0.280)	(0.277)	(0.310)		(0.276)	(0.308)
Change in military expenditure				-0.093			-0.091
				(0.221)			(0.220)
Military expenditure/soldier				-0.127			-0.126
				(0.084)			(0.084)
Military personnel (log)				-0.278***			-0.280***
				(0.091)			(0.092)
Military regime				0.353*			0.366*
				(0.190)			(0.199)
Democracy				-0.188			-0.174
				(0.236)			(0.249)
GDP/capita (log)				-0.266***			-0.268***
				(0.096)			(0.097)
Change in GDP/capita				-1.333**			-1.322**
				(0.627)			(0.637)
Recent revolution				-0.180			-0.177
				(0.305)			(0.303)

Instability			0.297*		0.301*
			(0.166)		(0.166)
Years since coup			−0.344***		−0.344***
			(0.070)		(0.070)
Constant	−2.978***	−2.935***	−2.978***	1.857*	−2.937***	−2.933***	1.848**
	(0.213)	(0.130)	(0.213)	(0.964)	(0.193)	(0.192)	(0.937)
Log likelihood	−1041.207	−1034.603	−1034.486	−725.271	−1041.519	−1034.602	−725.191
Pseudo R-squared	0.001	0.007	0.007	0.146	0.000	0.007	0.146
Observations	5,047	5,047	5,047	3,861	5,047	5,047	3,861

Notes: Robust standard errors clustered by country in parentheses. *** p<0.01, ** p<0.05, * p<0.1. Cubic splines are included in Models 4 and 7.

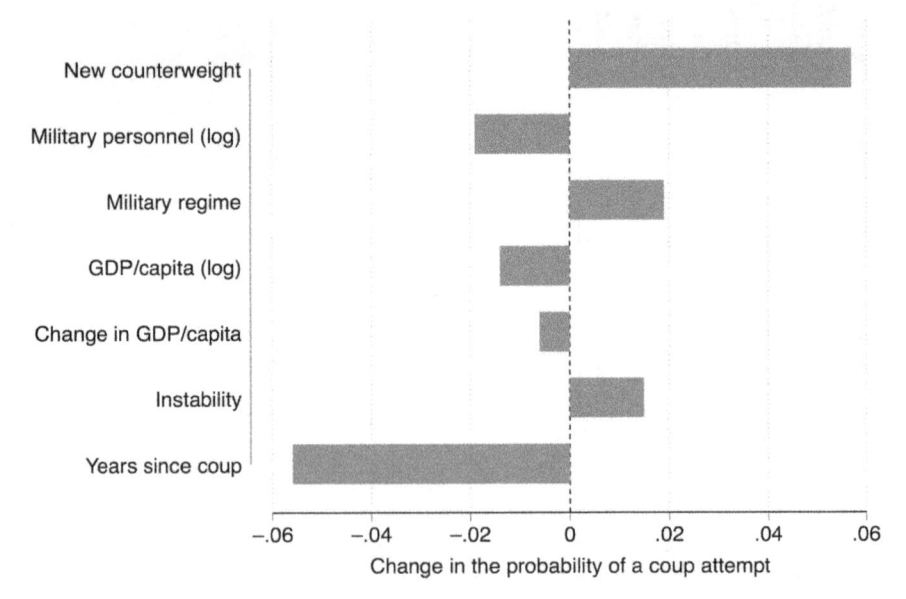

FIGURE 4.1. Marginal effect of selected variables on coup attempts (from table 4.3, model 4)

Note: For discrete variables, the marginal effect of a change from 0 to 1 is shown. For continuous variables, a change of one standard deviation is shown.

Survival Analysis

I next treat the data as time duration data. Event history analysis entails understanding not only if something happens, but when it happens. In other words, while the logistic model above can help us understand whether counterbalancing affects the incidence of coups, event history analysis can help us understand whether it affects the ability of regimes to survive in the long term. The dependent variable measures the length of time before a coup attempt occurs. In this case, we can examine whether the extent of counterbalancing that occurs or the creation of a new counterweight influences the length of the time before a coup attempt. I model years for every country until a coup attempt or "failure" occurs.[22] In this analysis, a country's survival rate is the probability of not experiencing a new coup attempt. This approach accounts for the effect of past coup attempts on the subsequent risk of a coup attempt. I use the conditional risk set model, a version of the semiparametric Cox model; unlike other event history models, the conditional risk set model does not make assumptions about how the risk changes over time but lets the data generate the level of risk. It also accounts for the possibility of multiple coup attempts. It measures time to each event from the time of the previous event.[23]

I first present bivariate Cox models with each independent variable, followed by a model containing all independent variables but not controls, and then a full model that contains all controls. Standard errors are clustered by country to account for potential heteroskedasticity in the data. In these models, the coefficients are parameterized in terms of the hazard rate. As a result, a positive coefficient indicates that the hazard increases as a function of the covariate (and survival time is decreasing). A negative coefficient indicates that the hazard is decreasing (and survival time is increasing). The results are presented in terms of the hazard ratios. I also include the size of the effect.

Table 4.4 shows the results of the survival analysis. It suggests that creating a new counterweight has a negative, statistically significant effect on the length of time a regime can survive without a coup attempt. The effect is substantively large: in the model with a full set of control variables, the creation of a new counterweight increases the risk of a coup by about 170 percent in the following year. Figure 4.2 graphs differing survival rates for two regimes: one that creates a new counterweight, and one that does not. Since repeated events Cox models do not allow for the estimation of survival functions, this figure is based on the traditional Cox model, which is a single-event model. It shows that regimes that create a new counterweight see an increased risk of a coup attempt that persists over time.

Alternative Arguments and Robustness Checks

The analysis in this chapter shows that creating a new counterweight is associated with an increased coup risk. I have argued that this association is a causal one—that counterbalancing can provoke the very coups it was intended to prevent. But the analysis thus far does not allow us to distinguish between this argument and an alternative one in which counterbalancing and coup attempts are both the function of elevated coup risk. It may be the case that rulers only create new counterweights when they perceive the risk of a coup attempt to be high, and thus that the correlation between new counterweights and coup attempts is spurious. In order to rule out this possibility, we need to know when rulers create counterweights. The idea that rulers would counterbalance when they face a heightened coup risk is intuitive. For instance, Aaron Belkin and Evan Schofer argue that "when the risk of a coup d'état is high, leaders almost always divide their armed forces into multiple organizations that check and balance each other."[24] Elsewhere, Belkin argues that "the possibility of a coup should almost always prompt regimes to pursue counterbalancing strategies."[25] Similarly, Ulrich

TABLE 4.4 Coup attempts: Survival analysis

	MODEL 1		MODEL 2		MODEL 3		MODEL 4	
	HAZARD RATIO	EFFECT	HAZARD RATIO	EFFECT	HAZARD RATIO	EFFECT	HAZARD RATIO	EFFECT
Counterbalancing	1.206	20.6%			1.132	13.2%	1.064	6.4%
	(0.199)				(0.185)		(0.199)	
New counterweight			2.625***	162.5%	2.497***	149.7%	2.703***	170.3%
			(0.686)		(0.645)		(0.828)	
Change in military expenditure							0.928	7.2%
							(0.196)	
Military personnel (log)							0.875	12.5%
							(0.789)	
Military regime							0.914	8.6%
							(0.178)	
Democracy							0.884	11.6%
							(0.205)	
GDP/capita (log)							0.982	1.8%
							(0.100)	
Change in GDP/capita							0.172***	82.8%
							(0.116)	
Recent revolution							0.873	12.7%
							(0.268)	
Instability							1.269	26.9%
							(0.228)	
Observations	5,047		5,047		5,047		3,997	
No. of countries	111		111		111		101	
No. of coup attempts	266		266		266		222	

Notes: Robust standard errors clustered by country in parentheses. *** $p<0.01$, ** $p<0.05$, * $p<0.1$. The effect represents the percentage increase or decrease in the likelihood of a future coup attempt.

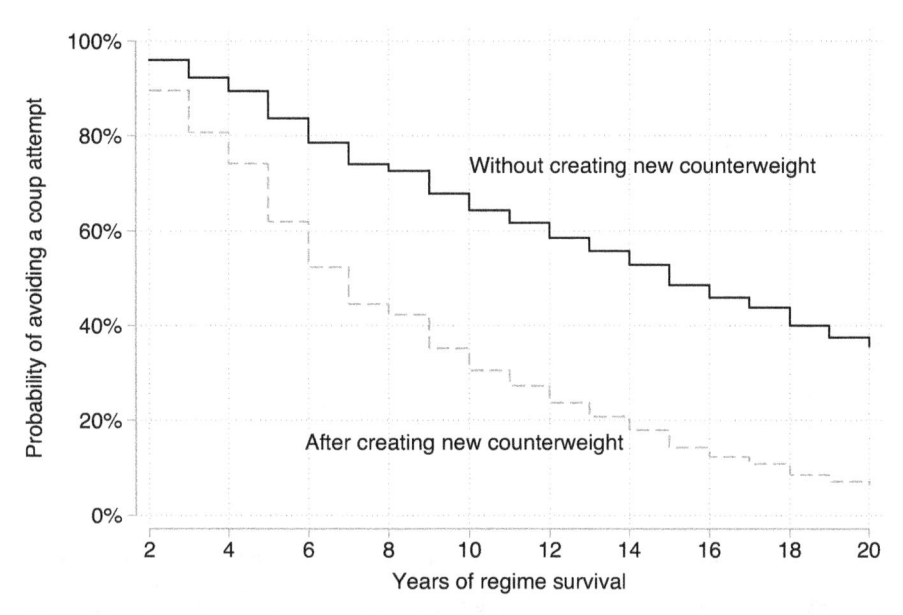

FIGURE 4.2. Change in coup risk with the creation of a new counterweight

Pilster and Tobias Böhmelt argue that autocracies are more likely to counterbalance the military than democracies because they face a higher risk of a coup.[26]

There are reasons to doubt this alternative argument, however. In particular, counterbalancing is most perilous where the risk of a coup is high. As Jun Koga Sudduth argues, where the risk of a coup is high, "leaders' efforts to coup-proof will provide only more grievances and discontent for the already dissatisfied officers and thus, a larger number will be willing to participate in a plot against the leader."[27] In contrast, where the risk of a coup is more moderate, rulers may be able to counterbalance without provoking a coup. Leaders at a particularly low risk of a coup might also be motivated to take steps to weaken the military and minimize its bargaining power. This is why earlier theorists of coup prevention theorized that rulers would only seek to create counterweights in narrow windows of opportunity following successful movements for national independence or successful revolutions.[28]

The empirical evidence in support of this alternative argument is weak. In her analysis, Sudduth finds that political leaders become less likely to counterbalance when the risk of a coup rises. In particular, she models coup risk as a function of several indicators capturing the military's willingness and ability to stage a coup, including GDP/capita (log), democracy, military regimes, and years since last coup—the variables most consistently associated with coup attempts in statistical analyses—and finds a strong, negative correlation between latent coup risk

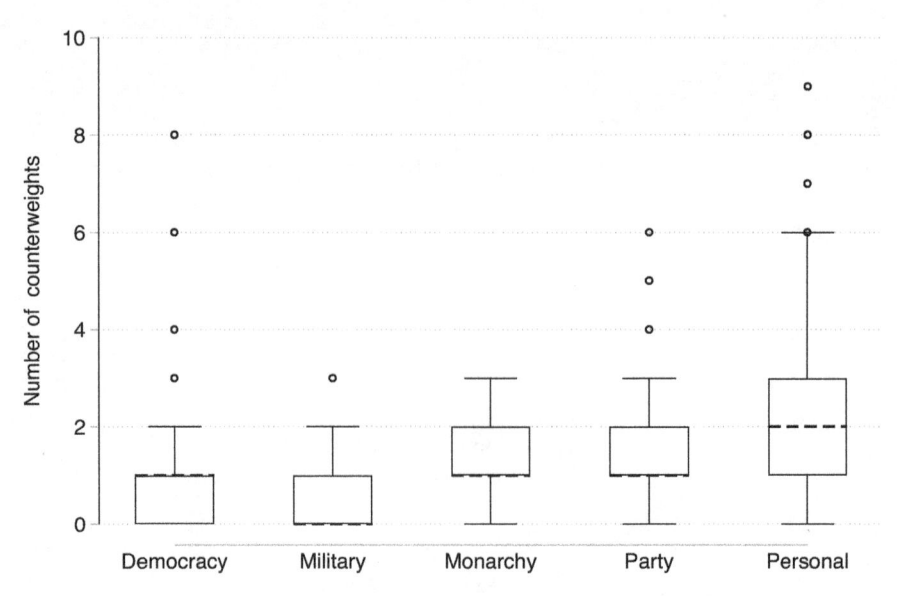

FIGURE 4.3. Counterbalancing by regime type

and counterbalancing. It is also the case that the most coup-prone types of regimes, military regimes, are the least likely to create counterweights. Figure 4.3 shows the average number of counterweights used by democracies, military regimes, monarchies, single-party regimes, and personalist dictatorships.[29] Military regimes are less likely than any other type of regime, including democracies, to counterbalance. Where military regimes inherit counterweights created under previous regimes, they frequently disband them or bring them under military control upon coming to power. For instance, Chile's carabineros were supervised by the Ministry of Interior until the 1973 military coup that deposed Salvador Allende, at which point they were brought under military control.[30] In short, there is little to suggest that coup risk is driving the association between the creation of a new counterweight and the incidence of coup attempts.

Another alternative argument posits that military strength or weakness can explain both coup attempts and the creation of counterweights. As with the alternative argument linking military strength to coup outcomes, however, that linking it to coup attempts is also weak. The argument could run in either direction: while some scholars contend that weaker militaries are more likely to stage coups, others contend that stronger militaries are more likely to do so. If military strength could explain coup attempts and counterweight creation, it should be negatively associated with both. However, as table 4.5 shows, the correlations between indicators of military strength and coup attempts are weak and inconsistent, while new counterweights and military strength are uncorrelated. This suggests that military

TABLE 4.5 Correlations: Coup attempts, new counterweights, and military strength

	COUP ATTEMPT	NEW COUNTERWEIGHT
Military expenditures (log)	−0.22	−0.02
Military personnel (log)	−0.17	0.00
Military regime	0.10	−0.02
Militarism index	0.16	0.03
Proportion of government active military	0.11	0.00

strength or weakness cannot explain why creating a new counterweight is so often followed by a coup attempt in the next year. As an additional robustness check, I confirm that the results hold when military regimes are excluded from the analysis (results not shown).

I next examine whether the relationship between new counterweights and coup attempts remains when selection in the extent of counterbalancing that a regime engages in is modeled explicitly. In the first stage, I include controls for a number of factors with theoretical links to counterbalancing, including whether the state is a former French colony or has a defense alliance with a major power.[31] I find that when selection into counterbalancing is accounted for, the creation of a new counterweight is still associated with a positive, statistically significant increase in coup attempts in the following year (results not shown). The correlation of errors between the selection and outcome equations is also insignificant. In short, coercive institutions exert powerful and independent effects that cannot be accounted for simply by the strength of the military, the extent of the coup threat faced by the regime, or the extent of existing counterbalancing.

It is reasonable to wonder whether the results are driven by temporal dynamics or time-invariant characteristics of states. Yet the positive association between the creation of a new counterweight and the incidence of coup attempts is robust to the inclusion of country and year fixed effects (results not shown). I examine whether particular coding decisions in the Center for Systemic Peace's coup data might be driving the results by re-estimating the main text models using only those coups that are also in Jonathan Powell and Clayton Thyne's coup dataset. The main results are unchanged (results not shown).

I next re-estimate the models after removing each control variable. The results remain unchanged in all twenty regressions in these tables, suggesting that the findings are not simply an artifact of including particular control variables (results not shown). In place of the indicator for domestic political instability, which captures the presence of riots, demonstrations, and strikes, I substitute more indirect measures of the threats facing political rulers, including the Gini coefficient and Theil statistic, which measure economic inequality (results not shown).[32] Finally, I re-estimate the results including controls for civil war and interstate conflict, which may potentially affect both counterbalancing and coups.[33] The central results remain unchanged (results not shown). All told, these efforts to address potential sources of spurious correlation and selection effects, and to ensure that the findings are not merely the result of particular coding decisions, modeling decisions, and control variables, should increase confidence that the results presented above are not illusory.

In contrast to prevailing theoretical expectations, this chapter demonstrates that counterbalancing does not insulate rulers from coup attempts. These findings are robust to a number of different estimation methods, modeling assumptions, and robustness checks. I argue that while the anticipation of failure should deter some potential coup plotters, counterbalancing also infringes on central institutional interests of the military, creating perceptions about a decline in status. As a result, the deterrent effect of counterbalancing is offset by the new grievances created. In fact, as this chapter shows, the creation of a new counterweight is associated with an increased risk of coups in the following year. The findings in this chapter emphasize some of the risks inherent in counterbalancing and suggest that rulers must exercise caution in establishing new counterweights.

5

CHALLENGES TO BUILDING COERCIVE INSTITUTIONS

The previous chapter established that counterbalancing does not deter soldiers from staging coup attempts. Indeed, establishing a new counterweight to the military is associated with an *increased* risk of a coup attempt in the following year. This raises a new puzzle: Why have some rulers been able to build new coercive institutions to counterbalance the military without provoking coup attempts, while others have not? Previous scholarship suggests that counterweights might be created without provoking a coup in the aftermath of successful revolutions or violent wars for independence in which the traditional military has been destroyed or incapacitated.[1] Yet counterweight creation is much more common than these theories would suggest. In order to understand the conditions under which counterweight creation is possible, this chapter compares successful efforts to counterbalance the military to failed ones that occurred in similar circumstances. I begin with Ghana, where Kwame Nkrumah's transformation of the President's Own Guard Regiment (POGR) from a largely ceremonial presidential guard unit within the regular military into a formidable counterweight ended up triggering the coup that ousted him from power in 1966. Nkrumah's case is one of the most well-known and widely cited examples of counterbalancing failure. This chapter traces in detail how Nkrumah's increasing dependence on the POGR generated resentment within the regular army, and how that resentment eventually provoked a coup attempt.

In contrast to Nkrumah, some leaders have been able to create new counterweights and then use them to fend off subsequent coup attempts. Here I compare Nkrumah's experience to that of three other leaders in very similar political and economic contexts: Siaka Stevens in Sierra Leone, Modibo Keita in Mali, and Fidel Castro in Cuba. In Mali, as in Ghana, the effort to establish a counterweight—in this case, a civilian militia—resulted in a coup attempt in which the military intervened to abolish it. Yet Stevens and Castro succeeded where Nkrumah and Keita failed. In Sierra Leone, Siaka Stevens established a paramilitary police force under his command, the Internal Security Unit, without triggering a coup attempt. And in Cuba, Fidel Castro succeeded in establishing Special Operations Troops under the Interior Ministry while retaining civilian control over the military (see table 5.1).

In comparing the experiences of these four leaders, the aim is both to explain the diverging outcomes in these specific cases and to inductively develop new hypotheses about the conditions under which building new counterweights will backfire. As such, the comparison is primarily an exercise in theory generation. Chapter 3 examined cases that were representative of the broader universe of cases from which they were drawn. In this chapter, in contrast, I use the structured comparisons of cases selected to hold constant important features of states thought to affect the likelihood of a coup attempt, including the type of political regime, the level of economic development, preexisting economic or political stability, and the level of military spending (see table 5.2). This allows me to focus instead on the strategic choices leaders make in designing their coup-proofing strategies. Each case involves a middle-income civilian dictatorship experiencing a modest decline in real GDP per capita, with similar levels of military spending and size. None experienced political instability in the form of strikes, riots, or demonstrations, or a revolution in the three years prior to the creation of a new counterweight (although Cuba experienced one four years before its creation of a new counterweight). The cases provide support for the proposed causal mechanism linking new counterweights to coup attempts developed in chapter 1 and suggests that the positive association between counterweight creation and coup attempts found in chapter 4 is a causal one: in each case, efforts to establish counterweights rankled officers in the regular military, who feared a decline in status, as anticipated.

The cases also shed light on the conditions under which building new counterweights is possible. The explanations presented here highlight the role of other

TABLE 5.1 Summary of case outcomes: New counterweights and coup attempts

COUNTRY	NEW COUNTERWEIGHT	COUP ATTEMPT
Ghana, 1960–66	President's Own Guard Regiment	Yes
Sierra Leone, 1968–74	Internal Security Unit	No
Mali, 1960–68	Popular Militia	Yes
Cuba, 1959–65	Special Operations Troops	No

TABLE 5.2 The context of counterweight creation in Ghana, Sierra Leone, Mali, and Cuba

COUNTRY	GHANA	SIERRA LEONE	MALI	CUBA
Year counterweight established	1966	1971	1964	1963
Military regime	No	No	No	No
Democracy	No	No	No	No
GDP/capita (log)	7.62	7.02	6.03	7.94
Change in GDP/capita	−0.05	−0.01	−0.24	−0.01
Change in military expenditure	0.14	0.19	0.09	0.00
Military expenditure/soldier	3.20	7.46	4.46	2.79
Military personnel (log)	3.22	1.10	2.08	4.38
Recent revolution	No	No	No	No
Instability	No	No	No	No
Years since last coup	N/A	3	N/A	6

coup-proofing strategies adopted in conjunction with counterbalancing. In contrast to Nkrumah and Keita, Stevens and Castro undertook counterbalancing in the wake of aggressive purges of the armed forces, combined with generous salaries and perks for senior officers who remained. In Sierra Leone, Stevens's effort to counterbalance came several years after he began stacking the military with co-ethnics and pushing others out. He lavished perks on senior officers, providing them with opportunities for economic enrichment, as well as political positions within his cabinet. At the same time, he worked to create obstacles to intervention: officers were rotated frequently through their posts, and the access of lower-ranked officers and enlisted men to weaponry was restricted. Meanwhile, in Cuba, Castro paired the creation of counterweights under a powerful Ministry of Interior with the purging of political opponents, expansion of the military's budget, and retention of military autonomy over defense matters. This analysis suggests that a fruitful direction for future research would be to examine how counterbalancing interacts with other strategies of coup-proofing.

The case comparison also suggests that the type of security force rulers establish to counterbalance the military may matter. In both cases in which counterbalancing proceeded without a coup, Sierra Leone and Cuba, the counterweight took the form of a militarized police force organized under the Interior Ministry. In Ghana and Mali, where counterbalancing provoked coup attempts, counterbalancing took the form of a presidential guard and civilian militia, respectively. Both were under the direct control of the executive. The final section of the chapter uses statistical analysis to test the hypothesis that officers are less likely to stage coups in response to the establishment of militarized police than in response to the creation of other types of counterweights. The analysis concludes that when counterbalancing is disaggregated by the type of counterweight created, new militias and secret police are associated with an increased likelihood of a coup attempt, while new presidential guards and militarized police are not. Thus while Nkrumah's example is frequently invoked as a cautionary tale, most rulers have an easier time counterbalancing with presidential guard forces than he did. These findings are important because they suggest that particular forms of counterbalancing may be less risky than others and highlight ways in which rulers might mitigate the costs of counterbalancing.

Failed Counterbalancing in Ghana, 1960–1966: The President's Own Guard Regiment

On February 24, 1966, a group of senior officers in Ghana's army and police ousted Kwame Nkrumah from power. The coup plotters objected to the country's drift toward socialism, Nkrumah's efforts to centralize political power, and—most forcefully—his efforts to build up parallel security forces as counterweights to the military.[2] When Nkrumah first came to power in Ghana, in 1957, he had widespread support inside and outside of the military. Early in his tenure, to promote rapid industrialization, he invested heavily in the construction of infrastructure and schools, factories and dams. He also moved toward a system of mechanized, state-run farms.[3] At the same time, Nkrumah invested in expanding and better equipping the armed forces. He raised an additional battalion for the army, and established naval and air forces. This investment was motivated, in part, by Nkrumah's desire to expand Ghana's influence abroad. He hoped that a stronger army could help support other free African states as well as provide for internal security.[4]

Yet Nkrumah soon came into conflict with military officers over his use of the army. His vision for Ghana's foreign policy included robust support for liberation movements elsewhere in Africa. The decision to send Ghanaian military and police units to the Congo under UN command in 1960–1961 turned many officers against his regime. What some came to see as Nkrumah's political meddling during the operation cast suspicion on the neutrality of Ghanaian troops and "made them victims of physical abuse and murder by the Congolese."[5] One senior officer described the intervention as part of a defense policy that "appeared to be determined in terms of prestige or in relation to some wild, political ambitions, rather than anything else."[6] Nkrumah used the military to help suppress strikes in September 1961. There were also ethnic tensions within the military. At independence, most infantry soldiers were northerners, while the officer corps was composed primarily of southerners including Ewe, Gã, and Ashani officers. Nkrumah's decision in 1961 to expel remaining British officers from Ghana opened up more opportunities for promotion within the armed forces, but also, many officers feared, would also free Nkrumah from constraints on using the military for his own purposes. Although he did not engage in ethnic stacking, there were perceptions that Nkrumah routinely passed over Ewe and Gã officers for promotion. A series of assassination attempts in 1962 and 1963 put Nkrumah on high alert.[7]

Nkrumah's growing concern for his personal safety prompted him to reorganize Ghana's security sector. In 1963, the National Security Service (NSS) Act organized a number of specialized intelligence and security units under Nkrumah's direct command. Military Intelligence, originally a small unit within the regular army, was transformed into a more robust secret police force under the NSS and was tasked with surveilling the army, navy, and air force. A new Special Intelligence Unit was also established under the NSS in 1963 focused on surveilling civilian opponents of Nkrumah's regime, while the Counter Intelligence Division (CID) kept an eye on the other security forces within the NSS. To command these new forces, Nkrumah increasingly turned to his small ethnic group, the Nzima, from western Ghana.[8]

But the most objectionable move, from the perspective of many officers, was Nkrumah's elevation of the POGR, which been a ceremonial presidential guard unit that served as a "relief post" for older soldiers, into an independent counterweight. In 1964, Nkrumah expanded it to battalion strength and commissioned new, luxurious flats for POGR officers. At the time, American embassy staff in Accra interpreted these changes as an indication that "Nkrumah is 'running scared' and believes he needs to insure the loyalty of the Guard by 'fringe benefits' far beyond what the average serviceman expects."[9] That year, Nkrumah also began a series of moves to centralize and consolidate his own political power. In January, he sponsored a constitutional referendum that made his political party, the Convention People's Party (CPP), the only legal political party in the country. Nkrumah had founded the CPP prior to Ghana's independence, and it remained popular. But the referendum itself was beset by fraud and intimidation; results showed an improbable 99.91 percent of voters in support.[10] Nkrumah also began to assert more control over army affairs. In June 1964, he proposed a plan to introduce political commissars into the army. The military resented the intrusion. One of the leaders of the 1966 coup that removed Nkrumah from power later described his impression that "for a long time, the Convention People's Party had made a steady assault on the Army with a determined programme to indoctrinate it with the ideology of Nkrumaism."[11] The following summer, Nkrumah dismissed the chief and deputy chief of the defense staff, reorganized the Ministry of Defense, and assumed direct personal responsibility for military affairs.[12]

Resentment within the military and the police service grew. Officers complained that they did not have enough resources to be able to fulfill the ambitious tasks they were being asked to perform. Soldiers had returned from the Congo mission with uniforms and equipment in need of repair. As one of the participants in the 1966 coup attempt put it, "Our clothes were virtually in tatters. We had no ammunition." At the same time, he continued, "we were also aware that members of the President's Own Guard Regiment were receiving kingly treatment."[13] Another recalled, "So it happened that naturally the rank and file of the Guard Regiment were envied because they had the best of everything! The best of equipment, the best of rations, the best of morale."[14]

The police, which had worked in close cooperation with the army in several matters of internal security, also resented being identified with the CPP's increasingly repressive policies.[15] Prior to independence, Nkrumah had been critical of the police force and its intelligence unit, the Special Branch, in particular. After a failed assassination attempt in 1964, Nkrumah blamed the police. In response, he "rendered the police a less effective counterweight to the army by disarming it, detaining eight of the most senior political officers, and then transferring the Special Branch from police to presidential control, an accusation of incompetence which angered the police."[16] Nkrumah later recalled, "I tried in these circumstances to build up a new security service which would be completely independent of the police," but it was dependent on personnel from the civil service, who he felt were hostile to his regime.[17] Meanwhile, police officers who remained were aware that members of the police who had been moved into the new NSS received higher salaries and better benefits. The 1965 Police Service Act made Nkrumah himself personally responsible for appointments within the service. These changes generated a great deal of resentment within the police.[18]

Nkrumah also pushed forward efforts to counterbalance the military. When Nkrumah announced, in July 1995, plans to form a second POGR battalion, soldiers attempted to oust him from power. When that attack failed, Nkrumah went forward with the plan, and the second battalion was trained under Soviet supervision. That same month, he officially moved operational control of the POGR from army command and put it directly under his control.[19] What Simon Baynham describes as a "simmering hostility" developed between the forces.[20] As one subsequent coup plotter recalled, there were "constant arguments" between the POGR commander and the chief of defense staff as to what the latter "could and what he could not do with the Regiment." In January 1966, Nkrumah met with staff officers to clarify that the military no longer had operational control over the presidential guard; instead it was "responsible directly to the Supreme Commander"—Nkrumah.[21] Nkrumah also floated proposals to arm members of two political organizations, the Ghana Young Pioneers and the Workers' Brigade.

Officers viewed these plans as evidence that Nkrumah was seeking to replace them.[22] In late 1966, he sought parliamentary authorization to form a new popular militia. While the stated rationale for the militia was to aid Rhodesian independence, it would also have been "separate from the army and designed as a counter to it."[23] Meanwhile, rumors that Nkrumah planned to enlarge the POGR yet again began to circulate.[24]

It was in this context that a coalition of coalition of Gã-Ewe officers in the military and police service staged the February 1966 coup that ousted Nkrumah from power. The coup attempt began when Colonel Emmanuel Kotoka, commander of the army's Second Brigade in Kumasi, north of the capital, began to move his troops toward Accra. It was timed to coincide with Nkrumah's trip abroad to Vietnam. The chief of defense staff and other top officers were also abroad in Addis Ababa for Organization of African Unity business. Coup forces quickly captured the presidential palace, as well as the Ministry of Defense, the radio station, and the post office.[25] In a speech explaining the coup, Police Commissioner John Harlley noted that Nkrumah had raised a "private army of his own at an annual cost of over half a million pounds in flagrant violation of a constitution which him himself had foisted on the country to serve as a counterpose to the Ghana Armed Forces."[26] He also complained that Nkrumah had armed the POGR "with the most modern and lethal weapons while the national army was neglected. Later, he decided secretly to disband [the] national army and replace it with a militia formed from fanatics."[27] The police, in turn, were instrumental in the execution of the coup. Their familiarity with other branches of the state security apparatus and access to a comprehensive internal communications system were used to neutralize potential opposition during the coup. While the army took on the POGR and seized key buildings in the capital, the police captured senior CPP officials.[28]

The coup plotters anticipated resistance from the POGR, Military Intelligence, and other counterbalancing units under the NSS. Plans were made to arrest the head of Military Intelligence and the POGR commander at the outset of the coup. The POGR, stationed at the presidential palace, defended it, exchanging fire with coup forces.[29] The POGR and other NSS forces "battled army units for ten hours," fighting desperately to keep the coup from succeeding.[30] In the end, however, Nkrumah's wife, fearing for her life, ordered guards at the palace to stand down. Coup forces quickly secured the rest of the city. By the next day, only a small group of presidential guards were still resisting. Three days of demonstrations in Accra and Kumasi followed the coup in support of the new National Liberation Council. Following the coup, the POGR was absorbed into the army.[31]

This case is one in which the grievances new counterweights created within the armed forces are clear. Reflecting on the causes of the coup, Baynham concludes:

"While a number of factors have been identified in explaining the widespread discontent existing within the Ghanaian army by 1966, there seems to be little doubt that Nkrumah's efforts to stem the emergence of internal military power by building up guards to guard guards was the most vital background feature to the coup. More than any other development, it was fear of being squeezed out of existence that united the army officers against the regime."[32] Kotoka, one of the coup plotters, put it simply: "Nkrumah was building a militia. Who can tolerate that?"[33]

Successful Counterbalancing in Sierra Leone, 1968–1974: The Internal Security Unit

Like the creation of the POGR in Ghana, that of the Internal Security Unit (ISU) in Sierra Leone generated resentment and frustration within the armed forces. But unlike in Ghana, officers did not attempt to stage a coup to disband it. In part, this is because by the time Siaka Stevens established the ISU, his multiyear effort to ethnically stack the military had largely concluded. Unlike Nkrumah, Stevens also combined counterbalancing with simultaneous efforts to bribe senior officers and create obstacles to revolts from the rank and file. While officers resented the creation of the ISU, these efforts helped assure senior officers that their status would not decline.

The first several years following Sierra Leone's independence in 1961 had featured multiparty competition. The country's first leader was Sir Milton Margai, who led the Sierra Leone People's Party (SLPP). The SLPP drew support mostly from Mende speakers in the south and east of the country, which represented around 30 percent of the country's population, and won the country's first two elections.[34] Under Margai's regime, existing inequalities between the more developed western, southern, and eastern provinces, on the one hand, and the northern provinces, on the other, became more pronounced. Margai also began to stack the army with Mende soldiers. At the same time, he co-opted some northern elites, appointing them to ministerial positions. The All-People's Congress (APC), which was formed by Siaka Stevens and represented predominantly Temne speakers in the north of the country, became the central opposition party to the SLPP. After Margai's death in 1964, his younger half-brother, Albert Margai, assumed power and accelerated ethnic stacking within the military. He focused on Africanizing the officer corps, replacing British officers with Mende ones.[35] Albert Margai also began to increase the prominence of officers in political life; some saw this "as part of his campaign to abandon the cautious policy of his late brother."[36] By 1966, the army was increasingly drawn into politics. In December of that year, a columnist writing for the newspaper *We Yone* observed, "Politics[,] which is of no concern of soldiers, has now reared its head within the military ranks."[37]

In the March 1967 elections the SLPP was defeated, despite widespread reports of fraud and intimidation, and Siaka Stevens, as head of the APC, was appointed prime minister. However, his appointment was halted by a military takeover. Mende officers within the army feared that the APC's electoral victory would threaten their status. The commander of the armed forces, Brigadier David Lansana, arrested Stevens and declared martial law.[38] But Lansana had trouble commanding the loyalty of his immediate subordinates, and Stevens's supporters rioted. A countercoup just days later established a military junta, the National Reformation Council (NRC), led by Brigadier Andrew Juxon-Smith, a senior officer who had been on leave in Britain at the time. One of the participants in the countercoup, Major Charles Blake, noted concern that Lansana would exclude the rest of the military from the government; as a result, he explained, other officers had "no alternative but to divest the Brigadier of control of this country."[39] Yet, while NRC leaders promised that its rule would not enrich its members, the gulf between senior officers and ordinary soldiers continued to widen. There were complaints about poor conditions in the barracks. New uniforms—which the NRC promised it would provide—never materialized. Meanwhile, senior officers appeared to be "basking in untold wealth."[40]

As a result, the NRC governed for just one year before another coup in April 1968, led by two warrant officers, Patrick Conteh and Emadu Rogers, returned Stevens to power.[41] In a radio broadcast announcing the coup, Conteh contended that "the rank and file of the army and police have been ignored" and accused the NRC of wanting to rule indefinitely even though "soldiers and police have no business running this country."[42] Another coup plotter, Private Morlai Kamara, emphasized the extent to which military rule had enriched senior officers: "The single objective of the enlisted men was financial: RSLMF [Royal Sierra Leone Military Forces] officers had benefited immensely from military rule, but the enlisted ranks had profited not at all."[43] During the coup attempt, coup plotters arrested and imprisoned a large number of senior officers. Outside the military, Stevens's return was greeted by widespread popular support. At that point, even some SLPP supporters had grown tired of military rule.[44]

But Stevens inherited a raft of political problems. These included "the inherited weak state, the economy with its over-reliance on diamonds, debt, corruption, politicized armed forces with a taste for power, a marginal electoral mandate inordinately skewed towards the North, a much more divided nation along the north-south axis, and an ambivalent relationship with the power in the countryside, the chiefs."[45] To add to these problems, during Stevens' tenure, Sierra Leone's economy contracted continuously. Tensions also surfaced within the APC between Stevens and other APC leaders who grew concerned that he was personalizing power; several resigned with public letters of dissent. In September, in the midst of public clashes, Stevens declared a state of emergency. A number of the APC ministers who resigned formed a new opposition party, the United Democratic Party (UDP), to contest his rule. Stevens retaliated by banning the UDP and detaining some thirty of its members under emergency powers.[46]

Stevens also remained concerned about the prospect of a military coup. Following the 1968 coup that brought him to power, noncommissioned officers and enlisted men "remained very restless."[47] Mende soldiers had opposed handing power to Stevens. He arrested those who had been closest to Margai and Lansana and took steps to reverse the ethnic stacking Margai had undertaken. In 1968 and 1969, Stevens purged Mende soldiers from all ranks of the armed forces.[48] As Thomas Cox writes: "Throughout 1968 and 1969, the APC eliminated as many Mendes as possible from the officer corps. Apart from those called upon to answer charges of treason, other Mendes were simply pensioned off without explanation. The result was that by the Fall of 1969 there remained a single Mende among the ten most senior army officers."[49] The purges were facilitated by the fact that the military Stevens inherited was largely missing its officer corps. As part of the 1968 coup that brought Stevens to power, soldiers and noncommissioned officers had imprisoned their commanding officers. Stevens began promoting junior officers through the ranks. In short order, northerners came to hold a disproportionate number of positions within the army.[50] Stevens paid remaining officers well. As Mac Dixon-Fyle describes, "The policy decided on was one which sought to patronize the army, improve its material circumstances and increase the Northern content of its officer cadre, while systematically cashiering Southerners whose loyalty was generally in doubt."[51]

Stevens also began to consider counterbalancing. In hiring for a riot unit within the police, the Special Army-Police Service (SAPS), Steven began to emphasize political allegiance. The hope was that in the event of a coup, he "might be able to rely on the support of some of the men of the riot police."[52] Meanwhile, plans to establish another security force took shape. In January 1971, the American ambassador reported, "The Prime Minister has not hidden from the Army the fact that he is having a special unit trained and that it could be used against the Army if need be."[53]

In March 1971, when Stevens attempted to narrow the ethnic profile of the military even further, restricting access to members of his own small Limba ethnic group, Temne officers revolted in a last-ditch effort to stave off ethnic stacking. Major Fallah Jawara, who had served briefly on the NRC, led a detachment into Stevens's residence early in the morning on March 23. The small band of Guinean bodyguards Stevens had brought back from exile defended him. Although the group was small, numbering between 150 and 300 troops, they managed to fend off the assault until the attackers ran out of ammunition and withdrew.[54] But by midday, the coup plotters regrouped and attacked the prime minister's office a second time. For several hours, coup plotters exchanged fire with loyalist troops. That afternoon, Brigadier John Bangura announced that the army had taken over the country, warning that "any undue outside interference will be viewed with disfavor."[55] But the coup's success was short-lived. A second broadcast that evening by Lieutenant Colonel Sam King contended that a substantial portion of the armed forces wished to disassociate themselves from the earlier broadcast, and that Stevens remained in power. Shortly thereafter, Stevens himself broadcast that he was well and that the situation had returned to normal. Over the course of the next few days, Brigadier Bangura was arrested, along with other officers alleged to have participated in the coup attempt. In the aftermath of the failed coup, Stevens accelerated the purges of non-northerners from the military, replacing them largely with Limba soldiers. He also increased military spending, both to compensate those solders that were dismissed and to convince those remaining not to object to the continued use of foreign troops.[56]

It was in this context—in the aftermath of a failed coup, following a multiyear effort to purge the military of non-co-ethnics, and at the same time as Stevens was increasing military pay—that he was able to establish the ISU without provoking another attempt. The various nicknames given to the force, including "Siaka Stevens' Dogs" and "ISU—I Shoot You," convey the extent to which it was perceived as loyal to Stevens and willing to target his opponents. Its members were recruited from among the ranks of ethnic minority groups such as the Koranko and Limba, and from APC strongholds.[57] As a report of the Truth and Reconciliation Commission (TRC) for Sierra Leone later noted, "Their loyalty to the APC and Siaka Stevens was unflinching."[58] The ISU reported to Stevens directly rather than to the inspector general of the police. In his testimony before Sierra Leone's Truth and Reconciliation Commission, the inspector general of the Police Service stated: "The [ISU] group was feared even by Police Commissioners, [which] eroded the basic rules of discipline within the force. A de facto 'force within a force' was created, which bore little or no allegiance to the Sierra Leone Police."[59]

Like the creation of the POGR in Ghana, the creation of the ISU in Sierra Leone generated resentment among the regular armed forces and anger about a perceived decline in status. Soldiers bristled at what they perceived as special treatment being bestowed on the ISU in the initial years after its creation. Despite the military's expanding budget, the ISU was perceived as being better armed and equipped than the regular army. Members received advanced training; one unit was trained by Israeli and British officers, while others were sent to Cuba. The military was "piqued by the attention" the ISU received."[60] Rumors that the army would be disbanded and replaced with the ISU began. As Dixon-Fyle describes: "ISU officers and men came to see themselves as the professional equals of the officers and men of the regular army. This affront the regular soldiers could not tolerate. They squared up to their ISU counterparts at the slightest provocation, and these confrontations were to grow with the years."[61]

Stevens took several steps to mollify soldiers concerned about the growing power of the ISU. First, he ramped up efforts to buy military loyalty by bringing army and police chiefs into the cabinet and providing copious opportunities for them to enrich themselves through economic ventures. In contrast, the opportunities for ISU members to extract bribes were more limited.[62] The army was "kept well supplied in the commodity staple rice, and military officers enjoyed car and housing loan terms not generally open to other members of the public service."[63] Stevens also began an arms buildup, importing antiaircraft guns, machine guns, ground-to-air ballistic missiles, and other weaponry, and put officers through a twelve-month training exercise. The defense budget soared in the years after the ISU was created. As a result, "fear of disbandment soon faded."[64] At the same time, Stevens worked to create practical obstacles to intervention. Within the senior ranks of the military, he rotated officers frequently. One observer described him as "the master of the shuffle" whose frequent appointments and dismissals "probably helped to ensure that those controlling profits from trade were not able to build up political constituencies or even private armies."[65] He made it more difficult for lower-ranked officers and enlisted men to access the arms they would need to seize power. As C. Magbaily Fyle states, "The military elite, which was now virtually part of the civilian government, enjoying lavish perks and kickbacks like their civilian counterparts, was in charge of the arms depot, kept under tight security."[66]

In short, Stevens succeeded where Nkrumah failed in part because he embraced ethnic stacking more wholeheartedly. By 1968, Steven had purged nearly all Mende officers, and he succeeded in the years following in restricting the ethnic base of the military even further, until it was dominated by fellow Limba. He also took advantage of failed coup attempts and plots to adopt coup-proofing strategies that would create grievances. As David Luke put it, "If luck and timing is everything in politics, Stevens had a lot of the former and a shrewd sense of the latter."[67] Stevens continued to expand the force in the years to come. In 1974, a small group of mainly Mende soldiers, along with primarily Temne civilians, were arrested for plotting a coup, but it never progressed past the plotting stage. That same year, Steven changed the name of the ISU to the Special Security Division (SSD) but retained its capacity to counterbalance the army.[68] In contrast to Nkrumah, Stevens did not equip the ISU/SSD at the expense of the regular military, instead lavishing financial perks on senior officers. Finally, Stevens took concrete steps to "harden the target," as Bruce Farcau puts it—creating obstacles to intervention by rotating senior officers through posts to prevent them from amassing their own base of political power, and restricting the access lower-ranking officers and enlisted men had to arms.[69] As a result, the creation of the ISU in 1971 occurred without provoking a coup attempt.

Failed Counterbalancing in Mali, 1960–1968: The Popular Militia

Like Nkrumah, Modibo Keita was ousted from power in large part because of his effort to counterbalance the military. Keita came to power in Mali in 1960. In the preceding years, he had established the Sudanese Bloc (Bloc Soudanais), which affiliated with the African Democratic Rally, a coalition of anticolonial parties, to become the Sudanese Union–African Democratic Rally (Union Soudanaise–Rassemblement Démocratique Africain, US-RDA). When Mali gained full independence, after an abortive effort to set up a union with Senegal, the US-RDA "had already swept away or absorbed all semblance of an opposition."[70] Under Keita's leadership, Mali soon became a one-party state headed by the National Political Bureau (Bureau Politique National, BPN).

At independence, Mali had a comparatively professional military. It was composed of veterans of the French colonial military and volunteers, and was initially charged solely with territorial defense. Heavy weaponry imported from Communist countries in Eastern Europe built up the army's supplies.[71] In addition to the regular armed forces, Keita formed a Popular Militia (Milice Populaire) in September 1960 as an auxiliary of the US-RDA. Its initial responsibilities included gathering intelligence and guarding national borders. In the mid-1960s, it was also used for agricultural labor in the countryside, establishing cooperative systems and harvesting collective fields where villagers resisted. At this point, the militia served largely as an agricultural workforce.[72]

Within a few years, the left-wing faction of the US-RDA emerged as the dominant one. Keita made several early moves to assert Mali's economic independence and associate the country with Communist nations. These included leaving the French monetary union and establishing a new currency, the Malian franc. These choices had unfortunate economic consequences. In response, neighboring Senegal cut off Mali's rail access to the ocean, which increased transportation costs and slowed exports. An alternative route through the Ivory Coast was eventually secured but at an increased cost. At the same time, France cut off economic subsidies. The result was several years of inflation and economic decline. Keita was forced to introduce austerity measures in 1964. He eventually had to sign a new currency accord with France, under the terms of which Mali's currency was devalued and government expenditures cut.[73] In 1967, an assessment concluded, "Modibo is likely to find himself under increasing pressure as a result of continuing economic strains, inevitable disappointments with the rate of economic recovery under the French Accords, and growing dissatisfaction of labor and youth with the prospects Modibo offers them."[74]

As the economic situation deteriorated, Keita came to depend more heavily on the military to quell internal dissent. Demonstrations by local business leaders were violently repressed.[75] When the Tuareg rebellion broke out in the north in 1963–1964, the army was sent to suppress it. The conflict turned into a "vicious, bitter struggle" that demoralized many of the soldiers who participated.[76] Increasingly, Keita asked the army to intimidate opponents inside and outside of government. The army resented taking on this new role.

In August 1967, Keita began a new campaign of "ideological purification" and anticorruption that came to be called the cultural revolution. As part of the campaign, he announced that he was dissolving the National Political Bureau; its powers would be taken over by the new National Committee for the Defense of the Revolution (Comité National de Défense de la Révolution, CNDR). The US-RDA, which had become a mass organization formally encompassing the majority of the country's population, organized a series of youth, labor, and women's demonstrations in support of Keita's new agenda over the course of the summer. In July, the army spokesman also lent the military's support for the campaign.[77]

Opponents were purged from government positions or intimidated into resigning. Importantly, however, and in contrast to Sierra Leone, the purges did not attempt to target the military, in part because Keita was concerned that doing so would provoke a coup. However, his purges of the civil service increasingly concerned military officers.[78] In an effort to retain military loyalty, Keita subjected the army to a series of political lectures on their new vocation, which was to involve political indoctrination and manual labor in the service of the state.[79] At the same time, "Keita's 'socialist option' and his close ties with Communist countries were most vehemently criticized within the Army."[80]

Over time, the Popular Militia came to play a larger role in Keita's cultural revolution. Modeling his efforts on the Red Guards in China, Keita reactivated and expanded the functions of the militia. He appointed his half-brother, Moussa Keita, to lead the force.[81] It began to attract volunteers with prior military service and to acquire better weaponry. Militia members "actively supported Keita, harassed merchants, enforced collectivization, and called for the ideological purification of just about everybody."[82] They also participated in the regime's use of torture against political opponents. By 1968, the Popular Militia had grown from three thousand to nine thousand—larger than the size of the regular military. It was also receiving what the army considered to be a "disproportionate share" of new equipment.[83] The political lectures that targeted military officers tried to convince the army to work together with the militia; the lectures encouraged military officers to view the militia "not [as] antagonists, but precious auxiliaries."[84]

But tensions between the military and the militia grew. Militia members were perceived as disrespectful toward army officers. As Michael Schatzberg describes, "Its members were no longer hesitant about insulting members of the army and, indeed, were doing so publicly."[85] At the same time, Keita began to float a proposal to redeploy army units to Bamako and other major cities abroad for training and to assist with cotton and rice projects. The idea was that in the interim, "newly-uniformed and equipped companies of the Milice populaire would occupy the barracks and receive additional military training."[86] Rumors also began circulating that he planned to arrest a number of army officers after his return from a conference in Mopti on November 20, 1968.[87] In response, senior army officers asked Keita directly to disband the militia or to place it under army command, but he refused. The stakes for the military were high. As Anton Bebler concludes, "The corporate existence of the army itself was at stake since Modibo Keita planned to replace it with the People's Militia.... The growth of the People's Militia as a rival and even a substitute, as well as the swelling security services, posed a very real threat to the army."[88] Officers became "increasingly jealous" of the liberties taken by militia members.[89]

On November 19, Lieutenant Moussa Traoré led a bloodless coup to depose Keita. Soldiers shouted, "Long live liberty, down with Modibo and the militia."[90] Traoré pointed to Keita's plan to move the militia into the barracks as the last straw for the military. The popular militia resisted the coup, but it was poorly trained in comparison to the regular army, and coup leaders were able to disarm them quickly. A number of more senior officers within the army opposed the intervention but did not use force to stop it. There was no other armed resistance to the coup, and it succeeded bloodlessly. The new regime's first act was to disband the militia. The move was a popular one. The day following the coup, civilian demonstrators roamed the streets, repeating coup-plotters' chants: "Down with Modibo, down with the militia."[91]

In sum, Keita's efforts to transform the Popular Militia from a largely rural force responsible for border security and agricultural labor into a substitute for the army did eventually provoke a military coup. As Bebler observes, "The Ghanaian coup that ousted Kwame Nkrumah had a strong echo in Mali."[92] In contrast to events in Sierra Leone, Keita's efforts did not take place in the wake of failed coup attempts. He did not combine counterbalancing with the other coup prevention strategies, such as purging or bribery, that helped Stevens reduce the risk of a coup while establishing a counterweight.

Successful Counterbalancing in Cuba, 1959–1965: Special Operations Troops

In Cuba, Fidel Castro was able to build up Ministry of Interior forces as counterweights to the regular military without provoking a coup attempt even though military officers, like those elsewhere, resented their creation. In part this was because, like Stevens, Castro had succeeded in purging the armed forces of potential opponents in the years preceding counterbalancing and had maintained high levels of military spending.

In 1959, when the Cuban Revolution brought Fidel Castro to power, he embarked on an effort to reorganize the military almost immediately. In the final years of Fulgencio Batista's rule, the morale of Cuba's armed forces had dropped precipitously. By the end, according to one observer, it was led by "a gaggle of corrupt, cruel and lazy officers without combat experience."[93] As one of his first moves in power, Castro had hundreds of soldiers and police tried and executed for their role in repression under Batista's regime. Castro established a new Ministry of the Revolutionary Armed Forces (MINFAR) to replace the existing defense department and installed new officers in the positions of minister of defense and chief of staff. He also replaced the majority of the army's officer corps. Some of those who had been in Batista's army were retained, but most were not.[94] Instead, the new Revolutionary Armed Forces (FAR) were staffed with members of the rebel army Castro had used to seize power, which numbered some three thousand soldiers, as well as with some members of other competing rebel and opposition groups. Many of the new soldiers had no prior military service. In the transition, the size of the armed forces was reduced from the thirty-nine thousand men it had been under Batista to approximately twenty thousand.[95]

Castro focused on rapidly bringing the military back up to strength. He sought equipment and advisers from the Soviet Union; aid began arriving in February 1960.[96] Castro envisioned the FAR as "the leading force to repel foreign enemies, namely counter-revolutionary landings or a US invasion."[97] At the same time, Castro mobilized civilian supporters into a volunteer militia, called the National Revolutionary Militia (MNR), to supplement the FAR until it was more militarily capable.[98] It was initially tasked with combating domestic counterrevolutionary movements. As a U.S. State Department assessment at the time noted, the militia units were, "in effect, units of a second, more politically-reliable army," better suited than the regular military for internal repression."[99] However, the militia remained under military command, and it was slowly phased out as the regular military increased capacity.[100]

While many officers in the FAR were personally loyal to Castro, having fought with him to overthrow Batista, the growing influence of communism, and the increasingly personal nature of Castro's rule, rapidly became a source of tension between him and the army. Castro decided to appoint his brother, Raul, to head MINFAR. In protest, fifteen high-ranking officers who had fought with Castro during the revolution resigned. Major Hubert Matos, commander of Camagüey Province, was a particularly outspoken critic of both the ideological drift of Castro's regime and his leadership style.[101] In his resignation letter, Matos expressed his desire not to "become an obstacle to the revolution."[102] He was arrested shortly thereafter and sentenced to twenty years in prison for "anti-revolutionary and anti-patriotic conduct."[103] The incident raised concerns that staffing the army with revolutionary fighters would not be enough to prevent a coup. As William LeoGrande notes, "The Matos incident raised for the first time the issue of the military's political loyalty to the leftward course of the revolution."[104] In the weeks and months that followed, a number of other prominent "anti-Batistianos" in high-level posts broke with Castro. The continued tensions between Castro and the Revolutionary Armed Forces he built to replace Bastia's army suggest that it was not a foregone conclusion that establishment of a counterweight would proceed without military intervention. At the same time, the United States, wary of a Communist regime so close to its own shores, began to explore a number of potential plots to assassinate Castro or encourage a military coup.[105]

Castro responded with aggressive purges in the armed forces. These targeted "officers and men who previously supported Castro against Batista but later became disillusioned."[106] Castro also began a program of political indoctrination classes within the army, which included lessons on Marxism, Cuban history, and new government policies. A new school, the Osvaldo Sanchez Cabrera School for Revolutionary Instructors, was established to train instructors for political courses in the military.[107] After some officers balked at the prospect of receiving instruction from civilians, the decision was made to switch to using only military personnel. As one observer described, "As the importance of the military grew, so did the emphasis accorded the creation of Communist Party cadres within it."[108]

At the same time, however, Castro took care to preserve important aspects of military autonomy. The need to retain a strong regular military was driven home by the April 1961 Bay of Pigs invasion, the failed military invasion of Cuba by U.S.-sponsored paramilitaries. Some twenty-five thousand FAR troops and two hundred thousand militia forces were sent to repel the invasion.[109] Castro chose not to implement the "dual command" system in place in the Soviet Union, through which the Communist Party exercised control within the military. Instead, the party played a supporting role within the armed forces. Phyllis Walker emphasizes that "in paying heed to the military's concern in preserving its domain, care was taken to emphasize the military's autonomy and to minimize party interference in professional military matters."[110] The aim was avoid undermining the military's capacity to repel invasion. Thus, while officers received ideological training, they retained control over important aspects of defense planning and staffing.

Castro also established, in 1961, an Internal Ministry, known as MININT, that could balance out MINFAR. Its first minister was a long-standing rival of Raul Castro's, Comandante Ramiro Valdés Menéndez. The new ministry was focused on domestic surveillance and policing. In the event of war, there was a provision for its subornation to the armed forces, but in peacetime it remained independent. By 1962, MININT had become an "increasingly powerful government entity."[111] Over time, tension between the two institutions grew, driven in part by personal clashes between Raul Castro and Ramiro Valdés.

The perks MININT officers received were also a source of bitterness within the FAR. As Frank Mora notes, "Perhaps because of MININT's special responsibilities and place in Fidel's heart, ministry officers had access to certain material benefits and operational opportunities that most people in FAR did not, helping to exacerbate resentment and disaffection between the institutions."[112] For example, even lower-ranking majors and captains in MININT had access to specialty vehicles, while senior officers in MINFAR went without. There was also the perception that, compared to MINFAR, officers in MININT lacked professional standards and were not subject to adequate supervision. Yet, at the same time, investments in force levels, training programs, and new equipment for the FAR meant that service in the regular armed forces remained prestigious.[113]

It was in this context that Castro established, in 1964, a new counterweight to the military in the form of a militarized police force called the Special Operations Troops. While under the administrative control of MININT, the Special Operations Troops were operationally under Castro's direct command.[114] They were "responsible for implementation and execution of counterinsurgency plans and for Castro's personal protection during crises."[115] They numbered between eight hundred and a thousand and were draw from "among the most highly skilled and disciplined Cuban military units."[116] A U.S. Defense Intelligence Agency assessment some years later noted that "personnel in the Special Troops are highly motivated, well educated and thoroughly indoctrinated."[117] While tensions between MINFAR and MININT remained for decades to come, the creation of the Special Operations Troops did not provoke a military coup.

In short, Castro's effort to counterbalance the military did not occur in isolation. Instead, Castro combined counterbalancing with several other measures of control. These included purges of political opponents and vigorous prosecution of officers who voiced criticism. Furthermore, while MININT officers often received more perks than MINFAR officers did, Castro did not neglect investment in the regular army, and took care that it retained autonomy over defense matters central to its portfolio. As a consequence, the military retained what Walker described as "an ascendant position in the new regime," and no coup attempt occurred in response to the creation of the Special Operations Troops.[118]

Discussion: Key Patterns across Cases

The cases illustrate that the creation of new counterweights is indeed likely to be met with fear and resentment among officers in the regular military. In Ghana and Mali, efforts to create counterweights to the military eventually provoked coup attempts that ousted rulers from power. In contrast, rulers in Sierra Leone and Cuba were able to avoid this fate. But in each case, tensions between military and civilian leaders were high, and were exacerbated by the creation of a counterweight. Military officers in Ghana were vocal about their displeasure, complaining repeatedly in the months leading up to the coup about what they perceived as preferential treatment for the President's Own Guard Regiment and attempting to reassert control over it. In Sierra Leone, officers in the ISU were also widely perceived as receiving special treatment, which gave rise to rumors that the military itself would be disbanded. In Mali, senior officers repeatedly asked Keita to disband the popular militia he had established. And in Cuba, a bitter rivalry formed between the officers in the regular armed forces and counterweights under the Ministry of Interior. These cases thus lend support to the proposed causal mechanism linking new counterweights to coup attempts.

The analysis also suggests that the *other* coup-proofing strategies rulers adopted alongside counterbalancing may explain the lack of coup attempts in Sierra Leone and Cuba. Table 5.3 summarizes the additional strategies employed by each ruler. The comparison highlights how frequent attempts at indoctrination were: each ruler installed political advisers or began ideological courses for military officers. As a result, the use of indoctrination cannot explain the different outcomes in the cases. Table 5.3 also highlights just how many different coup-proofing strategies Stevens employed in Sierra Leone at the same time: in addition to indoctrination, Stevens bought off high-ranking officers by giving them access to sources of economic revenue and political posts, while also rotating them frequently through different posts, preventing any from developing a loyal constituency, and restricted the access of junior officers and enlisted men to arms. Stevens also undertook counterbalancing only after he had effectively stacked the military with co-ethnics, purging others from its ranks. Given the sheer number of different strategies Stevens used, his political survival may have been overdetermined. However, when we compare across cases to see what factors varied along with the outcomes in each case, there are two that cannot be eliminated: bribery and purges of the armed forces. Both Stevens and Castro combined counterbalancing with bribery and purges, whereas rulers in the two cases in which coups

TABLE 5.3 Comparing coup-proofing strategies and forms of counterbalancing

COUNTRY	OTHER COUP-PROOFING STRATEGIES	TYPE OF COUNTERWEIGHT
FAILED CASES (COUP ATTEMPT)		
Ghana, 1960–66	Indoctrination	Presidential guard
Mali, 1960–68	Indoctrination	Militia
SUCCESSFUL CASES (NO COUP ATTEMPT)		
Sierra Leone, 1968–74	Indoctrination, bribery, purges, ethnic stacking, officer rotation, arms restrictions	Interior Ministry troops
Cuba, 1959–65	Indoctrination, bribery, purges	Interior Ministry troops

occurred did not. Their experiences suggest that where rulers combine counterbalancing with these strategies, it may be less likely to provoke coup attempts.

Finally, the cases suggest that the type of security force rulers use to counterbalance the military might affect the extent of grievances it creates within the armed forces. In the two cases in which rulers successfully created new counterweights, Sierra Leone and Cuba, rulers established paramilitary police forces that were under the administrative control of interior ministries. In contrast, the counterweights established in Ghana and Mali were a presidential guard and popular militia, respectively; both forces were organized directly under presidential command. This raises the possibility that military officers may view the use of presidential guard forces and militia as counterweights as more threatening than the use of militarized police. It may be that police have a more clearly delineated mission, distinct from that of the armed forces, while militia and presidential guard forces do not. In Ghana and Mali coup plotters publicly voiced concerns about *replacement* in a way that officers in Sierra Leone and Cuba did not. Because military officers in Ghana and Mali led successful coups, and thus made a number of public statements justifying their actions, more material is available in these cases. As a result, I cannot eliminate the possibility that the extent of grievances generated was the same.

However, I can test the hypothesis that the form of counterbalancing matters with large-n data. In order to test whether the type of security force created affects the propensity of the military to rebel, I divide the security forces used as counterweights into four categories: presidential guards, militarized police and interior troops, militias, and intelligence services or secret police. Table 5.4 replicates the analysis in the preceding chapter with these disaggregated indicators for the creation of new counterweights. In this statistical analysis, the creation of two types of counterweights is associated with an increased risk of a coup attempt in the following year: new militia forces and new intelligence services or secret police. This suggests that Keita's experience establishing a counterweight militia

TABLE 5.4 Coup attempts: Logit results with forms of counterbalancing disaggregated

	MODEL 1	MODEL 2	MODEL 3	MODEL 4
Counterbalancing	0.144	0.133	0.123	0.114
	(0.178)	(0.179)	(0.179)	(0.179)
New presidential guard	−1.111			
	(1.133)			
New interior troops/militarized police		0.294		
		(0.692)		
New militia			1.045**	
			(0.502)	
New intelligence service				1.566**
				(0.750)
Change in military expenditure	−0.060	−0.068	−0.069	−0.071
	(0.219)	(0.22)	(0.222)	(0.222)
Military expenditure/soldier	−0.122	−0.127	−0.131	−0.125
	(0.086)	(0.087)	(0.085)	(0.086)
Military personnel (log)	−0.274***	−0.276***	−0.282***	−0.281***
	(0.095)	(0.095)	(0.095)	(0.095)
Military regime	0.320*	0.328*	0.320*	0.333*
	(0.186)	(0.187)	(0.185)	(0.187)
Democracy	−0.173	−0.173	−0.171	−0.214
	(0.239)	(0.241)	(0.239)	(0.235)
GDP/capita (log)	−0.264***	−0.261***	−0.266***	−0.255***
	(0.099)	(0.099)	(0.098)	(0.097)
Change in GDP/capita	−1.514**	−1.510**	−1.410**	−1.428**
	(0.659)	(0.651)	(0.645)	(0.656)
Recent revolution	−0.139	−0.135	−0.172	−0.153
	(0.304)	(0.304)	(0.310)	(0.302)
Instability	0.300*	0.294*	0.309*	0.319*
	(0.171)	(0.169)	(0.171)	(0.171)
Years since coup	−0.357***	−0.352***	−0.346***	−0.344***
	(0.075)	(0.073)	(0.073)	(0.073)
Constant	1.843*	1.829*	1.892*	1.780*
	(1.026)	(1.017)	(1.011)	(1.000)
Log likelihood	−722.010	−722.659	−720.958	−720.479
Pseudo R-squared	0.143	0.142	0.144	0.145
Observations	3,840	3,840	3,840	3,840
Number of new forces	26	32	36	15

Notes: Robust standard errors clustered by country in parentheses. *** p<0.01, ** p<0.05, * p<0.1. Cubic splines are included in all models.

is not a unique one. In contrast, even though Nkrumah's effort to use his presidential guard as a counterweight was cited as one of the central reasons for the 1966 coup attempt that ousted him from power, most militaries do not intervene in response to the creation of counterweights in the form of presidential guard units. Militarized police forces, like the ISU in Sierra Leone or Special Operations Troops in Cuba, are not systematically associated with an increase in the incidence of coup attempts. These findings suggest that on average counterbalancing the military with presidential guards and interior troops or militarized police may be less risky than counterbalancing with militia and secret police.

Like Nkrumah, many leaders have found that the creation of new coercive institutions to counterbalance the military threatens the interests of officers and soldiers in the regular armed forces—frequently provoking the very coups counterbalancing was intended to prevent. Yet some rulers are able to establish new counterweights without triggering a coup attempt, while others are not. This chapter compared four rulers in similar circumstances who each attempted to counterbalance the military. Efforts by Kwame Nkrumah in Ghana and Modibo Keita in Mali eventually resulted in successful coups to disband the new counterweight, while those by Siaka Stevens in Sierra Leone and Fidel Castro in Cuba did not. In comparing these cases, the aim was to both to explain their diverging outcomes and to inductively develop new hypotheses about the conditions under which establishing counterweights is feasible. The comparative analysis highlights the role of the broader set of coup-proofing strategies rulers employed along with counterbalancing. In Sierra Leone, Stevens aimed to counteract the military grievances about the new Internal Security Unit with remuneration and political posts for senior officers. As important, his effort to counterbalance came in the final stage of a multiyear effort to pack the military with co-ethnics and purge others from the armed forces. Similarly, in Cuba, Castro combined purges of the military and political indoctrination with concrete efforts to ensure that the military retained autonomy in defense affairs and sufficient resources to defend the nation from external threats. The case comparison in this chapter also raised the possibility that some forms of counterbalancing may be more threatening to the military than others; in particular, the two successful cases of counterweight creation featured the use of militarized police forces rather than presidential guards, secret police, or civilian militia. Statistical analysis of patterns of coup attempts suggests that, on average, the creation of new militias or intelligence forces is more likely to backfire, provoking a coup attempt, than the creation of militarized police or presidential guards. These findings are important because they suggest that there are concrete ways in which rulers may be able to mitigate some of the potential hazards of counterbalancing.

6

HOW COUPS D'ÉTAT ESCALATE TO CIVIL WAR

For military coup plotters, the ideal coup is a bloodless one. As Samuel Finer argues, the "whole point" of a coup "is to carry out the displacement or the supplantment [of the current regime] with the minimum of bloodshed."[1] Even Edward Luttwak, who describes coups as being akin to other military operations ("only more so"), emphasizes that they should "not result in much actual combat."[2] This is in part because violence has the potential to undermine support for the coup. It may be seen as a sign of weakness, which drives uncommitted soldiers to the other side. After all, stronger actors should have no need to use violence to achieve their aims.[3] Coup plotters are also thought to avoid violence during a coup because intramilitary violence can undermine the unity and cohesion of the armed forces, as well as the morale of individual officers and soldiers forced to kill those with whom they have lived, worked, and trained.[4] As a result, even after threatening to use violence, coup plotters usually take great care to avoid it.

Yet many coups do turn violent—and some escalate to the sustained, high level violence characteristic of civil war. This chapter shows that one of the unintended consequences of counterbalancing is that it increases the risk of such escalation. It compares three coup attempts, exploring in detail how the organization of coercive institutions affected the extent to which the coup escalated to broader conflict. First, the chapter compares two coup attempts in the Dominican Republic, which occurred in similar political, cultural, and economic contexts, but which resulted in different levels of violence: the first coup attempt, in 1963, was bloodless, while the second, in 1965, escalated to over two thousand fatalities. The analysis shows that a key difference was that in the two years between the coup attempts, the

115

TABLE 6.1 Summary of case outcomes: Counterbalancing and the escalation of coups to civil war

COUP ATTEMPT	USE OF COUNTERWEIGHTS	ESCALATED TO CIVIL WAR	CAUSAL MECHANISM
Dominican Republic, 1963	No	No	N/A
Dominican Republic, 1965	Yes	Yes	More resistance to the coup
Yemen, 1962	Yes	Yes	Fewer organizational barriers to rebellion

Dominican government built up a riot squad within the National Police, the *cascos blancos*, to serve as a counterweight to the military. The creation of a counterweight was not sufficient for the coup to escalate—after all, counterbalancing is common, while civil wars are rare. But a close analysis of how the coup attempt unfolded shows that counterbalancing prevented the coup plotters from achieving a rapid victory. Their resistance prompted other factions within the armed forces, which had previously been content to sit on the sidelines, to intervene. The presence of an armed counterweight also motivated the coup's supporters to begin distributing weapons to civilians, which broadened the conflict from an intraregime one to one that involved nonstate actors as well.

After comparing the differing trajectories of the two coups in the Dominican Republic, I turn to a third coup in a markedly different setting: the 1962 coup in Yemen, which touched off a six-year-long civil war that resulted in the deaths of some two hundred thousand people—4 percent of the country's population.[5] The comparison between Yemen in 1962 and the Dominican Republic in 1965 illustrates how very different types of counterweights, used in very different circumstances, similarly facilitated the escalation of coups to civil war. In this case, the use of tribal militias as counterweights helped Imam Muhammad al-Badr, who was ousted from power in the 1962 coup, to overcome logistical and organizational challenges inherent in starting a rebellion. Table 6.1 summarizes the case outcomes. The analysis provides preliminary support for the book's fourth hypothesis, which posits that coup attempts are more likely to escalate to civil war when they are staged against regimes that counterbalance than when they are staged against regimes that do not.

Background: The Dominican Republic after Trujillo

In 1961, Rafael Trujillo, who had ruled the Dominican Republic for three decades, was assassinated. His death threw the country into a prolonged period of instability. In the last years of his life, facing international pressure to democratize, Trujillo had appointed Joaquín Balaguer to serve as president. Yet Trujillo retained power. At the time, American Consul General Henry Dearborn noted in a memo to Washington that Trujillo would retain "his political domination whether he is President or dogcatcher."[6] After Trujillo's death, Balaguer officially continued as president, while Trujillo's son Ramfis ruled from behind the scenes. Balaguer took some initial steps toward liberalizing the regime, including allowing the return of some exiled groups and the organization of opposition parties. These steps angered both Trujillo's surviving family members, who thought the reforms went too far, and their opponents, for whom the reforms did not go far enough.[7]

In January 1962, the opposition party, the National Civic Union (UCN), which represented the business community, led a general strike to protest Balaguer's rule. The United States helped mediate an agreement for Balaguer to share power with a seven-member Council of State, with elections to be held the following year. Once the Council began to operate, the military threatened to stage a coup unless Balaguer remained president. The U.S. State Department offered to mediate but informed UCN leaders privately that they retained American support; the United States also kept naval units visible as a coup deterrent.[8] A military coup that same month, led by air force general Pedro Rodríguez Echavarría, dissolved the Council, but failed to secure the support of other senior officers, and the Council was restored in a countercoup two days later. The country's first democratic elections went forward as planned in December. Juan Bosch Gaviño, head of the leftist Dominican Revolutionary Party (PRD), won the support of most rural and working-class voters, who carried him to an overwhelming but unexpected electoral victory.[9] Senior officers were satisfied with the outcome.[10]

But Bosch's regime soon faced criticism from businessmen and religious leaders on the right. The UCN had trouble reconciling itself to an unanticipated defeat, and business elites were concerned that the program of economic reform Bosch had campaigned on would be to their detriment. Church leaders also criticized the secular tilt of Bosch's regime.[11] In response, Bosch's critics began what a CIA memorandum at the time described as a "concerted campaign to discredit Bosch by charging that he is himself a crypto-Communist engaged in establishing a Communist dictatorship, or else that his ineptitude will lead to a Communist take over in the Dominican Republic."[12] Since coming to office, Bosch had continued Balaguer's policy of allowing formerly exiled opponents of the regime to return. Many joined existing leftist parties or formed new ones.[13] At the same time, Bosch was "obsessed with avoiding . . . giving the impression that he was a puppet of the Americans."[14] He argued that cracking down on Communist organizing would only push them toward violence. The bigger threat to the republic, Bosch contended, was the possibility of a reactionary coup.[15]

When Bosch came to power, he inherited the military Trujillo had built largely intact. It was an institution with deep internal divisions, which Trujillo had deliberately fostered in order to prevent officers from coordinating to oust him from power. He appointed his son Ramfis as chief of the armed forces. Ramfis lavished funds and equipment on the air force and placed a special tank corps under its command—an unusual step that enabled it to counter the army's ground power.[16] Intraservice rivalries ran deep. Yet in the few months Bosch was in office, he refrained from attempting to reform the armed forces. The United States discouraged him from purging holdovers from Trujillo's regime. The concern, as Theodore Draper argues, was that "a much-needed purge of the top leadership would immediately trigger a coup."[17] Within the army, many officers were staunchly anticommunist. They believed that the recent revolution in Cuba brought about the "destruction of the armed forces and death to the officers," and were concerned that Bosch was not doing enough to prevent the possibility of one in the Dominican Republic.[18] Military officers were also concerned that Bosch's ambitious reform programs threatened to cut into the military budget. He also seemed to be threatening to involve the military in a dispute with Haiti. Finally, officers were increasingly concerned that in lieu of reform, Bosch would attempt to counterbalance the military. According to G. Pope Atkins and Larman Wilson, "Unfounded rumors that Bosch was creating his own rival military force increased the military's fear and suspicion."[19] In testimony before a subcommittee of the U.S. Senate Committee on the Judiciary, General Elías Wessin y Wessin, who helped lead the countercoup in 1962, recalled the military's belief that Bosch was forming a peasant militia under the pretext of guarding cane fields and that his real purpose "was to use them as a substitute for the Armed Forces at the opportune moment."[20]

Rumors of an impending coup also began to circulate. In July, a group of military leaders issued an ultimatum to Bosch, which demanded he take stronger action against leftists.[21] He refused, stating, "I did not return here to shed blood."[22] In the context of rising tensions with the military, several prominent politicians—on the left and the right—became concerned enough about the prospect of a coup that they publicly declared their intent to oppose one should it be staged. The PRD, Bosch's own party, declared that it would respond with a general strike. As Gall describes the situation, "Week after week," the PRD "brought its supporters into the street to demonstrate against a coup, while American diplomats tried repeatedly to persuade the plotters to call it off."[23] The United States wanted a stable, noncommunist government in the Dominican Republic. While it would have preferred Bosch take a stronger stance on communism, it also did not want the first elected president of the Dominican Republic to be overthrown.[24] The American ambassador to the Dominican Republic, John Barlow Martin, reported in mid-September his impression that "the military is restless."[25]

The Bloodless 1963 Coup in Santo Domingo

When the coup finally came, it was swift and bloodless. A group of high-ranking officers entered the presidential residence at 3 a.m. on September 25 and arrested President Bosch. Wessin, a colonel at the time, and commander of the Armed Forces Training Center (CEFA) at San Isidro, just outside the capital, led the attempt. Twenty-five high-ranking officers in the Dominican military and National Police signed a communiqué backing the coup.[26] In a broadcast over Santo Domingo radio, coup leaders described Bosch's regime as corrupt, procommunist, and inefficient, charging him with "contempt for the constitution" and economic mismanagement; the broadcast also announced that the legislature had been dissolved and that the constitution Bosch had signed into law in July had been overturned.[27] It concluded with a warning for people to stay home because "groups sympathetic to Premier Fidel Castro of Cuba and pro-Bosch elements were allegedly organizing in several parts of the city."[28]

The joint communiqué announcing the coup masked a great deal of division within the armed forces. The military remained the site of what Abraham Lowenthal depicts as "competing cliques that had been struggling for predominance ever since Trujillo's death."[29] The day after the coup, Ambassador Martin emphasized in a telegram to the State Department that "persistent rumors of serious split within military continue."[30] A number of officers supported Bosch remaining in office. But those who opposed the coup "were surrounded by the great mass of officers who were unwilling to 'get their feet wet'" in his defense.[31]

The response from Bosch's party and from the politicians who had declared their opposition in advance was also muted. As a subsequent U.S. National Intelligence Estimate noted, given the extent of this opposition, "the coup provoked surprisingly little popular reaction."[32] The apparent unity of the military likely limited resistance from other sectors. It was not until coup leaders invited the members of rightist parties to the palace to form a provisional government that protests began. Even then, they were largely limited to left-wing students, who began to barricade streets near the city center. Policemen dispersed the protests; one woman was injured, but there were no fatalities. Among the first acts of the provisional government were to outlaw Communist parties and to begin to round up leftist leaders. In the days following the coup, thirty-one people were arrested on suspicions of being Communists.[33] There was no other resistance to the coup. As Norman Gall summarizes, "Bosch's party collapsed."[34]

From the National Palace, Bosch tried to reach out to friendly foreign governments for support, but there was little they could do.[35] The United States suspended diplomatic relations and cut off economic and military assistance to the Dominican Republic. It may have been willing to do more—President John F. Kennedy briefly contemplated the possibility of a military intervention—but Bosch did not want to risk bloodshed.[36] The presidents of Mexico, Costa Rica, and Venezuela, the governor of Puerto Rico, and the chairman of the Council of the Organization of American States also received Bosch's calls sympathetically. Without armed resistance to the coup, however, there were limits to what outside pressure could accomplish. Bosch refused to sign a statement of resignation that would have lent the junta legal cover and remained a political prisoner while the swearing in of the new government took place. He was forced into exile in Puerto Rico on September 29. By December, the United States had resumed diplomatic relations with the Dominican Republic, and an economic assistance package was in the works.[37]

Civil-Military Relations and Coup-Proofing under Reid

Donald Reid Cabral eventually emerged as the dominant figure in the new regime. He inherited a country in economic crisis. In an effort to forestall economic collapse, Reid initiated a series of unpopular austerity measures. He also announced that he would cancel upcoming elections.[38] In taking these steps, Reid initially had the military's support. Particularly important was the support of Wessin, who had been promoted to general following the 1963 coup, and who retained command of the CEFA force in San Isidro. As one account described, "Whoever controlled San Isidro controlled the country."[39] Over time, however, Reid's relationship with the armed forces deteriorated. He began to purge the military of suspected opponents and sought to leverage existing divisions and rivalries for his own gain. By the summer of 1964, multiple factions within the armed forces were "restless and discontented"; senior army officers in San Cristobal grew concerned about Reid delaying elections, while junior officers complained of "unfair promotion policies, disgust with graft and incompetence of senior officers, and pressures exerted by politicians."[40] In conversation with American officials that year, Reid made clear that he was "in no hurry to begin the electoral process."[41] The United States decided to refrain from pressuring him to do so; the State Department argued that how the country returned to democracy was a "strictly internal problem."[42]

As part of his effort to retain control over the military, Reid also invested in building a counterweight within the National Police. Efforts to increase police capacity had begun the year prior to Reid's assumption of power, in 1962, when two detectives from the Los Angeles Police Department were sent to establish a riot control squad within the police. The new formation was equipped with heavy weaponry, and its commanders were sent to a training course in the United States. It eventually came to be known as the cascos blancos for the white helmets its officers wore.[43] The cascos blancos were initially under military command. Members of Bosch's cabinet argued that giving the police more independence from the military would be "unconstitutional and dictatorial." Reid felt differently. As part of his military reform effort, Reid moved the police, including the cascos blancos, "under his personal jurisdiction."[44] In doing so, the hope was that it would come to "serve as a counterweight to the other Trujillista-dominated services," as well as repress regime opponents.[45] While American officials later recognized the need to reassure the military that a "build-up of the police forces does not constitute a move against the military," Reid's changes to the unit's chain of command were interpreted as such at the time.[46] Within the first year of Reid's tenure, the cascos blancos had grown to around five hundred men, stationed in the capital at Fortaleza Ozama.[47]

By the spring of 1965, when it became clear that Reid intended to continue to postpone elections or to rig them to remain in power, he began to face more widespread public opposition and protest. At least four different factions within the military were rumored to be plotting to overthrow him.[48] On April 22, Reid dismissed seven officers believed to be involved in a plot to seize power. The remaining conspirators decided to make their move. On April 25, 1965, they ousted Reid from power.[49] Their stated aim was to return to the 1963 constitution and restore Bosch to office.

How the 1965 Coup Escalated to Civil War

When the 1965 coup began, on April 25, few observers anticipated that it would be any different from previous ones in the Dominican Republic. As Bryant Wedge explains, "To the very last moment it seemed that the coup would probably fail but that, at most, it might result in just another fairly orderly change in government."[50] Most of the "constitutionalist" conspirators had been taken by surprise by the decision to go forward with the attempt. Nonetheless, on the first day of the coup, some fifteen hundred soldiers from the army battalions located just north of the city joined. Rebellious officers led by Colonel Francisco Caamaño seized control of army headquarters in Santo Domingo, but had not yet moved on the palace to capture Reid. Eight of the officers who had signed the communiqué removing Bosch from power just two years earlier reversed course and now supported his reinstatement.[51] José Francisco Peña Gómez, head of the PRD, got word of the attempt while in the middle of a radio address. He announced that the attempt had succeed and called on Bosch's remaining supporters to come into the streets to celebrate. Members of Reid's regime countered over the government radio station that Reid remained in office, and ordered a 6:00 p.m. curfew for all residents.

Meanwhile, Reid personally appealed to General Wessin and other members of the armed forces not yet in revolt to defend his regime. It quickly became clear, however, that no one within the Dominican military was willing to defend Reid from the coup.[52] As Lowenthal concludes, most officers "failed to support Reid Cabral during the crucial first hours of the coup, thus assuring his regime's fall."[53] The commander of the National Police, General Despradel Brache, also initially declared that his force was an "apolitical" one, and would not get involved.[54] The coup plotters were thus able to move through the capital and take the National Palace unimpeded. They placed Reid under arrest.

Within the military, however, there were conflicting opinions about what should happen after Reid's ouster. Soldiers were of three main views: some wanted to reinstate Bosch without holding elections; some advocated a temporary junta to hold elections in which both Bosch and Balaguer could compete; and still others thought a military junta was the best solution.

As a consequence, "inside the Palace, confusion prevailed. Some military men, who had rebelled because they were anti-Reid, or anti-Wessin, or pro-Balaguer, were leaving, having discovered the rebellion was pro-Bosch. Still, armed civilians and military men crowded the corridors, some drinking."[55] Wessin later recalled: "One side wanted a military junta and elections within 3 months. This included myself. The other side wanted the return of Juan Bosch to the presidency. And this we did not accept."[56] The State Department concluded on April 25 that "failure to resolve the dissension among the military would cause a dangerous situation. However, it seems likely that quarrels can be patched up on the basis of self-interest in preserving the armed forces as an institution."[57] That may well have been the case had the cascos blancos not intervened.

While General Brache had initially announced that the police would not take sides, he reversed course within the span of a few hours under pressure from subordinates, and ordered the cascos blancos to resist.[58] Members of the riot squad almost uniformly opposed the attempt to oust Reid. Police officers feared that their own status, which had improved under Reid, would fall with a military takeover.[59] Police units retook the radio station, arresting Peña Gómez and other constitutionalist rebels there; they then broadcast an announcement denying that the regime had been overthrown and imposing their own curfew. As more and more Bosch supporters began amassing at the palace, however, the police retreated to their headquarters at Fortaleza Ozama.[60]

Police opposition provided space for Wessin, who had neglected to defend Reid's regime, to formulate his own post-coup plan—one that did not involve Bosch's return. Under Wessin's direction, the air force announced from San Isidro that it would begin bombing the palace unless a military junta was established. Military officers and civilian supporters gathered in the palace were shocked when Wessin carried through with the threat. The navy, which had initially supported Wessin, objected to the bombing and went over to the side of the newly formed government.[61] Even after the bombing, however, most observers thought the coup would not escalate to further violence. Briefing President Lyndon B. Johnson on the morning of April 26, U.S. Under Secretary of State for Economic Affairs Thomas Mann argued, "They are not likely to do too much shooting—at least they never have in the past. Either the troops on one side or the other are likely to cave."[62]

Meanwhile, the PRD and other leftist organizations remained concerned that the police would crush the revolt. As Piero Gleijeses describes it, the police represented "a hostile force within the heart of the constitutionalist zone, a force that at any moment could stir and strike the rebels in the back, while they faced an attack from San Isidro."[63] In response, they began distributing weapons to civilians; "on Sunday, and on Monday and Tuesday, they hauled several thousand guns—estimates go as high as seven thousand—into downtown Santo Domingo."[64] The result was that "armed bands of civilians began to roam the streets."[65] Machine guns and hand grenades were taken from the barracks of the army training center in Santo Domingo.[66] Where weapons could not be found, they were improvised. Martin reports, "Rebels were forcing filling station operators to fill Coca-Cola bottles with gasoline for anybody on the street; they made Molotov cocktails from them."[67] While such forces were no match for the cascos blancos or the armed forces, their presence raised the prospect that consolidating power would involve heavy civilian casualties.

From there, the conflict escalated rapidly. Although Wessin's forces gained control of the palace, Bosch supporters outnumbered them. Wessin was reluctant "to risk his depleted forces, and especially his precious tank units (which come close to representing the real source of power in the Dominican Republic) in the crowded, narrow, rebel-infested streets of downtown Santo Domingo."[68] By April 26, however, newly armed groups of civilians had begun to attack police stations. In the hope of reducing the attacks, the police tried to make their opposition to Wessin clear. A committee of police officers went on Radio Santo Domingo that morning to announce that the police were "'on the side of the people'—and against San Isidro."[69] At this point, the situation, as the State Department explained to Johnson, was one in which "the Wessin group and the Air Force are in one camp; a large part of the Army that is in Santo Domingo, the capital itself, is supporting the rebel government and the loyalties of the troops outside the capital are still uncertain."[70] At times during the following days, the pro-Bosch forces appeared to have the upper hand.

Caamaño organized a particularly violent attack on the cascos blancos remaining at the Fortaleza Ozama. Brian Bosch describes how "many of the cascos blancos were slaughtered as they tried to escape across the Ozama River to the rear of the colonial fortress."[71] One of soldiers fighting with Caamaño recalled, "We had to go with a tank, mortars, bazookas, and have men climbing on rooftops. It lasted really about 24 hours."[72] It fell to the pro-Bosch rebels.[73] At this point, the police chief informed the American embassy that his "mopping up operations have met such violent resistance he can no longer continue."[74] By April 28, rebels were rounding up the remaining cascos blancos police squads. A report in *La Nacion* (Santo Domingo) described the scene: "With their hands raised above their heads and in undershirts, the members of the 'Cascos Blancos' were paraded by the Constitutionalists through various streets of the city so that people could identify them, and then locked up.... A large number of others were found two days later, drowned, on the banks of the Ozama estuary."[75] At this point, "the police were no longer effective, and the junta forces, tired and disorganized, began to crumble."[76] At the same time, loyalists and constitutionalists continued to clash outside of Santo Domingo.

The incipient civil war ended when the United States intervened. The American ambassador to the Dominican Republic, William Bennett, sent a series of increasingly dire cables about the situation. One noted, "Logically, the [Loyalist] forces should be able to control the situation. But the situation is not really very logical and a test of nerves is in progress."[77] Fearing that Communists would prevail and risk encouraging left-wing revolts in neighboring states, President Lyndon B. Johnson sent U.S. troops to occupy Santo Domingo.[78] Some fourteen thousand marines arrived on May 1. The American intervention turned the tide. Pro-Bosch forces "did not at any time contemplate actually fighting the U.S. troops."[79] To do so would have been suicidal. Instead, they agreed to a cease-fire and to begin negotiations to end the conflict. In the meantime, Wessin's forces continued to engage pro-Bosch rebels; they defeated them militarily by June 15. By the time the conflict ended, the death toll reached over two thousand.[80]

Explaining the Diverging Outcomes of the Two Dominican Coups

What explains why the 1965 coup escalated to civil war, while the 1963 coup did not? Many of the factors that seemingly made the Dominican Republic ripe for civil war in 1965—including the recent legacy of Trujillo's dictatorship, the country's deep ideological divisions, weak political institutions, and conflict-ridden civil-military relations—were present in 1963 as well. In both cases, multiple coup plots were brewing when the attempt got off the ground. If anything, widespread public opposition appeared *more* likely in advance of the first coup, when multiple parties explicitly declared their intent to oppose a coup, than in advance of the second. And as Lowenthal emphasizes, the military itself was as internally divided in 1963 as it was in 1965.[81]

In their initial hours, the dynamics of the two coup attempts themselves were also very similar. The ranks of the coup leaders were similar: high-ranking officers led both coups, which should have discouraged resistance.[82] Both attempts also initially appeared to succeed. In both cases, the president was captured without a fight. The responses of officers uncommitted at the outset of the coup were identical: in neither case did army, navy, or air force officers move to defend the ousted executive. When the armed forces declined to defend them, neither Bosch nor Reid received military assistance from abroad.

The difference, in 1965, was the opposition to the coup mounted by the cascos blancos riot squad of the National Police. While Bosch had explicitly declined to use the force as a counterweight to the army, in the period between the two attempts, Reid removed the National Police from army command and brought them under his personal control. While the presence of a counterweight did not deter the military from staging a coup, it stopped it from becoming "just another fairly orderly change in government," as most observers had expected.[83] The cascos blancos launched a violent counterattack that prevented the constitutionalists from achieving a rapid victory. Their resistance was motivated in part by fears about their fate under the new, coup-appointed regime. In dragging the coup out, the police opened space for other factions within the military—most notably Wessin's air force units, which did not want to return to the 1963 constitution—to fight for their own aims. The resistance of the cascos blancos and other police to the coup is also what prompted the PRD to begin arming civilian supporters. This step broadened the conflict from an intra-regime fight to one in which civilians were involved—in short, it turned the conflict into a civil war.

Counterbalancing and the Origins of the Civil War in Yemen

Counterbalancing also facilitated in the escalation of the 1962 coup in Yemen into a civil war. On September 26, a group of young officers in the Yemeni military staged a coup to overthrow Imam Muhammad al-Badr. With the help of his presidential guard, the Imam escaped capture. Tribal militias, which had long been used as counterweights to the regular military, could not stop the initial attack, but served as the core of the rebel force the ousted Imam used to challenge the coup plotters' hold on power.

The 1962 coup was the last in a series of attempts to overthrow the monarchy in Yemen. When the Ottoman Empire dissolved in 1918, Imam Yahya Muhammad Hamid ed-Din took power in the territory that became Yemen. The population in the majority of the territory was part of the Zaydi religious sect. During his rule, Imam Yahya established Yemen's first military. He also created two parallel armies: the Army of Defense, staffed by conscripts, and the Desert Army, composed of Zaydi tribal militias. The idea was that the tribal army would "act as a buffer against the regular and defense armies, and create a balance in the new military institutions."[84] Imam Yahya also had two battalions of royal guards for his person protection. Opposition to his rule—and to hereditary rule more generally—grew until a 1948 coup. Yahya was killed in the coup but was succeeded by his son Ahmad. Ahmad presided over the country's joining with Egypt and Syria to form the United Arab States between 1958 and 1961. Over time, his reign grew increasingly repressive.[85] He survived an assassination attempt in April 1961. In November of that year, Ahmad announced that he had uncovered another plot against his life, and arrested a number of alleged conspirators.[86] He also added members to the royal guard, which grew to about three thousand or four thousand men, and then merged it with the Army of Defense to form the core of a new military. The tribal militias Yahya had organized into the Desert Army remained an independent military force of some three thousand to five thousand soldiers. They were recruited, trained, and commanded by local sheikhs, and their command structure was decentralized and entirely separate from that of the army. They were equipped with light weapons only.[87]

At the time of Ahmad's death, in September 1962, several distinct coup plots were brewing. Ahmad had sent some officers abroad to Iraq for military training. While there, many picked up republican ideals and, upon their return, formed a Free Officer movement along the lines of those in Egypt and Sudan. In an effort to hobble potential coup plotters, the Imam restricted bullets available to soldiers.[88] Ahmad's successor, al-Badr, came to power with plans for gradual reform, but after meeting with senior members of the former administration, signaled in a speech his intent to continue most of his father's policies.[89] A State Department paper at the time of his ascension to power noted, "Crown Prince Badr has neither exhibited the stature of the Imam, nor commanded much of an internal following nor displayed qualities of leadership."[90]

A small group of army officers went forward with their plot to seize power, despite the change in executive, surprising al-Badr with an attack on the palace on September 26, less than one week after he assumed power. Al-Badr had been warned of the coup in advance. He surrounded himself with bodyguards.[91] While members of the guard were thought to be loyal, they were organized as part of the regular military, rather than as a counterweight. At the time of the coup, tribal militias, which remained independent, were camped on the outskirts of town.[92] The coup plotters attempted to recruit within al-Badr's bodyguard but anticipated resistance from both the majority of the guard and from tribal militias, which they assumed would remain loyal to the monarchy. Civilian supporters were also recruited in an attempt to exert pressure on tribal forces to accept the new regime.[93]

The evening of the coup, al-Badr held a late meeting of his Council of Ministers in the palace. One of his bodyguards attempted to shoot him, but the rifle jammed. It was not clear yet that the attack was part of an attempted coup. Over the course of the next few hours, the coup plotters seized control of radio station and airfield in Sana'a. A radio address announced the overthrow of what coup plotters described as the Imam's "corrupt, reactionary," and "criminal" regime, and told civilians to remain in their homes or they would be shot.[94] Once the coup was under way, the young officers leading it approached Colonel Abdullah al-Sallal, who had been a member of the presidential guard; he agreed to take charge.[95]

The coup plotters then moved toward the palace, where a firefight ensued. Most of the presidential guard remained loyal, defending the Imam and his family. Their efforts were aided by the fact that the streets surrounding the building were too narrow for tanks to approach closely. This meant that the gunners had to fire over the tops of buildings, and only the top floors of the palace were shelled.[96] Victoria Clark chronicles the effort to defend the palace: "After sending some loyal guards out through the firing line in search of any remaining loyal officers, the Imam had organized others to fetch sandbags, douse them with petrol, set them alight and hurl them down onto the tanks, while he and his father-in law manned the third floor balcony with their submachine gun."[97] Tanks, light artillery, and machine guns were employed.[98]

Eventually, the Imam decided to try to escape the palace and directed the soldiers remaining with him to meet in Gabi al Kaflir, a village two miles northwest of Sana'a. He exited through a door in the garden wall that remained unguarded; in the nearby home of a friend, he disguised himself in an army uniform, and made his way through side streets to the western edge of the city. From there, he walked to Gabi al Kaflir.[99] Meanwhile, in the capital, the coup plotters had taken care to station troops outside the main army barracks to deter any soldiers who might have been inclined to resist from doing so. Within the capital, Edgar O'Ballance concludes, "it was largely a matter of where the Yemeni soldiers happened to be at the time that governed the side they opted for."[100] Meanwhile, youth groups began marching through the streets with banners in support of the revolution. In advance of the coup, a couple of prominent merchants had stockpiled arms that were intended for civilians supporters; given the limited supply of ammunition available to rebellion soldiers, however, they were instead turned over to members of the army when the coup was under way.[101]

The bloodiest battle in the first few hours of the coup occurred around the military stores at al Qalah, on the eastern side of town, as coup plotters tried to liberate additional weapons and munitions. The three hundred officers guarding the al Qalah supply refused to open the stores except on direct orders from al-Badr. Some eighty men were killed. Meanwhile, the tribal militias stationed outside the capital missed much of the action in the first night of the coup.[102]

By morning, the rebels had taken the capital. They claimed that al-Badr was killed in the shelling of the palace. Over the radio, al-Sallal announced the abolition of the Imamate and the founding of a new Yemeni Arab Republic (YAR). Following al-Sallal's broadcast, the "streets soon became filled with cheering citizens, and the remainder of the army and militia" in Sana'a "threw in their lot with him."[103] The Imam's remaining relatives in Sana'a were executed, along with several members of his government.[104] The Imam's uncle, Prince Hassan bin Hussein, who had been in New York serving as Yemen's delegate to the United Nations, claimed legal succession to the Imamate and formed a government in exile, with the support of Saudi Arabia and Jordan. He returned to Yemen in early October in an attempt to assert his authority.[105]

The new regime requested support from Cairo. Within forty-eight hours of the coup, Egyptian troops began to land. Within a week, an estimated three thousand had entered the country.[106] It initially looked like the Republican government would consolidate power. At the time of the coup, some seventy tribal sheikhs were in Sana'a to pledge loyalty to al-Badr. The coup plotters approached several on the eve of the revolt. Those who agreed to join were appointed to a defense council, given ministerial salaries, and sent home to maintain order. The new government also tried to retain military loyalty by doubling the salaries of all enlisted men and providing a one-month bonus.[107] But rumors that al-Badr had survived the coup attempt persisted. Al-Sallal could not produce his body, though the coup plotters had produced those of several of his relatives and cabinet members. Foreign journalists became more vocal in pointing out that only the top floors of the palace were damaged, casting doubt on al-Sallal's claims.[108]

Finally, in mid-October the Imam resurfaced and began reaching out to potential supporters abroad, detailing his escape and rallying of loyalist tribes, and requesting backing.[109] On November 10, the Imam held a public press conference from the northwest corner of Yemen, announcing his intent to continue to fight for the crown. Although there was some bad blood between Hassan and al-Badr—Hassan had previously indicated he thought al-Badr was "unfit to be Imam"—Hassan recused himself from the contest and threw his support behind al-Bahr as soon as it became clear al-Badr was alive.[110] The new regime sent soldiers in pursuit of al-Badr, while the few army units that remained intact were deployed around the capital.[111]

Tribal militias that had fled during the coup regrouped and formed the locus of the royalist forces. The Imam's core support came from two tribal confederations in the north, Hashid and Bakil, both of which had a long history of cooperation with the Imamate.[112] At al-Badr's press conference, he claimed that he had the support of tribal militias that totaled over twenty thousand men. These included "an army of tribesmen under his personal command to the west of Sada, and that his uncle, Prince Hassan, had another army to the east of Sana, and that there was yet another near Harib, in the southeast."[113] Former members of the Imam's presidential guard who had escaped formed another core of his support.[114]

In the months immediately following al-Badr's press conference, the royalists appeared to have the upper hand. Al-Badr's forces eventually grew to include some fourteen thousand soldiers that had split off from the regular army to support the Imam, and an estimated thirty thousand to eighty thousand tribal forces.[115] Rebel forces held control in cities, but did not control the roads between them or in most rural areas. The new regime in Sana'a, led by al-Sallal, recruited volunteers to take the place of those who had deserted to form a new national guard in the urban centers of Sana'a, Taiz, Hodeida, and Hakka. While the hope was to raise funds to train and equip them properly, the national guard units "were sent to fight with no training and thousands, perhaps, were slaughtered."[116] The Republicans also tried to win over the support of uncommitted tribes by supplying arms and funding.[117] While, the royalists won several early, important battles, foreign intervention, beginning with Egypt, helped turn the tide.[118] Fred Halliday notes that, "the Egyptian intervention spared the YAR from a probable rapid defeat by northern tribes."[119] Eventually, the Soviet Union and China also provided support to the Republican side, while the royalists were aided by Britain and Saudi Arabia. Both the new regime in Sana'a and its external patrons began providing subsidies to tribes to lure them away from the rebellion; many tribes managed to collect fees from both sides of the conflict.[120] The conflict ended shortly after Egyptian troops withdrew in 1967.

In short, while the 1962 coup in Yemen escalated through a different mechanism than the 1965 coup in the Dominican Republic, counterbalancing also affected its outcome. The Dominican coup faced immediate resistance from the police riot squad. Battles between the police and regular military units, and between the police and civilians who took up arms in the days following the coup, resulted in the largest number of fatalities. In contrast, in Yemen, al-Badr's tribal militias did not resist the initial attack. Stationed on the outskirts of the capital, they were too far way to come to his defense when the palace was under siege. Compared to the regular army units, the tribal militias were also poorly equipped. Nonetheless, when the Imam escaped and declared his intent to challenge the new coup-appointed government, he was able to draw on the tribal militias to serve as the core of his rebel army. Eventually, individual soldiers and units from the regular armed forces split with the Republican government and peeled off to join the Imam as well. But the tribal militias formed the bulk of his armed forces. Their presence helped al-Badr quickly overcome the logistical and organizational challenges of organizing a rebellion to challenge the coup-installed government. Thus while the context of the coup in Yemen, and the way in which it unfolded, differed in important ways from that of the 1965 Dominican coup, counterweights played a central role in the escalation of both.

Civil wars, particularly civil wars that escalate from coups, are rare events. The vast majority of coup attempts will not escalate to broader violence. But the presence of an armed counterweight to the military increases the risk that they will do so. The analysis in this chapter showed how counterbalancing can facilitate the escalation of coups to civil war. The chapter first compared the 1963 coup in the Dominican Republic, which remained bloodless, with the violent coup just two years later, in 1965, which escalated to civil war. The contexts of the two coups were very similar. Yet in the short period between the two attempts, Reid built up a counterweight, the cascos blancos riot squad, within the police and brought it under his personal command. In part because of fears about their fate should the coup succeed, the cascos blancos violently resisted the 1965 coup when officers in the regular military would not. This resistance prevented coup plotters from achieving a quick and bloodless victory and prompted actors both within and outside of the armed forces to enter the fray. The 1962 coup in Yemen occurred in very different circumstances. It also developed in a different way, with the ousted Imam escaping alive. Yet in this case too counterbalancing facilitated the escalation of the coup to a civil war: once outside the capital, the Imam was able to draw upon tribal militias, which had long served as counterweights to the regular military, to serve as a ready-made rebel army, and use them to successfully challenge the new government brought to power in the coup. The evidence from these cases thus suggests that counterweights can facilitate the escalation of coup attempts into civil wars.

CONCLUSION
Coercive Institutions and Regime Survival

For leaders across the globe, preventing military intervention in politics remains one of the central challenges of governance. Although coups d'état have become less common over the past few decades, they remain frequent and destabilizing events. In some places, democratic institutions have persisted despite the best efforts of soldiers who have sought to undermine them. Elsewhere, coups have ousted would-be democrats from power, setting back reforms. This variation can be explained, in part, by the choices rulers make in organizing their presidential guards, police, and other coercive institutions. In their efforts to prevent coups, rulers from Jawaharlal Nehru in India to Hugo Chávez in Venezuela and Nouri al-Maliki in Iraq have counterbalanced the regular military with independent security forces. The aim of this book has been to understand the consequences of that decision. In order to do so, it addressed three interrelated questions. First, does counterbalancing work? Is it associated with fewer coup attempts, or less successful ones? Second, *how* does it work? What are the mechanisms through which it affects the incidence and outcomes of coup attempts? Finally, what are the implications of counterbalancing for the risk that coups d'état will escalate to broader violence?

The evidence examined in this book shows that counterbalancing increases the risk that coup attempts will fail in ousting rulers from power by creating incentives for police and paramilitary forces to resist the coup. When a coup attempt begins, most military officers are not yet committed to one side or the other. Whether it succeeds or fails depends on how those in the vicinity of coup targets, including broadcast stations and symbolic seats of political power, choose to respond. Because the consequences for being on the losing side of a coup attempt are harsh, officers are apt to throw their lot in with the side that appears to be winning, or to remain on the sidelines the entire time. However, when rulers organize presidential guards, militarized police, and other security forces outside military command, the calculus for their officers changes. Because their presence impinges on core institutional interests of the military, coup plotters from within the armed forces cannot credibly commit to maintain the status or even the existence of other security forces following a successful coup. This gives officers and soldiers in counterbalancing forces powerful incentives to interpose themselves between coup plotters and their targets or to launch counterattacks to recapture those that have already been seized. Such actions undermine coup plotters' ability to make the coup's success appear inevitable.

Chapter 2 tests the observable implications of this argument. Drawing on new data on state security forces in 110 states between 1960 and 2010, statistical tests demonstrated that coup attempts fail more often when rulers counterbalance. The effect is substantively large: when rulers do not counterbalance, coup attempts against them succeed about half of the time. Where they employ three or more counterweights, counterbalancing cuts the risk that a coup will succeed in half. The association between counterbalancing and failed coups remains when accounting for potential confounding factors that might affect both the use of counterweights and the outcomes of coup attempts. I also carefully consider alternative arguments, showing that the association between counterbalancing and coup failure cannot be explained by the political strength or weakness of the military in relation to civilian authorities, and that the findings are not driven by particular subsets of states such as military regimes or by particular coding decisions. Chapter 3 examines evidence on the causal mechanisms linking counterbalancing to coup failure. While common narratives about counterbalancing suggest that it creates obstacles to coordination during a coup attempt, a close analysis of coup attempts in sixteen different cases, including the 1982 coup in Kenya, the 1971 coup in Morocco, and the 1989 coup in Panama, suggests that counterbalancing is associated with failed coups because counterweights violently resist.

Even as counterbalancing helps to prevent successful interventions, however, the fear and resentment it generates within the regular military can provoke new coups attempts. Chapter 4 examines patterns in coup attempts in a cross-national sample. The analysis demonstrates that counterbalancing does not deter coup attempts. On the contrary, creating a new counterweight *increases* the risk of a coup in the following year. This is because organizing security forces outside of military command infringes on a central institutional interest of the regular armed forces: their monopoly on the state's use of military power. As failed efforts by Kwame Nkrumah in Ghana and Modibo Keita in Mali illustrate, the consequences for individual leaders can be severe. Yet the book also points to examples of efforts by rulers in similar political and economic situations, such as Siaka Stevens in Sierra Leone and Fidel Castro in Cuba, that were more successful. This comparison suggests that counterweights may be less likely to trigger a coup attempt where leaders embed counterbalancing in broader strategies of coup prevention that include increased remuneration for the regular military and purges of political opponents. It also suggests that the use of militarized police may be viewed with less hostility than other types of counterweights.

Disentangling the mechanisms through which counterbalancing works is important because different mechanisms have different implications for the extent of violence associated with coups. In particular, I argue that one of the unintended consequences of counterbalancing is that it increases the risk that coup attempts will escalate into the more sustained violence that characterizes civil war. The evidence presented in chapter 6 lends support to this argument. The comparison of two coup attempts in the Dominican Republic, just two years apart, suggests that whether the regime engaged in counterbalancing affected the different levels of violence associated with the coups. During the 1962 coup in North Yemen, counterweights similarly facilitated the escalation of a coup attempt to civil war. In short, rulers who counterbalance may be trading the threat of a successful coup for that of civil war.

Theoretical Implications

The findings in this book have implications for a number of different areas of research in political science. To begin with, there are implications for theories about the military and democratization. Given the frequency with which rulers establish coercive institutions outside the military—and the central role of state security forces in theories of democratization—the rarity with which counterbalancing has been the subject of scholarly attention is surprising.[1] Indeed, democratic consolidation is often defined by a lack of military intervention in politics. Daron Acemoglu and James Robinson, for example, describe a consolidated democracy as one in which "there is never any effective coup threat."[2] Understanding the conditions under which democratic regimes consolidate thus requires understanding the conditions under which coups occur. Much existing research focuses on long-term, structural features of states, such as their level of economic development or legacies of colonial rule. This book advances existing research on democratization by emphasizing the conditions under which individual leaders can use counterbalancing to reduce the risk of successful coups themselves and by providing new data with which to test theories about whether and how counterbalancing works. For those already convinced of the importance of coercive institutions in preventing coups, the book's framework improves our understanding of exactly how their design affects regime survival.

That said, the findings here do not suggest that counterbalancing is necessarily good for democracy. Indeed, they suggest important reasons for caution in using counterbalancing. As the preceding chapters have shown, counterbalancing is a coup prevention strategy that aims to make coups harder to carry out, rather than to change underlying beliefs about the rule of law or the legitimacy of democratic procedures. To the extent that rulers are investing in restricting opportunities to stage a coup to the exclusion of efforts to build more durable political institutions, their actions are not likely to bring about long-term change. As troubling, the findings also indicate that coups that occur in the presence of counterweights are more likely to escalate to civil war than those that do not. More broadly, this book highlights some of the trade-offs leaders face in attempting to address multiple threats to their power. While counterbalancing is effective in impeding successful coups, it can provoke new coup attempts and increase the risk that such attempts will escalate to civil war. In highlighting these trade-offs, the book joins a growing literature on the unintended consequences of coup prevention strategies, which have thus far emphasized its effects on military effectiveness and the durability of regimes in the face of mass protests.[3]

There are also implications for scholars of civil war. There are important reasons to think that different causal processes underlie the escalation of coups to civil wars and the organization of insurgency. Yet theories about the onset of civil war are almost entirely theories about the conditions that favor insurgency. Furthermore, studies of civil war typically lump together conflicts that originate with rebellion by nonstate actors and those that originate in coups or other splits within the military, without examining whether the factors that cause them are the same. This book contributes to our understanding of civil war by exploring the origins of coup-related civil wars and theorizing an alternate causal pathway to civil war beyond that of insurgency. Deploying case studies and structured comparisons to generate new theoretical claims, it posits that counterbalancing increases the risk of civil war by creating incentives for armed resistance to coup attempts and enabling ousted rulers to overcome the challenges of recruiting and organizing rebel forces with which they can challenge the coup-installed regime.

More broadly, this book emphasizes the importance of opening up the "black box" of the state's security sector to examine how states organize, staff, equip, and deploy their security forces. Many studies of international conflict and civil war have tended to assume that contestation takes place between two sides—state A and state B, or incumbents and insurgents. Empirically, however, neither states nor rebels are unified actors. In the context of civil war, a growing body of research examines the consequences of having multiple armed actors challenging the state.[4] New work has also shed light on the role of militias, paramilitaries, and self-defense forces that may be "pro-government" but that are not an official part of the state's security sector.[5] This book emphasizes corresponding variations in the number and type of coercive institutions that can be present *within* a state's security sector. In emphasizing the role of state security forces beyond the military in underpinning political stability, this research thus contributes to an emerging research agenda on "third actors" in conflicts. Within the field of civil-military relations, scholars have begun to explore divisions between junior and senior officers, between different generations of officers, and between those with different regional backgrounds.[6] This book suggests that further efforts to disaggregate intra-military and intra–security sector divisions are likely to bear fruit.

The theory and evidence in this book also suggest a number of other directions for future research. While the central aim of the book is to test whether and how counterbalancing works, it also provides a more general framework to explain the dynamics of coup attempts, which emphasizes actors' perceptions about the likelihood the coup will succeed, the costs of defeat, and the costs of violence, that can guide future research. Branching out from the study of military and security forces, subsequent studies might examine how other actors, such as international organizations, foreign powers, or civilian elites, influence these parameters. In many coup-prone countries, rulers depend on foreign troops in addition to their own. For instance, France remained heavily involved in domestic political developments in post-colonial Africa. By one count, France intervened militarily to protect French nationals and defend incumbent regimes against uprisings nineteen times between 1962 and 1995.[7] The presence of foreign troops might decrease estimates about the costs of using violence during a coup, resulting in less successful—and more violent—coup attempts. While the central dynamics of coups occur largely within the armed forces, rapid condemnation of the coup from international actors might affect officers' estimates of the costs of the coup succeeding. Future research might thus productively theorize about how such actors might affect estimates of the likelihood a coup will succeed, the costs of it doing so, and the costs of using violence.

The arguments developed here emphasize the incentives rulers have to foster competition between their security forces, so as to increase the odds that a coup originating within one force will be opposed by others. Yet the book also identifies cases, like that of the Civil Guard in Peru, and of the Leopards and Dessalines Battalions in Haiti, in which counterweights partnered with segments of the regular military against the regime. As Risa Brooks points out, military and police frequently have both competing and complementary interests.[8] Future work might attempt to theorize more concretely about the variety of relationships that exist between different military and security forces that can comprise a state's security sector, and the conditions under which they may be expected to perceive their interests as aligned.

Finally, while recent work has emphasized that the choice of coercive institutions reflects the balance of threats rulers face, we know little about how and why rulers make the particular choices they do.[9] In particular, the analysis in chapters 2 and 4 showed that neither the extent of coup risk rulers face nor the preexisting strength of the military does a good job of explaining where rulers will counterbalance. The case comparisons in chapter 5 suggested that new counterweights might be easiest to establish in the context of a more comprehensive coup prevention strategy. As strides are made in documenting how the use of other coup-proofing strategies, such as ethnic stacking, purges, and bribery, varies over time and space, future research may test this hypothesis in a larger number of cases. Future research may also seek to develop a more comprehensive theory about the origins of coercive institutions. Why do some of the most coup-prone types of regimes refrain from counterbalancing? Among those that counterbalance, why do some rulers invest in presidential guards, while others build secret police forces? Why do some create a single, powerful counterweight, while others fragment their coercive institutions into a complex patchwork of overlapping forces? Does the way in which a regime comes to power influence the coercive institutions that it builds? How does external sponsorship shape the trajectory of a state's coercive institutions? Thus far, too little is known about the factors that influence the design of coercive institutions.

Policy Implications

While there are no simple policy solutions that follow from this book, the results can offer some guidance to policymakers interested in shoring up civilian control over the military and in preventing coups from escalating to higher levels of violence. The findings also offer an analytic lens through which policymakers can better understand contemporary conflicts between military and civilian elites, and help them to better predict when coup attempts will occur, whether they will succeed, and how violent they are likely to be.

Where rulers have successfully established counterweights to the military, the likelihood that a military coup will oust them from power is low. Take the case of the unrest in Venezuela in the spring of 2019, when opposition leader Juan Guaidó called on the military to join him in ousting President Nicolás Maduro from power. U.S. policymakers publicly supported the effort, but grew frustrated when the attempt failed.[10] Attention to the use of counterweights can help policymakers better predict the likelihood that efforts to oust leaders from power in a coup will succeed. Both Maduro and his predecessor, Hugo Chávez, had counterbalanced the military with paramilitary and militia forces. After a failed coup in 2002, Chávez created the Bolivarian National Militia, a civilian paramilitary force, to deter subsequent attempts. In 2017, Maduro added paramilitary Special Actions Forces to the ranks of the national police, and recruited and trained armed bands of civilians to suppress regime opponents. The presence of these counterweights suggests that the prospects for a successful coup in contemporary Venezuela are slim.[11]

The findings in this book also highlight the dangers of attempting to build new coercive institutions to counterbalance the military. Policymakers interested in preventing coup attempts should be on alert that coup attempts are more likely to occur when rulers reorganize their security sectors. In particular, efforts to establish new coercive institutions to counterbalance the military can backfire. At the same time, this book suggests some ways in which the risk that building new coercive institutions will provoke a coup can be mitigated. In contrast to broader, structural factors that may influence the incidence and outcomes of coup attempts, policymakers do have some leverage over the structure of a state's security sector. Where new security forces are deemed necessary, they can be designed in a way that reduces the risk they will provoke military intervention in politics. In particular, security forces that are organized under military command are likely to be less destabilizing than those that are independent. As the examples of counterbalancing in Sierra Leone and Cuba illustrate, embedding counterbalancing in a broader strategy of coup-proofing may also mitigate some of the risks. Counterbalancing the military with militarized police also seems to be a safer option than using civilian militia or secret police.

While the analysis in this book does suggest that counterbalancing is effective in stopping coups, it also emphasizes that the risks of counterbalancing remain high. Fragmented, exclusionary security sectors may increase the odds that there will be resistance to a coup attempt. But they do not deter soldiers from attempting to seize power. The creation of new counterweights can provoke military intervention in politics. And, as chapter 6 shows, counterbalancing increases the risk that a coup attempt will escalate to civil war. These findings add to a raft of prior research on the costs of counterbalancing. Where the state's coercive institutions are more fragmented, it creates barriers to communication and coordination that undermine military effectiveness.[12] In Sudan, for instance, the Economist Intelligence Unit describes how the Peoples' Defense Force (PDF) undermined the effectiveness of the national military: "not only because ill-trained conscripts to the PDF are a liability on the battlefield but also because they act as informers" for the government.[13] Counterbalancing is also associated with high levels of repression against civilians.

In short, counterbalancing is a coup prevention strategy with important downsides. As such, policymakers concerned with building stable, democratic regimes should not be encouraged to make it a centerpiece of their coup prevention efforts. At the same time, it does not make sense to vilify individual leaders who turn to counterbalancing. Rulers in countries with a long history of coup attempts are likely to face strong temptations to fragment their security forces, as are those in post-conflict settings, particularly where peace agreements encourage them to incorporate former combatants into the military. Instead, a more realistic appraisal of the incentives rulers have to fragment their security forces can help focus resources where they will be of the most use.

Overall, the arguments and findings in this book suggest that there are important limitations to current policies that aim to prevent coups. International efforts to reduce military intervention in politics focus primarily on fostering norms of democratic, civilian control of the military. American policymakers in particular devote significant efforts to training and building up the capacity of security forces overseas. The United States spends an estimated $200 million per year on military training to promote more democratic civil-military relations.[14] The results of these efforts have been mixed at best. While such training may provide soldiers with prolonged exposure to the workings of a professional and nonpolitical military, it can also impart valuable resources to individual officers in the form of military expertise and social capital that can be turned against the state.[15] To the extent that rulers channel these resources to counterweights rather than the regular military, investments in training and capacity-building might also exacerbate military grievances. As a result, international efforts to prevent coups are unlikely to succeed where they do not take into account how rulers structure their coercive institutions and allocate resources between them.

Finally, the presence of counterweights should alert policymakers of the potential for the coup to escalate to broader violence. Coup attempts that occur where rulers counterbalance bring with them the risk of escalation to civil war. If the factors that cause coups to escalate to civil war are distinct from those that facilitate insurgency, as this book argues, this suggests a different set of tools to policymakers seeking to prevent civil war. In particular, knowing that having more security forces increases the risk that coups will escalate should give pause to policymakers currently advocating their creation in post-conflict settings as a method to quickly incorporate rebel forces and militia. Instead, security sector reform efforts may have more success where nonstate armed groups can be incorporated into the traditional army.

The preceding pages have sought to unpack the motivations and mechanisms that drive coups d'état. By focusing on how states structure their coercive institutions, this book has argued, we can better understand the incentives facing soldiers and the threat that they pose to civilian rule. It has offered insight into the conditions under which coup attempts occur, whether they will succeed, and how much violence they will entail. International actors cannot remove the threat of a coup. But by recognizing the competing pressures that rulers face, and the ways in which counterbalancing works, they may be able to mitigate some of the costs.

Appendix
COUNTERBALANCING DATA

TABLE A.1 Coup attempts included in the statistical analysis

COUNTRY	YEAR	SUCCESS	COUNTER-BALANCING	NO. OF COUNTERWEIGHTS
Afghanistan	1973	Yes	Yes	1
Afghanistan	1978	Yes	Yes	2
Afghanistan	1979	Yes	Yes	3
Afghanistan	1990	No	Yes	3
Afghanistan	1992	Yes	Yes	3
Afghanistan	2002	No	Yes	1
Algeria	1965	Yes	Yes	1
Algeria	1967	No	Yes	1
Angola	1977	No	Yes	1
Argentina	1961	No	No	0
Argentina	1962	Yes	No	0
Argentina	1963	No	No	0
Argentina	1966	Yes	No	0
Argentina	1970	Yes	No	0
Argentina	1971	Yes	No	0
Argentina	1976	Yes	No	0
Argentina	1990	No	No	0
Azerbaijan	1994	No	Yes	3
Azerbaijan	1995	No	Yes	3
Bangladesh	1975	Yes	Yes	2

(continued)

TABLE A.1 (Continued)

COUNTRY	YEAR	SUCCESS	COUNTER-BALANCING	NO. OF COUNTERWEIGHTS
Bangladesh	1976	Yes	Yes	2
Bangladesh	1977	No	Yes	2
Bangladesh	1980	No	Yes	2
Bangladesh	1981	No	Yes	2
Bangladesh	1982	Yes	Yes	2
Bangladesh	1996	No	Yes	2
Bangladesh	2007	Yes	Yes	3
Benin	1963	Yes	No	0
Benin	1965	Yes	No	0
Benin	1967	Yes	No	0
Benin	1969	Yes	No	0
Benin	1972	No	No	0
Benin	1975	No	No	0
Benin	1977	No	No	0
Benin	1988	No	Yes	2
Benin	1992	No	Yes	2
Benin	1995	No	No	0
Bolivia	1964	Yes	Yes	1
Bolivia	1968	No	Yes	1
Bolivia	1969	Yes	Yes	1
Bolivia	1970	No	Yes	1
Bolivia	1971	No	Yes	1
Bolivia	1974	No	Yes	1
Bolivia	1978	Yes	No	0
Bolivia	1979	Yes	No	0
Bolivia	1980	Yes	No	0
Bolivia	1981	No	No	0
Bolivia	1984	No	No	0
Brazil	1964	Yes	Yes	1
Burma (Myanmar)	1962	Yes	No	0
Burma (Myanmar)	1988	Yes	No	0
Burundi	1965	No	Yes	1
Burundi	1966	No	Yes	1
Burundi	1976	Yes	No	0
Burundi	1987	Yes	Yes	1
Burundi	1992	No	Yes	1
Burundi	1993	No	Yes	1
Burundi	1994	No	Yes	1
Burundi	1996	Yes	Yes	1
Burundi	2001	No	Yes	1
Cambodia	1970	Yes	No	0

COUNTRY	YEAR	SUCCESS	COUNTER-BALANCING	NO. OF COUNTERWEIGHTS
Cambodia	1975	No	No	0
Cambodia	1976	No	No	0
Cambodia	1977	No	No	0
Cambodia	1978	No	No	0
Cambodia	1991	No	No	0
Cambodia	1997	Yes	No	0
Cambodia	2000	No	No	0
Cameroon	1984	No	Yes	1
Central African Republic	1966	Yes	Yes	2
Central African Republic	1969	No	Yes	1
Central African Republic	1974	No	Yes	1
Central African Republic	1979	Yes	Yes	1
Central African Republic	1981	Yes	Yes	1
Central African Republic	1983	No	Yes	1
Central African Republic	1996	No	Yes	1
Central African Republic	2001	No	Yes	2
Central African Republic	2003	Yes	Yes	2
Chad	1971	No	Yes	1
Chad	1975	Yes	Yes	2
Chad	1976	No	Yes	2
Chad	1977	No	Yes	1
Chad	1982	Yes	No	0
Chad	1989	No	Yes	2
Chad	1990	Yes	Yes	2
Chad	1991	No	Yes	3
Chad	1992	No	Yes	3
Chad	1993	No	Yes	2
Chad	2006	No	Yes	2
Chad	2008	No	Yes	2
Chile	1973	No	Yes	1
Cote d'Ivoire	1980	No	Yes	2
Cote d'Ivoire	1991	No	Yes	2
Cote d'Ivoire	1995	No	Yes	2
Cote d'Ivoire	1999	Yes	Yes	2
Cote d'Ivoire	2000	No	Yes	2
Cote d'Ivoire	2001	No	Yes	2
Djibouti	1991	No	Yes	1
Djibouti	2000	No	Yes	1
Dominican Republic	1961	No	No	0
Dominican Republic	1962	No	No	0
Dominican Republic	1963	Yes	Yes	1
Dominican Republic	1965	Yes	Yes	1

(continued)

TABLE A.1 (Continued)

COUNTRY	YEAR	SUCCESS	COUNTER-BALANCING	NO. OF COUNTERWEIGHTS
East Timor	2008	No	Yes	1
Ecuador	1963	Yes	Yes	1
Ecuador	1966	Yes	Yes	1
Ecuador	1972	Yes	Yes	1
Ecuador	1975	No	Yes	1
Ecuador	1976	Yes	Yes	1
Ecuador	2000	No	Yes	1
Ecuador	2010	No	Yes	1
El Salvador	1961	Yes	No	0
El Salvador	1972	No	No	0
El Salvador	1979	Yes	No	0
Ethiopia	1974	Yes	No	0
Ethiopia	1977	Yes	No	0
Ethiopia	1989	No	No	0
Fiji	1987	Yes	No	0
Fiji	2000	No	No	0
Fiji	2006	Yes	Yes	1
Georgia	2009	No	Yes	3
Ghana	1962	No	No	0
Ghana	1966	Yes	Yes	1
Ghana	1967	No	Yes	1
Ghana	1972	Yes	No	0
Ghana	1977	No	No	0
Ghana	1978	Yes	No	0
Ghana	1979	No	No	0
Ghana	1981	Yes	No	0
Ghana	1982	No	No	0
Ghana	1983	No	No	0
Greece	1967	Yes	No	0
Greece	1973	Yes	No	0
Guatemala	1963	Yes	Yes	2
Guatemala	1982	Yes	Yes	2
Guatemala	1983	Yes	Yes	2
Guatemala	1988	No	Yes	2
Guatemala	1989	No	Yes	2
Guatemala	1993	No	Yes	2
Haiti	1968	No	Yes	3
Haiti	1970	No	Yes	3
Haiti	1986	No	Yes	3
Haiti	1988	Yes	Yes	2
Haiti	1989	No	Yes	2

COUNTRY	YEAR	SUCCESS	COUNTER-BALANCING	NO. OF COUNTERWEIGHTS
Haiti	1991	No	Yes	1
Haiti	2000	No	Yes	1
Honduras	1963	Yes	Yes	1
Honduras	1972	Yes	No	0
Honduras	1975	Yes	No	0
Honduras	1977	No	No	0
Honduras	1978	Yes	No	0
Honduras	1999	No	No	0
Indonesia	1965	No	Yes	2
Indonesia	1966	Yes	Yes	2
Iran	1980	No	Yes	2
Iran	1982	No	Yes	3
Iran	1984	No	Yes	3
Iraq	1963	Yes	No	0
Iraq	1964	No	No	0
Iraq	1965	No	Yes	1
Iraq	1966	No	Yes	1
Iraq	1968	Yes	Yes	1
Iraq	1973	No	Yes	2
Iraq	1979	No	Yes	2
Iraq	1984	No	Yes	2
Iraq	1991	No	Yes	1
Iraq	1992	No	Yes	1
Iraq	1995	No	Yes	2
Lebanon	1961	No	Yes	2
Lebanon	1976	No	Yes	2
Liberia	1980	Yes	No	0
Liberia	1985	No	Yes	1
Liberia	1994	Yes	No	0
Libya	1969	Yes	Yes	2
Libya	1993	No	Yes	2
Mali	1968	Yes	Yes	3
Mali	1969	No	Yes	2
Mali	1978	No	Yes	1
Mali	1991	No	Yes	1
Morocco	1971	No	Yes	2
Morocco	1972	No	Yes	2
Nepal	2002	Yes	Yes	1
Nicaragua	1967	No	No	0
Nicaragua	1978	No	No	0
Nicaragua	1980	No	Yes	2
Niger	1974	Yes	Yes	2

(continued)

TABLE A.1 (Continued)

COUNTRY	YEAR	SUCCESS	COUNTER-BALANCING	NO. OF COUNTERWEIGHTS
Niger	1976	No	No	0
Niger	1983	No	No	0
Niger	1996	No	No	0
Niger	2010	Yes	Yes	1
Nigeria	1966	Yes	Yes	1
Nigeria	1975	Yes	Yes	1
Nigeria	1976	No	Yes	1
Nigeria	1983	Yes	Yes	1
Nigeria	1985	Yes	Yes	1
Nigeria	1990	No	Yes	1
Nigeria	1993	Yes	Yes	2
Pakistan	1977	Yes	Yes	1
Pakistan	1984	No	No	0
Pakistan	1999	Yes	No	0
Panama	1968	Yes	No	0
Panama	1969	No	No	0
Panama	1988	No	No	0
Panama	1989	No	Yes	1
Peru	1962	Yes	Yes	2
Peru	1963	Yes	Yes	2
Peru	1968	Yes	Yes	2
Peru	1975	Yes	Yes	2
Peru	1992	No	Yes	1
Philippines	1986	No	Yes	4
Philippines	1987	No	Yes	3
Philippines	1989	No	Yes	1
Philippines	1990	No	Yes	1
Philippines	2007	No	Yes	1
Poland	1981	Yes	Yes	2
Portugal	1974	Yes	Yes	4
Portugal	1975	No	Yes	2
Russia (Soviet Union)	1991	No	Yes	2
Rwanda	1973	Yes	No	0
Sierra Leone	1967	Yes	No	0
Sierra Leone	1968	Yes	No	0
Sierra Leone	1971	No	No	0
Sierra Leone	1987	No	Yes	1
Sierra Leone	1992	Yes	Yes	1
Sierra Leone	1995	No	Yes	1
Sierra Leone	1996	Yes	Yes	1
Sierra Leone	1997	Yes	Yes	1

COUNTRY	YEAR	SUCCESS	COUNTER-BALANCING	NO. OF COUNTERWEIGHTS
South Korea	1961	Yes	No	0
South Korea	1979	No	No	0
Spain	1981	No	Yes	1
Sudan	1966	No	Yes	2
Sudan	1969	Yes	Yes	2
Sudan	1970	No	Yes	3
Sudan	1971	No	Yes	3
Sudan	1975	No	Yes	3
Sudan	1976	No	Yes	3
Sudan	1977	No	Yes	3
Sudan	1985	Yes	Yes	3
Sudan	1989	Yes	Yes	2
Sudan	1990	No	Yes	4
Sudan	2008	No	Yes	4
Swaziland	1984	No	Yes	1
Syria	1962	No	Yes	1
Syria	1963	Yes	Yes	1
Syria	1966	Yes	Yes	2
Syria	1970	Yes	Yes	3
Syria	1982	No	Yes	6
Tajikistan	1992	No	No	0
Tanzania	1964	No	Yes	1
Tanzania	1980	No	Yes	2
Tunisia	1987	Yes	Yes	3
Turkey	1962	No	Yes	1
Turkey	1963	No	Yes	1
Turkey	1971	Yes	No	0
Turkey	1980	Yes	No	0
Uganda	1971	Yes	Yes	2
Uganda	1974	No	Yes	2
Uganda	1975	No	Yes	2
Uganda	1980	Yes	Yes	2
Uganda	1985	Yes	Yes	2
Venezuela	1992	No	No	0
Venezuela	2002	No	No	0
Yemen (Yemen Arab Republic)	1962	Yes	Yes	1
Yemen (Yemen Arab Republic)	1967	Yes	No	0
Yemen (Yemen Arab Republic)	1974	Yes	No	0
Yemen (Yemen Arab Republic)	1978	No	No	0

Coup Narratives: Counterbalancing and Coup Outcomes

This appendix provides short narratives of the coup attempts listed in table 3.1 not already explored in depth in other chapters of the book.

Afghanistan, 3/7/1990

On March 7, 1990, Afghanistan's defense minister, Shah Nawaz Tanai, launched a coup to depose President Mohammed Najibullah. The coup was supported by sections of the army and air force, as well as by Gulbuddin Hekmatyar, a mujahideen leader.[1] It began with an aerial attack on Najibullah's presidential palace. On the ground, skirmishes between coup forces and those loyal to the president occurred near the airport, the Defense Ministry, and the government radio station. Resistance from within the military was minimal. According to Steve Coll, "A large portion of the air force either defected to Tanai or decided to wait out the coup attempt before taking sides."[2] Instead, coup forces marching on the palace were intercepted by the military police (sarandoy) and secret police (KhaD). The police, which were under the command of General Mohammed Aslam Watanjar at the Ministry of Interior, had been built up as counterweights to the military during the 1980s, along with a presidential guard force and Communist Party militia.[3] They successfully blocked the army from seizing the palace, and by March 8, coup forces had been pushed out of the capital. Najibullah appointed General Watanjar as the new defense minister, and he gave a radio address ordering the army to capture General Tanai "dead or alive." Tanai fled to Pakistan, although sporadic fighting continued for several days.[4]

Chad, 4/13/2006

In late March, 2006, the rebel alliance United Front for Democratic Change (FUC), which united eight different rebel groups in conflict with Idriss Déby's regime, began an offensive in eastern Chad. On April 11 they announced their intention to capture the capital, N'Djamena, and remove Déby, who had ruled for sixteen years at that point, from power.[5] The attack on the capital began on April 13. Members of Déby's Zaghawa tribe from within the armed forces had begun defecting to join (or form their own) rebel groups in the months leading up to the coup. When FUC rebels entered the capital, several hundred more soldiers and police abandoned the regime to join them.[6] Many had clashed with Déby over his refusal to openly back rebel groups Darfur, where the Sudanese government and proxy militia were targeting Zaghawa; they also opposed Déby's choice of his son Brahim as successor. While the coup was under way, there was some confusion among coup plotters about how to locate their targets, but this was due to the inclusion of some Sudanese troops, who needed directions, in the attempt, rather than to coordination problems between different Chadian security forces caused by counterbalancing.[7] Coup forces advanced through the capital, confronting loyal troops from the Chadian army in front of the National Assembly in a skirmish that lasted several hours. At the time, Déby had several potential counterweights at his disposal, including the Zaghawa-dominated DGSSIE unit (Direction Générale de Sécurité des Services et des Institutions de l'État), which had replaced his Republican Guard the previous year, and ANS (Agence Nationale de Sécurité), both of which reported directly to him, as well as the National Police, which were under the Ministry of Public Security.[8] However, since the coup attempt was organized by a rebel group rather than by the military, Déby was able to call on the regular army to defend him.[9] They were aided by the French government, which "provided intelligence and airlift capabilities to help Déby fend off the attack."[10] The rebels, who were armed with surface-to-air missiles and machine guns, shelled buildings and battled army troops for several hours, but were eventually overpowered. Some 350 were killed. Military and internal security forces helped secure the city in the hours that followed.[11]

Haiti, 4/2/1989

On April 2, 1989, colonels in two elite battalions of the Haitian army, the Leopards and Dessalines battalions, stationed in Port-au-Prince, revolted. Former president Jean-Claude Duvalier (1957–1986) had created both battalions, along with the Presidential Guard, to serve as counterweights to the regular army. All three circumvented the army chain of command to report directly to Duvalier.[12] After Duvalier's resignation in 1986, the country cycled through four governments in as many years. President Prosper Avril, former chief of the Presidential Guard, came to power in a 1988 coup. Under his tenure, the Leopards and Dessalines battalions grew increasingly restless. As Julia Preston notes, "The Dessalines barracks, which stands in the shadow of the elegant National Palace, had long been a nest for officers sympathetic to the Duvalierists' tenacious campaign to stage a comeback."[13] That spring, Avril's government had been "slowly advancing toward democratic elections in which, it seemed, allies of the deposed Duvalier family dictatorship would be barred as candidates."[14] In late March, the army dismissed four high-ranking officers, including the head of the Leopards battalion, on charges of drug trafficking. As the coup got under way, members of the Leopards battalion, supported by the Dessalines, arrested President Avril at his home and subsequently took over government television and radio stations, demanding the restoration of the 1987 constitution and the release of the Leopards' commander. In a public press conference, the coup plotters emphasized their desire to avoid violence. They claimed they were acting in conjunction with members of other units from within the army and appealed to the Presidential Guard to join them. The commander of the Presidential Guard, Colonel Philippe Biamby, defected to the side of the coup plotters, but other members of the Presidential Guard did not, and moved quickly to free President Avril.[15] On April 5, soldiers from the Dessalines battalion clashed with the Presidential Guard troops that had defended Avril's regime. The forces exchanged "intense rifle and artillery fire."[16] By April 9, after some thirty-five people were killed, the Presidential Guard had defeated the Dessalines battalion, and remaining rebel forces indicated that they were willing to negotiate a surrender. Both the Leopards and Dessalines battalions were disbanded as a result of the coup.[17]

Iraq, 6/14/1995

On June 14, 1995, Turki Ismail al-Dulaimi, commander of the Iraqi Republican Guard's July 14 Tank Battalion, led a failed coup to depose President Saddam Hussein that was put down by the Special Republican Guard. The Republican Guard had long been used by Ba'ath Party leaders for regime maintenance. However, after Iraq's poor performance in the Iran-Iraq War, Saddam followed the advice of military commanders and began to recruit and staff the force on the basis of merit rather than loyalty. Growing tensions within the regime led to a series of coup attempts from Republican Guard officers and others within the military, of which the June 1994 coup was one.[18] The coup attempt occurred in the midst of ongoing riots in the city of Ramadi, which began in mid-May when members of the al-Dulaimi tribe protested in response to the return of the mutilated body of former Air Force general Mohammed Mazlum al-Dulaimi to his family. Mazlum al-Dulaimi was arrested in late 1994 along with several other high-ranking military officers for allegedly attempting to organize a coup. Members of the al-Dulaimi tribe, one of the largest Sunni tribes in Iraq and one that had long been considered loyal to Saddam's regime, said that Saddam had originally promised to pardon Mazlum but went back on his word.[19] Internal security forces were tasked with suppressing the riots, which continued into mid-June.[20] In the midst of ongoing unrest, Ismail al-Dulaimi led his Republican Guard troops in an attack on the radio station in Abu Ghraib, in the western district of Baghdad, in an effort to free prisoners held in the prison complex there.[21] The Special Republican Guard, which had at this time come to replace the Republican Guard as the regime's primary counterweight, responded quickly, exchanging fire with coup plotters and securing the area. The Special Republican Guard's swift response deterred other units that planned to provide air support for the coup attempt from participating.[22] As he watched his battalion decimated, al-Dulaimi committed suicide, and the remaining coup participants were crushed. The Fedayeen Saddam, a civilian paramilitary under the command of Saddam's son, was responsible for rounding up suspected participants; some 150 were executed.[23]

Libya, 10/11/1993

On October 11, 1993, disaffected soldiers in units based just to the south and east of the Libyan capital of Tripoli revolted against the regime of Muammar el-Qaddafi. Although Qaddafi initially gave the military a privileged role in his regime, in 1973 he initiated a "popular revolution" in which citizens purportedly exercised direct control of society, and created two counterweights: the Revolutionary Guards, an elite force tasked with regime protection, and the People's Militia.[24] These forces were a "set of praetorian-guard like organizations," used to protect regime officials and suppress internal dissent.[25] Each force "reported directly to Qaddafi and his top security advisors."[26] By the early 1990s, tensions with the military grew. The 1993 coup was staged by members of the Warfalla tribe, which had long been considered loyal to the regime. Many blamed Qaddafi for Libya's embarrassing defeat in the final phase of the Chadian-Libyan conflict, which ended in 1987. International sanctions "crippled the military because of a lack of spare parts."[27] An additional motive for Warfalla coup participants may have been rivalry with the Magarha tribe for positions within the government and security forces.[28] Newspaper and academic coverage of the coup is not detailed enough to ascertain how, precisely, the coup unfolded, or whether coup plotters faced coordination problems. However, multiple sources report that Qaddafi's Revolutionary Guards, from which the Warfalla were excluded, were responsible for violently suppressing the coup; doing so took three days. After the October 1993 coup attempt failed, Qaddafi increasingly depended on the Revolutionary Guards instead of the military for regime maintenance.[29]

Sudan, 7/2/1976

The July 2, 1976, coup in Sudan was launched as President Gaafar al-Nimeiry was landing at Khartoum's airport. The effort was led by former prime minister Sadiq al-Mahdi and former finance minister Hussein al-Hindi, both of whom had been recently expelled from the government, backed by soldiers in the Sudanese army, who came primarily from Sudan's western provinces of Darfur and Kordofan, "where there existed massive discontent over the continued lack of development."[30] The coup was described as well organized; participants arrived with detailed instructions about what buildings to seize and who to kill. In their initial attack, coup leaders seized government facilities in Khartoum and the primary radio station in Omdurman. However, Nimeiry eluded capture because his flight departed an hour earlier than anticipated. Technicians at the radio station also refused to help the coup plotters broadcast.[31] Having escaped capture, Nimeiry called on the Central Reserve Police (CRP) force as well as loyal army units in nearby Damazin and Shendi to retake the captured targets. The CRP, created in 1974 by combining various riot squads within the police into one body, and which had received military training in Egypt, played a crucial role.[32] The result was "several days of bloody street-fighting in the capital" that ended with coup plotters being assassinated.[33] Minister of Culture and Information Bona Malwal aided in the suppression of the coup by using the Sudan News Agency and Radio Juba to broadcast in support of the regime, which undercut the narrative presented by coup plotters. After the attempt collapsed, several of the coup plotters were executed. In recognition of the CRP's central role in defeating the coup, Nimeiry also moved it from the Ministry of Interior to his direct control.[34]

Thailand, 4/1/1981

On the morning of April 1, 1981, a faction within the Thai military seized control of the capital in a coup attempt that came to be known as the "April Fools' coup." The attempt was organized by a group of mid-ranking officers referred to as the Young Turks, members of the 1960 graduating class of the Chulachomklao Military Academy. Although the Young Turks had previously supported Prem Tinsulanonda's government, they had become disillusioned with corruption in the regime and the military.[35] The April Fools' coup began on the evening of March 31, when Young Turk leaders Manoon Roopkachorn and Prachak Savangchit asked Prem to dismiss parliament and step down from power. According to several sources, Prem asked to meet with the king to give his resignation but ended up fleeing with the royal family to the Nakhon Ratchasima army base north of Bangkok. General Sant Chitpatima, a longtime friend of Prem, whose career advancement was stalled by Prem's successful effort to get parliament to approve an extension of his own term in office, agreed to serve as the head of the new coup-appointed government. Military forces under Sant's command seized control of the capital without facing resistance from troops or police stationed there. Sant addressed the country over Radio Thailand, citing the "deteriorating situation" in Thailand as the cause of the coup and criticizing Prem for getting parliament to approve an extension of his term five years past the mandatory retirement age of sixty. The next morning, however, with the king's backing, Prem began broadcasting from Nakhon Ratchasima, announcing that he had survived the coup attempt and ordering coup plotters to return to the barracks.[36]

Opinions within the military were split. As Suchit Bunbongkarn describes, "A number of senior officers seemed reluctant and some had joined the coup before defecting to the government side."[37] Scholarly and journalistic accounts do not suggest that Prem had independent security forces on which he could draw to repress the coup. Although some scholars identify Thailand as heavily coup-proofed during this period,[38] Prem's primary strategy was to foment divisions primarily *within* the Thai military, which was organized into five autonomous military regions. There was a National Police Force, which was independent of the military, and during the first night of the coup, its leader defected to the regime; crucially, however, the National Police were not militarized—they lacked the military-style command and control centers, heavy weaponry, or specialized riot squads that would have enabled them to resist the coup militarily. As a result, while the chief of police's defection was important in signaling high-profile opposition to the coup, police officers were of little use in suppressing the coup.

Instead, it was troops from the Second Army region that Prem called on to retake Bangkok; they did so largely unopposed, seizing the airport, radio and television stations, and government headquarters without opposition. According to Larry Niksch, "As loyalist troops seized positions in the city, rebel troops surrendered en masse, leaders fled or gave themselves up, and General Sant departed for Burma."[39] The only holdouts were three hundred soldiers at army headquarters who engaged in a two-hour standoff with loyal forces, but eventually gave up as well. Prem was able to return to Bangkok on April 4; he eventually offered amnesty for the coup plotters.[40]

Notes

INTRODUCTION

1. D. Scott Bennett and Allan C. Stam, "Predicting the Length of the 2003 U.S.-Iraq War," *Foreign Policy Analysis* 2 (2006): 101–116.

2. Caitlin Talmadge, *The Dictator's Army: Battlefield Effectiveness in Authoritarian Regimes* (Ithaca, NY: Cornell University Press, 2015); Kevin M. Woods, with Michael R. Pease, Mark E. Stout, Williamson Murray, and James G. Lacey, *Iraqi Perspectives Project: A View of Operation Iraqi Freedom from Saddam's Senior Leadership* (Norfolk, VA: United States Joint Forces Command, 2008).

3. Erica De Bruin, "Coup-Proofing for Dummies: The Benefits of Following the Maliki Playbook," *Foreign Affairs* Snapshot, July 27, 2014; Robert Tollast, "Maliki's Private Army," *The National Interest*, December 31, 2012; Marisa Sullivan, "Maliki's Authoritarian Regime," *Middle East Security Report* 10 (Washington, DC: Institute for the Study of War, 2013). On the costs of rebuilding the Iraqi army, see Special Inspector for Iraq Reconstruction, *Learning from Iraq: A Final Report from the Special Inspector General for Iraq Reconstruction*, March 2013, https://www.globalsecurity.org/military/library/report/2013/sigir-learning-from-iraq.pdf.

4. See, for example, Omar Al-Nidawi, "How Maliki Lost Iraq: The Slow Motion Collapse of a Sectarian Truce," *Foreign Affairs* Snapshot, June 18, 2014; Ali Khedery, "Why We Stuck with Maliki—and Lost Iraq," *Washington Post*, July 3, 2014; Zaid Al-Ali, "How Maliki Lost Iraq," *Foreign Policy*, June 19, 2014.

5. Philip Roessler, "The Enemy Within: Personal Rule, Coups, and Civil War in Africa," *World Politics* 63, no. 2 (2011): 308; Philip Roessler, *Ethnic Politics and State Power in Africa: The Logic of the Coup-Civil War Trap* (Cambridge: Cambridge University Press, 2016). On the post-coup fate of rulers, see the online appendix for Erica De Bruin, "Will There Be Blood? The Determinants of Violence during Coups d'État," *Journal of Peace Research* 56, no. 6 (2019): 797–811.

6. On these and other strategies of coup prevention, see David Goldsworthy, "Civilian Control of the Military in Black Africa," *African Affairs* 80, no. 318 (1981): 49–74; Donald Horowitz, *Ethnic Groups in Conflict* (Berkeley: University of California Press, 1985), 532–559; Samuel Decalo, *The Stable Minority: Civilian Rule in Africa, 1960–1990* (Gainesville: Florida Academic Press, 1998), 19–30; Risa Brooks, *Political-Military Relations and the Stability of Arab Regimes*, Adelphi Paper No. 324 (London: International Institute for Strategic Studies, 1998); James T. Quinlivan, "Coup-Proofing: Its Practice and Consequence in the Middle East," *International Security* 24, no. 2 (1999): 131–165.

7. Aaron Belkin, *United We Stand? Divide-and-Conquer Politics and the Logic of International Hostility* (Albany: State University of New York Press, 2005); Erica De Bruin, "Preventing Coups d'État: How Counterbalancing Works," *Journal of Conflict Resolution* 62, no. 7 (2018): 1433–1458.

8. Peter D. Feaver, "Civil-Military Relations," *Annual Review of Political Science* 2 (1999): 225. Throughout, I use the terms "military" and "armed forces" to refer to the army, navy, and air force that comprise a traditional military. In addition to the military, a state's coercive institutions may include presidential guards, militarized police, secret police or intelligence

agencies with law enforcement powers, state-run militia, and border guards; I use the terms "coercive institutions" and "security forces" interchangeably to refer to them.

9. Edward Luttwak, *Coup d'État: A Practical Handbook* (Cambridge, MA: Harvard University Press, 1979); Naunihal Singh, *Seizing Power: The Strategic Logic of Military Coups* (Baltimore: Johns Hopkins University Press, 2014).

10. This figure comes from the Global Instances of Coups Data Set, v.2018.07.18, available at http://www.jonathanpowell.com/coup-detat-dataset.html (accessed October 3, 2018). See Jonathan M. Powell and Clayton L. Thyne, "Global Instances of Coups from 1950 to 2010: A New Dataset," *Journal of Peace Research* 48, no. 2 (2011): 249–259.

11. Barbara Geddes, Joseph Wright, and Erica Frantz, *How Dictatorships Work: Power, Personalization, and Collapse* (Cambridge: Cambridge University Press, 2018); Curtis Bell, "Coup d'État and Democracy," *Comparative Political Studies* 49, no. 9 (2016): 1167–1200; Curtis Bell and Jonathan Powell, "Turkey's Coup Attempt Was Unusual, but Not for the Reasons You Might Expect," *Washington Post*, Monkey Cage, July 22, 2016, https://www.washingtonpost.com/news/monkey-cage/wp/2016/07/22/turkeys-coup-was-unusual-but-not-for-the-reasons-you-might-expect/?utm_term=.4d67ca0520e0.

12. Jonathan Powell, "Determinants of the Attempting and Outcome of Coups d'État," *Journal of Conflict Resolution* 56, no. 6 (2012): 1017–1040; De Bruin, "Preventing Coups d'État"; Bell, "Coup d'État and Democracy."

13. Nikolay Marinov and Hein Goemans, "Coups and Democracy," *British Journal of Political Science* 44, no. 4 (2014): 799–825; Amnesty International, *Amnesty International Report 2016/2017: The State of the World's Human Rights* (London: Amnesty International, 2017).

14. Clayton L. Thyne and Jonathan M. Powell, "Coup d'État or Coup d'Autocracy? How Coups Impact Democratization, 1950–2008," *Foreign Policy Analysis* 12, no. 2 (2016): 192–213.

15. George Derpanopoulos, Erica Frantz, Barbara Geddes, and Joseph Wright, "Are Coups Good for Democracy?," *Research and Politics* 3, no. 1 (2016): 1–7; Andrea Kendall-Taylor and Erica Frantz, "How Autocracies Fall," *Washington Quarterly* 37, no. 1 (2014): 35–47; Oisin Tansey, "The Limits of the 'Democratic Coup' Thesis: International Politics and Post-Coup Authoritarianism," *Journal of Global Security Studies* 1, no. 3 (2016): 220–234; Kevin Koehler and Holger Albrecht, "Revolutions and the Military: Endgame Coups, Instability, and Prospects for Democracy," *Armed Forces and Society*, doi 10.1177/0095327X198881747.

16. Jonathan Powell, Mwita Chacha, and Gary E. Smith, "Failed Coups, Democratization, and Authoritarian Entrenchment: Opening Up or Digging In?," *African Affairs* 118, no. 471 (2019): 239; Travis B. Curtice and Daniel Arnon, "Deterring Threats and Settling Scores: How Coups Influence Respect for Physical Integrity Rights," *Conflict Management and Peace Science*, doi 10.1177/0738894219843240

17. Ben Hubbard, Tim Arango, and Ceylan Yeginsu, "Failed Turkish Coup Accelerated a Purge Years in the Making," *New York Times*, July 22, 2016; Elif Shafak, "Turkey's Future Is Moving Backward," *New York Times*, September 19, 2017.

18. De Bruin, "Will There Be Blood?"; Tim Arango and Ceylan Yeginsu, "Turkey Rounds Up Thousands of Military Personnel," *New York Times*, July 16, 2016.

19. Theodore McLauchlin, "Explaining the Origins of Military Rebellions" (paper presented at the International Studies Association Annual Meeting, Baltimore, 2017). McLauchlin includes as military rebellions armed conflicts in the Uppsala Conflict Data Program/Peace Research Institute Oslo (UCDP/PRIO) Armed Conflict Actor Database, 1956–2011, in which the rebel forces originate within the state security forces. See also James D. Fearon, "Why Do Some Civil Wars Last So Much Longer Than Others?," *Journal of Peace Research* 41, no. 3 (2004): 275–301.

20. On Chile, see Gregory Bart Weeks, *The Military and Politics in Postauthoritarian Chile* (Tuscaloosa: University of Alabama Press, 2003); Patricio Silva, "Searching for Civilian

Supremacy: The Concertacion Governments and the Military in Chile," *Bulletin of Latin American Research* 21, no. 3 (2002): 375–395; Mary Helen Spooner, *Soldiers in a Narrow Land: The Pinochet Regime in Chile* (Berkeley: University of California Press, 1999). On Libya, see Jonathan Bearman, *Qadhafi's Libya* (Atlantic Highlands, NJ: Zed Books, 1986); Paola De Maio, "From Soldiers to Policemen: Qadhafi's Army in the New Century," *Journal of Middle Eastern Geopolitics* 2, no. 3 (2006): 17–26; Dirk Vandewalle, *A History of Modern Libya* (Cambridge: Cambridge University Press, 2006).

21. Ariel I. Ahram, *Proxy Warriors: The Rise and Fall of State-Sponsored Militias* (Stanford, CA: Stanford University Press, 2011); Sheena Greitens, *Dictators and Their Secret Police: Coercive Institutions and State Violence* (New York: Oxford University Press, 2018); Caitlin Talmadge, "The Puzzle of Personalist Performance: Iraqi Battlefield Effectiveness in the Iran-Iraq War," *Security Studies* 22, no. 2 (2013): 180–221; Talmadge, *The Dictator's Army*. Talmadge, for instance, shows that over the course of the Iran-Iraq War, as the threat from Iran became more pressing, Saddam Hussein shifted from military organizational practices best for coup prevention to those that optimized battlefield effectiveness—and then reverted to back to coup-proofing at the end of the war. Ahram also emphasizes the path-dependent nature of security sector organization.

22. Robert I. Rotberg, *Haiti: The Politics of Squalor* (Boston: Houghton Mifflin, 1971), 203; Robert Fatton, *Haiti's Predatory Republic: The Unending Transition to Democracy* (Boulder, CO: Lynne Rienner, 2002); Michel-Rolph Trouillot, *Haiti, State against Nation: The Origins and Legacy of Duvalierism* (New York: Monthly Review Press, 1990); Elizabeth Abbott, *Haiti: The Duvaliers and Their Legacy* (New York: McGraw-Hill, 1988).

23. Abbott A. Brayton, "Stability and Modernization: The Ivory Coast Model," *World Affairs* 141, no. 3 (1979): 243.

24. Jens Gieseke, *The History of the Stasi: East Germany's Secret Police, 1945–1990*, trans. David Burnett (New York: Berghahn Books, 2014).

25. See, for instance: Stephen Biddle and Robert Zirkle, "Technology, Civil-Military Relations, and Warfare in the Developing World," *Journal of Strategic Studies* 19, no. 2 (1996): 171–212; Risa Brooks, *Political-Military Relations*; Herbert M. Howe, *Ambiguous Order: Military Forces in African States* (Boulder, CO: Lynne Rienner, 2001), 45; Risa Brooks, "An Autocracy at War: Explaining Egypt's Military Effectiveness, 1967 and 1973," *Security Studies* 15, no. 3 (2006): 396–430; Ulrich Pilster and Tobias Böhmelt, "Coup-Proofing and Military Effectiveness in Interstate Wars, 1967–99," *Conflict Management and Peace Science* 28, no. 4 (2011): 331–350; Talmadge, *The Dictator's Army*; R. Blake McMahon and Branislav L. Slantchev, "The Guardianship Dilemma: Regime Security through and from the Armed Forces," *American Political Science Review* 109, no. 2 (2015): 297–313.

26. Zoltan Barany, "The Role of the Military," *Journal of Democracy* 22, no. 4 (2011): 24–35; Michael Makara, "Coup-Proofing, Military Defection, and the Arab Spring," *Democracy and Security* 9, no. 4 (2013): 334–359; Hicham Bou Nassif, "Generals and Autocrats: How Coup-Proofing Behavior Predetermined the Military Elite's Behavior in the Arab Spring," *Political Science Quarterly* 130, no. 2 (2015): 245–275; Julien Morency-Laflamme, "Regime Crises in Africa: A Study of the Armed Forces' Behavior" (Ph.D. diss., Department of Political Science, University of Montreal, 2016); Julien Morency-Laflamme, "A Question of Trust: Military Defection during Regime Crises in Benin and Togo," *Democratization* 25, no. 3 (2018): 464–480; Philipp M. Lutscher, "The More Fragmented the Better? The Impact of Armed Forces Structure on Defection during Nonviolent Popular Uprisings," *International Interactions* 42, no. 2 (2016): 350–375; Terrence Lee, "Military Cohesion and Regime Maintenance: Explaining the Military in 1989 China and 1998 Indonesia," *Armed Forces and Society* 32, no. 1 (2005): 80–104.

27. Greitens, *Dictators and Their Secret Police*, 5.

28. For a survey of the political science literature, see Risa A. Brooks, "Integrating the Civil-Military Relations Subfield," *Annual Review of Political Science* 22 (2019): 379–398.

29. This wave of research began with Brooks's 1998 Adelphi Paper, *Political-Military Relations*, and Quinlivan's 1999 article "Coup-Proofing: Its Practice and Consequences in the Middle East." Other recent, relevant work includes Belkin, *United We Stand?*; Aaron Belkin and Evan Schofer, "Toward a Structural Understanding of Coup Risk," *Journal of Conflict Resolution* 47, no. 5 (2003): 594–620; Barbara Geddes, "How Autocrats Defend Themselves against Armed Rivals" (paper presented at the American Political Science Association Annual Meeting, Toronto, Canada, 2009); Tobias Böhmelt and Ulrich Pilster, "The Impact of Institutional Coup-Proofing on Coup Attempts and Coup Outcomes," *International Interactions* 41, no. 1 (2015): 158–182; Pilster and Böhmelt, "Coup-Proofing and Military Effectiveness"; De Bruin, "Preventing Coups d'État." Earlier theorists of civil-military relations that discuss counterbalancing include Eric A. Nordlinger, *Soldiers in Politics: Military Coups and Governments* (Englewood Cliffs, NJ: Prentice-Hall, 1977); Horowitz, *Ethnic Groups in Conflict*; Jendayi Elizabeth J. Frazer, "Sustaining Civilian Control: Armed Counterweights in Regime Stability in Africa" (PhD diss., Stanford University, 1994); and Bruce W. Farcau, *The Coup: Tactics in the Seizure of Power* (Westport, CT: Praeger, 1994). Although he does not refer to counterbalancing by name, Luttwak also discusses the police, intelligence, and other security forces that must be neutralized, co-opted, or overcome for a successful coup in *Coup d'État*.

30. Horowitz, for instance, includes counterbalancing in his catalogue of strategies to counter a coup but does not develop a causal argument about how it is supposed to work. Quinlivan similarly describes the use of what he calls "parallel militaries" in the Middle East but does not spell out the mechanisms by which they might prevent coups.

31. Frazer, *Sustaining Civilian Control*; Robert H. Bruce, "Keeping the Military at Bay with Countervailing Force: The Utility of Indonesian Civilian Leaders' Use of Paramilitary Police," Indian Ocean Centre for Peace Studies Occasional Paper No. 20 (Nedlands, Western Australia: Indian Ocean Centre for Peace Studies, 1992); Quinlivan, "Coup-Proofing"; Belkin, *United We Stand?*

32. Nordlinger, *Soldiers in Politics*; Farcau, *The Coup*; Geddes, "How Autocrats Defend Themselves."

33. In "Determinants of the Attempting and Outcome," for instance, Powell finds that counterbalancing reduces both the number of coup attempts rulers see and how likely those attempts are to succeed, but the results are significant in only half the specifications presented. In "The Impact of Institutional Coup-Proofing," Böhmelt and Pilster find evidence of a U-shaped relationship between counterbalancing and coup attempts, but not coup outcomes.

34. Barbara Geddes, "How the Cases You Choose Affect the Answers You Get: Selection Bias in Comparative Politics," *Political Analysis* 2, no. 1 (1990): 131–150; Alexander L. George and Andrew Bennett, *Case Studies and Theory Development in the Social Sciences* (Cambridge, MA: MIT Press, 2005). In "Coup-Proofing," Quinlivan, for example, focuses on Saudi Arabia, Iraq, and Syria precisely because their leaders were able to prevent coups for decades. Frazer's *Sustaining Civilian Control* similarly focuses on Kenya because it was an outlier in Africa, having maintained civilian rule for decades at the time of her writing.

35. E.g., Clare Mundy and Dan Smith, "'Facts' about the Military," *Journal of Peace Research* 17, no. 3 (1980): 261–267; John T. Ostrich Jr., and William C. Green, "Methodological Problems Associated with the IISS Military Balance," *Comparative Strategy* 3, no. 2 (1981): 151–171; Milton Leitenberg, "The Numbers Game or 'Who's on First?,'" *Bulletin of the Atomic Scientists* 38, no. 6 (1982): 27–32; Jeff Colgan, "Venezuela and Military Expenditure Data," *Journal of Peace Research* 48, no. 4 (2011): 547–556; Erica De Bruin, "Mapping Coercive Institutions: The State Security Forces Dataset, 1960–2010" (unpublished

manuscript, October 17, 2019), https://papers.ssrn.com/sol3/papers.cfm?abstract_id =3317127.

36. E.g., International Institute for Strategic Studies [hereafter IISS], *The Military Balance* (London: IISS, 2010), 6–7. The reason for this caution is that prior editions of the review are not updated when new information becomes available. This can result in large fluctuations in reported force size from year to year.

37. Powell and Thyne, "Global Instances of Coups."

38. In practice, military officers lead the overwhelming majority of coup attempts. Some 95 percent of coup attempts since 1950 were staged from within the armed forces. See Curtis Bell and Jun Koga Sudduth, "The Causes and Outcomes of Coups during Civil War," *Journal of Conflict Resolution* 61, no. 7: 1432–1455.

39. Singh, *Seizing Power*; Luttwak, *Coup d'État*.

40. Harvey G. Kebschull, "Operation 'Just Missed': Lessons From Failed Coup Attempts," *Armed Forces and Society* 20, no. 4 (1994): 565–579.

41. Barbara Geddes, "What Do We Know about Democratization after Twenty Years?," *Annual Review of Political Science* 2, no. 1 (1999): 126; Samuel E. Finer, *The Man on Horseback: The Role of the Military in Politics* (New York: Praeger, 2002); Luttwak, *Coup d'État*; Nordlinger, *Soldiers in Politics*; Alfred C. Stepan, *The Military in Politics: Changing Patterns in Brazil* (Princeton, NJ: Princeton University Press, 1971).

42. Singh, *Seizing Power*, 6.

43. De Bruin, "Will There Be Blood?," 802.

44. Horowitz, *Ethnic Groups in Conflict*, 547; Kristen A. Harkness, "The Ethnic Army and the State: Explaining Coup Traps and the Difficulties of Democratization in Africa," *Journal of Conflict Resolution* 60, no. 4 (2016): 587–616; Kristen A. Harkness, *When Soldiers Rebel: Ethnic Armies and Political Instability in Africa* (Cambridge: Cambridge University Press, 2018).

45. Peter D. Feaver, *Armed Servants: Agency, Oversight, and Civil-Military Relations* (Cambridge, MA: Harvard University Press, 2003), 83.

46. Martin C. Needler, "Military Motivations in the Seizure of Power," *Latin American Research Review* 10, no. 3 (1975): 63–79; Nordlinger, *Soldiers in Politics*.

47. Robert H. Bruce, "Paramilitary Police as Political Resources in Civil-Military Crisis: The Mobile Brigade between Sukarno and the Army in Indonesia," *Asian Profile* 14, no. 5 (1986): 474.

48. Christopher S. Clapham, *Transformation and Continuity in Revolutionary Ethiopia*, African Studies Series 61 (Cambridge: Cambridge University Press, 1988). The data presented in chapter 2 suggests that coercive institutions outside the regular military played a lead role in only 4 percent of the coup attempts staged by members of the state's military and security forces.

49. Simon J. Baynham, "Quis Custodiet Ipsos Custodes? The Case of Nkrumah's National Security Service," *Journal of Modern African Studies* 23, no. 1 (1985): 87–103; H. M. Howe, *Ambiguous Order: Military Forces in African States* (Boulder, CO: Lynne Rienner, 2004).

50. Albert Kwesi Ocran, *A Myth Is Broken: An Account of the Ghana Coup d'État of 24 February 1966* (New York: Humanities Press, 1968), 37.

51. Accra Ghana Broadcasting Corporation, "Radio Ghana Reports National Guard Dissolved," Federal Broadcast Information Service Daily Report, FBIS-AFR-93-208, October 29, 1993.

52. Saeed Shafqat, *Civil-Military Relations in Pakistan: From Zulfikar Ali Bhutto to Benazir Bhutto* (Boulder, CO: Westview Press, 1997), 718; Steven I. Wilkinson, *Army and Nation: The Military and Indian Democracy since Independence* (Cambridge, MA: Harvard University Press, 2015), 215–216. In *The Coup*, Farcau cites several additional examples

from Latin America of the creation of counterweights leading to coups, including Guatemala (1954), Argentina (1955), Bolivia (1971), and Chile (1973).

1. THE LOGIC OF COUNTERBALANCING

1. Jonathan M. Powell and Clayton L. Thyne, "Global Instances of Coups from 1950 to 2010: A New Dataset," *Journal of Peace Research* 48, no. 2 (2011): 249–259; Erica De Bruin, "Will There Be Blood? The Determinants of Violence during Coups d'État," *Journal of Peace Research* 56, no. 6 (2019): 797–811. The data presented in chapter 2 suggests that 82 percent of coup attempts are led by members of the state's military and security forces; of these, 90 percent are led by the army in particular.

2. Naunihal Singh, *Seizing Power: The Strategic Logic of Military Coups* (Baltimore: Johns Hopkins University Press, 2014); Barbara Geddes, "What Do We Know about Democratization after Twenty Years?," *Annual Review of Political Science* 2, no. 1 (1999): 115–144; Barbara Geddes, "Authoritarian Breakdown" (unpublished manuscript, January 2004), PDF, http://citeseerx.ist.psu.edu/viewdoc/download?doi=10.1.1.659.7165&rep=rep1&type=pdf; Andrew T. Little, "Coordination, Learning, and Coups," *Journal of Conflict Resolution* 61, no. 1 (2017): 204–234; Brett A. Casper and Scott A. Tyson, "Popular Protest and Elite Coordination in a Coup d'État," *Journal of Politics* 76, no. 2 (2014): 548–564; Jaclyn Johnson and Clayton L. Thyne, "Squeaky Wheels and Troop Loyalty: How Domestic Protests Influence Coups d'État, 1951–2005," *Journal of Conflict Resolution* 62, no. 3 (2018): 597–625.

3. Singh, *Seizing Power*, 8.

4. Donald J. Goodspeed, *The Conspirators: A Study of the Coup d'État* (London: Macmillan, 1962), 220–238. Other central works include Curzio Malaparte, *Coup d'État: The Technique of Revolution*, trans. Sylvia Saunders (New York: E. P. Dutton, 1932); Edward Luttwak, *Coup d'État: A Practical Handbook* (Cambridge, MA: Harvard University Press, 1979); Gregor Ferguson, *Coup d'État: A Practical Manual* (Poole, Dorset: Arms and Armour Press, 1987).

5. Singh, *Seizing Power*, 82–85; Holger Albrecht and Ferdinand Eibl, "How to Keep Officers in the Barracks: Causes, Agents, and Types of Military Coups," *International Studies Quarterly* 62, no. 2 (2018): 315–328.

6. David D. Kirkpatrick, "Mubarak Out: Egypt Erupts in Jubilation," *New York Times*, February 12, 2011.

7. Luttwak, *Coup d'État*, 153; Eric A. Nordlinger, *Soldiers in Politics: Military Coups and Governments* (Englewood Cliffs, NJ: Prentice-Hall, 1977).

8. Luttwak, 21. In practice, of course, the effective chain of command "may skip one or more levels, particularly in regard to 'political' sorts of orders." See Bruce W. Farcau, *The Coup: Tactics in the Seizure of Power* (Westport, CT: Praeger, 1994), 46.

9. Jeffrey Moyo and Norimitsu Onishi, "Robert Mugabe under House Arrest as Rule over Zimbabwe Teeters," *New York Times*, November 15, 2017.

10. Aaron Belkin, *United We Stand? Divide-and-Conquer Politics and the Logic of International Hostility* (Albany: State University of New York Press, 2005), 20.

11. Zaya Yeebo, *Ghana: The Struggle for Popular Power* (London: New Beacon Books, 1991), 47.

12. Luttwak, *Coup d'État*, 58.

13. Geddes, "What Do We Know about Democratization," 126.

14. Morris Janowitz, *The Professional Soldier* (Glencoe, IL: Free Press, 1960); Morris Janowitz, *Military Institutions and Coercion in the Developing Nations* (Chicago: University of Chicago Press, 1977); Samuel E. Finer, *The Man on Horseback: The Role of the Military in Politics* (New York: Praeger, 2002); Samuel Decalo, *Coups and Army Rule in Africa: Studies in Military Style* (New Haven, CT: Yale University Press, 1976); Nordlinger, *Soldiers in Politics*.

15. Terrence Lee, "Military Cohesion and Regime Maintenance: Explaining the Military in 1989 China and 1998 Indonesia," *Armed Forces and Society* 32, no. 1 (2005): 86; Erving Goffman, *Asylums: Essays on the Social Situation of Mental Patients and Other Inmates* (Garden City, NY: Anchor, 1961), 1–124; John P. Lovell and Judith Hicks Stiehm, "Military Service and Political Socialization," in *Political Learning in Adulthood*, ed. Roberta S. Sigel (Chicago: University of Chicago Press, 1989), 172–202.

16. Martin C. Needler, "Military Motivations in the Seizure of Power," *Latin American Research Review* 10, no. 3 (1975): 63–79.

17. Geddes, "What Do We Know about Democratization," 126.

18. Harvey G. Kebschull, "Operation 'Just Missed': Lessons from Failed Coup Attempts," *Armed Forces and Society* 20, no. 4 (1994): 565–579.

19. Luttwak, *Coup d'État*, 74.

20. E.g., James D. Fearon, "Rationalist Explanations for War," *International Organization* 49, no. 3 (1995): 379–414; Robert Powell, "Bargaining Theory and International Conflict," *Annual Review of Political Science* 5, no. 1 (2002): 1–30; Darren Filson and Suzanne Werner, "A Bargaining Model of War and Peace: Anticipating the Onset, Duration, and Outcome of War," *American Journal of Political Science* 46, no. 4 (2002): 819–837; Dan Reiter, "Exploring the Bargaining Model of War," *Perspectives on Politics* 1, no. 1 (2003): 27–43; Alastair Smith and Allan C. Stam, "Bargaining and the Nature of War," *Journal of Conflict Resolution* 48, no. 6 (2004): 783–813; Andrew H. Kydd, "Rationalist Approaches to Conflict Prevention and Resolution," *Annual Review of Political Science* 13 (2010): 101–121.

21. Singh, *Seizing Power*, 30–31.

22. Steven R. David, "Coup and Anti-Coup," *Washington Quarterly* 5, no. 4 (1982): 195.

23. Suchit Bunbongkarn, *The Military in Thai Politics, 1981–86* (Singapore: Institute of Southeast Asian Studies, 1987), 19.

24. Singh, *Seizing Power*.

25. Jaimie Bleck and Kristin Michelitch, "Capturing the Airwaves, Capturing the Nation? A Field Experiment on State-Run Media Effects in the Wake of a Coup," *Journal of Politics* 79, no. 3 (2017): 873–889. Newspapers may also be targeted. During the 2015 coup in Burundi, for instance, several papers stopped publishing under pressure from coup plotters; the manager of one newspaper reported that the coup plotters "don't want people to know what is happening." Isma'il Kushkush, "Burundi President, Surviving Coup, Warns of a Threat from Shabab," *New York Times*, May 27, 2015.

26. Farcau, *The Coup*, 180.

27. Hein Goemans, Kristian Skrede Gleditsch, and Giacomo Chiozza, "Introducing Archigos: A Dataset of Political Leaders," *Journal of Peace Research* 46, no. 2 (2009): 269–283.

28. Brian D. Taylor, *Politics and the Russian Army: Civil-Military Relations, 1689–2000* (Cambridge: Cambridge University Press, 2003), 246.

29. Singh, *Seizing Power*, 6.

30. Kebschull, "Operation 'Just Missed.'"

31. Singh, *Seizing Power*; Luttwak, *Coup d'État*; Stepan, *The Military in Politics*; Janowitz, *The Professional Soldier*; Finer, *The Man on Horseback*; Nordlinger, *Soldiers in Politics*.

32. John Roosa, *Pretext for Mass Murder: The September 30th Movement and Suharto's Coup d'État in Indonesia* (Madison: University of Wisconsin Press, 2006), 210.

33. John Neagle, "Haiti: President Avril Asked to Step Down by Soldiers from Dessalines Barracks," April 6, 1989, https://digitalrepository.unm.edu/notisur/2959.

34. Nordlinger, *Soldiers in Politics*, 106.

35. Singh, *Seizing Power*, 82.

36. Singh, 28–29.

37. Albrecht and Eibl, "How to Keep Officers in the Barracks," 319. Albrecht and Eibl argue that the inability to meet in advance with commanders of counterbalancing forces should deter elite officers from staging coup attempts in the first place.

38. Singh, *Seizing Power*, 82–84.

39. Joseph Takougang, *Democracy and Democratization in Cameroon: Living with the Dual Heritage* (Aldershot, UK: Ashgate, 1998), 78–79.

40. Michael S. Hooper, *Duvalierism since Duvalier: A Report on the Human Rights Situation in Haiti since February 7, 1986* (New York: National Coalition for Haitian Refugees, 1986), 16.

41. Barbara Geddes, Joseph Wright, and Erica Frantz, *How Dictatorships Work: Power, Personalization, and Collapse* (Cambridge: Cambridge University Press, 2018), 160.

42. Samuel Decalo, *The Stable Minority: Civilian Rule in Africa, 1960–1990* (Gainesville: Florida Academic Press, 1998), 22.

43. Jonathan Powell, "Determinants of the Attempting and Outcome of Coups d'État," *Journal of Conflict Resolution* 56, no. 6 (2012): 1017–1040; Tobias Böhmelt and Ulrich Pilster, "The Impact of Institutional Coup-Proofing on Coup Attempts and Coup Outcomes," *International Interactions* 41, no. 1 (2015): 158–182.

44. E.g., Stephen Biddle and Robert Zirkle, "Technology, Civil-Military Relations, and Warfare in the Developing World," *Journal of Strategic Studies* 19, no. 2 (1996): 171–212; Risa Brooks, *Political-Military Relations and the Stability of Arab Regimes*, Adelphi Paper No. 324 (London: International Institute for Strategic Studies, 1998); Risa Brooks, "An Autocracy at War: Explaining Egypt's Military Effectiveness, 1967 and 1973," *Security Studies* 15, no. 3 (2006): 396–430; Ulrich Pilster and Tobias Böhmelt, "Coup-Proofing and Military Effectiveness in Interstate Wars, 1967–99," *Conflict Management and Peace Science* 28, no. 4 (2011): 331–350; Caitlin Talmadge, *The Dictator's Army: Battlefield Effectiveness in Authoritarian Regimes* (Ithaca, NY: Cornell University Press, 2015); R. Blake McMahon and Branislav L. Slantchev, "The Guardianship Dilemma: Regime Security through and from the Armed Forces," *American Political Science Review* 109, no. 2 (2015): 297–313.

45. Brooks, *Political-Military Relations*, 48.

46. Luttwak, *Coup d'État*, 149.

47. J. Powell, "Determinants of the Attempting and Outcome," 1024.

48. Donald Horowitz, *Ethnic Groups in Conflict* (Berkeley: University of California Press, 1985), 547; Kristen A. Harkness, "The Ethnic Army and the State: Explaining Coup Traps and the Difficulties of Democratization in Africa," *Journal of Conflict Resolution* 60, no. 4 (2016): 587–616; Kristen A. Harkness, *When Soldiers Rebel: Ethnic Armies and Political Instability in Africa* (Cambridge: Cambridge University Press, 2018).

49. Geddes, Wright, and Frantz, *How Dictatorships Work*, 164; the authors take the view that resistance is more important than coordination as a mechanism: "We see the coup deterrence value of loyalist paramilitary forces as arising from their staffing by officers and men from groups identified with the dictator who expect to share his fate if he is overthrown."

50. Bhuian Md. Monoar Kabir, *Politics and Development of the Jamaat-e-Islami, Bangladesh* (Delhi: South Asian Publishers, 2006), 44.

51. Peter D. Feaver, *Armed Servants: Agency, Oversight, and Civil-Military Relations* (Cambridge, MA: Harvard University Press, 2003), 83.

52. Needler, "Military Motivations"; Nordlinger, *Soldiers in Politics*.

53. Horowitz, *Ethnic Groups in Conflict*, 547.

54. Farcau, *The Coup*, 67.

55. Decalo, *The Stable Minority*.

56. John F. Burns, "In Power Still, Afghan Can Thank His 4-Star Aide," *New York Times*, May 10, 1990; Mark Fineman, "Afghanistan Army Units Attempt Coup; President Najibullah Declares Rebellion Was Crushed by Loyal Forces," *New York Times*, March 7, 1990.

57. John Henderson, "Pacific Island States," in *International Security and the United States: An Encyclopedia*, vol. 1, ed. Karl DeRouen and Paul Bellamy (Westport, CT: Praeger Security International, 2008), 588.

58. Brett A. Woods, *The Causes of Fiji's 5 December 2006 Coup* (master's thesis, University of Canterbury, 2008), 120.

59. Randall Parish, Mark Peceny, and Justin Delacour, "Venezuela and the Collective Defence of Democracy Regime in the Americas," *Democratization* 14, no. 2 (2007): 207–231; Jon Beasley-Murray, "Media and Multitude: Chronicle of a Coup Unforetold," *Journal of Iberian and Latin American Research* 8, no. 1 (2002): 105–116. The lesson was not lost on Chávez. In the years following the failed coup, he strengthened the presidential guard and created a second security force, a national militia, to deter subsequent coup attempts.

60. Farcau, *The Coup*, 192.

61. Horowitz, *Ethnic Groups in Conflict*, 542–543.

62. Albrecht and Eibl, "How to Keep Officers in the Barracks," 319.

63. Farcau, *The Coup*, 67

64. Because coup plots are particularly difficult to track, I cannot systematically test whether counterbalancing impedes coup plots from escalating to coup attempts. Importantly, however, this argument would attenuate the estimated effect of counterbalancing on coup failure. That I find, in chapter 2, a negative and statistically significant effect despite this expectation should increase our confidence that the relationship between counterbalancing and coup failure is not a spurious one.

65. Singh, *Seizing Power*.

66. Finer, *The Man on Horseback*; Peter D. Feaver, "The Civil-Military Problematique: Huntington, Janowitz, and the Question of Civilian Control," *Armed Forces and Society* 23, no. 2 (1996): 146–178.

67. Samuel Huntington, *The Soldier and the State* (New York: Vintage Books, 1957).

68. Claude Welch, *Civilian Control of the Military: Theory and Cases from Developing Countries* (Albany: State University of New York Press, 1976).

69. John B. Londregan and Keith T. Poole, "Poverty, the Coup Trap, and the Seizure of Executive Power," *World Politics* 42, no. 2 (1990): 151–183.

70. Finer, *The Man on Horseback*; Aaron Belkin and Evan Schofer, "Toward a Structural Understanding of Coup Risk," *Journal of Conflict Resolution* 47, no. 5 (2003): 594–620.

71. E.g., Needler, "Military Motivations"; Nordlinger, *Soldiers in Politics*; William R. Thompson, *The Grievances of Military Coup-Makers* (London: Sage, 1973).

72. Farcau, *The Coup*, 192.

73. Drew Holland Kinney, "Politicians at Arms: Civilian Recruitment of Soldiers for Middle Eastern Coups," *Armed Forces and Society* 45, no. 4 (2018): 681–701.

74. Robert Fatton, *The Roots of Haitian Despotism* (Boulder, CO: Lynne Rienner, 2007), 107.

75. Decalo, *The Stable Minority*, 22.

76. Janowitz, *Military Institutions and Coercion*; Nordlinger, *Soldiers in Politics*; Zoltan Barany, "The Role of the Military," *Journal of Democracy* 22, no. 4 (2011): 24–35.

77. Decalo, *The Stable Minority*, 88.

78. Taylor, *Politics and the Russian Army*, 265.

79. Juan Linz and Alfred Stepan, *Problems of Democratic Transition and Consolidation* (Baltimore: Johns Hopkins University Press, 1996), 209–11; see also Brooks, *Political-Military Relations*.

80. Steven I. Wilkinson, *Army and Nation: The Military and Indian Democracy since Independence* (Cambridge, MA: Harvard University Press, 2015), 145–146.

81. Nordlinger, *Soldiers in Politics*, 67.
82. Farcau, *The Coup*, 182. Other cases include Ghana in 1966, Algeria in 1965, Mali in 1968, Honduras in 1963, and Chile in 1973. See Nordlinger, *Soldiers in Politics*, 75–78.
83. Nordlinger, *Soldiers in Politics*, 75; Needler, "Military Motivations"; Thompson, *Grievances of Military Coup-Makers*.
84. Quoted in Martin C. Needler, "The Latin American Military: Predatory Reactionaries or Modernizing Patriots?," *Journal of Inter-American Studies* 11, no. 2 (1969): 241.
85. Farcau, *The Coup*, 192.
86. Decalo, *The Stable Minority*, 22.
87. Farcau, *The Coup*, 192.
88. Geddes, Wright, and Frantz, *How Dictatorships Work*, 159.
89. Belkin, *United We Stand?*, 76.
90. Steven R. David, "Coup and Anti-Coup," *Washington Quarterly* 5, no. 4 (1982): 200
91. Geddes, Wright, and Frantz, *How Dictatorships Work*, 167.
92. Jendayi Elizabeth J. Frazer, "Sustaining Civilian Control: Armed Counterweights in Regime Stability in Africa" (PhD diss., Stanford University, 1994); Farcau, *The Coup*. Others note that counterbalancing might be easier in particular types of states. Former French colonies, which inherited relatively fragmented security sectors at independence, might find it easier to repurpose existing forces as counterweights, as might states that have a tradition of using tribal levies. See Horowitz, *Ethnic Groups in Conflict*, 548–549.
93. E.g., Egil Fossum, "Some Attributes of the Latin American Military Coup," *Proceedings of the International Peace Research Association, Second Conference*, vol. 2 (Assen: van Gorcum, 1968): 269–293; William R. Thompson, "Organizational Cohesion and Military Coup Outcomes," *Comparative Political Studies* 9, no. 3 (1976): 255–276.
94. Finer, *The Man on Horseback*.
95. Belkin and Evan Schofer, "Toward a Structural Understanding," 603.
96. Stathis N. Kalyvas, *The Logic of Violence in Civil War* (Cambridge: Cambridge University Press, 2006).
97. James D. Fearon, "Why Do Some Civil Wars Last So Much Longer Than Others?," *Journal of Peace Research* 41, no. 3 (2004): 275–301; Theodore McLauchlin, "Explaining the Origins of Military Rebellions" (paper presented at the International Studies Association Annual Meeting, Baltimore, 2017)
98. Goodspeed, *The Conspirators*, 233.
99. Geddes, "Authoritarian Breakdown," 9.
100. James D. Fearon and David D. Laitin, "Ethnicity, Insurgency, and Civil War," *American Political Science Review* 9, no. 1 (2003): 75–90.
101. Paul Collier and Anke Hoeffler, "Greed and Grievance in Civil War," *Oxford Economic Papers* 56, no. 4 (2004): 563–595.
102. Fearon, "Why Do Some Civil Wars Last So Much Longer Than Others?," 275–301.
103. E.g., Nicholas Sambanis, "Do Ethnic and Nonethnic Civil Wars Have the Same Causes? A Theoretical and Empirical Inquiry (Part 1)," *Journal of Conflict Resolution* 45, no. 3 (2001): 259–282; Lars-Erik Cederman, Andreas Wimmer, and Brian Min, "Why Do Ethnic Groups Rebel? New Data and Analysis," *World Politics* 62, no. 1 (2010): 87–119. One exception is Theodore McLauchlin, "Explaining the Origins of Military Rebellions" (paper presented at the Annual Meeting of the International Studies Association, Baltimore, February, 2017).
104. Nicholas Sambanis, "Using Case Studies to Expand Economic Models of Civil War," *Perspectives on Politics* 2, no. 2 (2004): 260.
105. Sheena Greitens, *Dictators and Their Secret Police: Coercive Institutions and State Violence* (New York: Oxford University Press, 2018).

106. Philip Roessler, "The Enemy Within: Personal Rule, Coups, and Civil War in Africa," *World Politics* 63, no. 2 (2011): 300–346.

107. Kalyvas, *The Logic of Violence*, 17.

108. In practice, researchers typically adopt a numerical threshold of deaths to distinguish civil wars from coups. Kalyvas, for example, notes that "civil wars are distinguished from coups when a certain fatality threshold is crossed, entailing significant military operations" (*The Logic of Violence*, 19).

109. Jeremy Weinstein, *Inside Rebellion* (New York: Cambridge University Press, 2007), 7.

110. McLauchlin, "Explaining the Origins," 4–5.

111. Evan S. Lieberman, "Nested Analysis as a Mixed-Method Strategy for Comparative Research," *American Political Science Review* 99, no. 3 (2005): 435–452.

112. Harry Eckstein, "Case Studies and Theory in Political Science," in *Handbook of Political Science*, vol. 7, ed. Fred Greenstein and Nelson Polsby (New York: Addison-Wesley), 79–138.

113. Arendt Lijphart, "Comparative Politics and the Comparative Method," *American Political Science Review* 65, no. 3 (1971): 682–693; Alexander L. George and Andrew Bennett, *Case Studies and Theory Development in the Social Sciences* (Cambridge, MA: MIT Press, 2005); Jason Seawright and John Gerring, "Case Selection Techniques in Case Study Research: A Menu of Qualitative and Quantitative Options," *Political Research Quarterly* 61, no. 2 (2008): 294–308.

2. COUNTERBALANCING AND COUP FAILURE

1. Judith Miller, "Saddam Hussein's Neighbors Grow Bolder, Tentatively," *New York Times*, September 29, 1991.

2. Ahmed Hashim, "Saddam Husayn and Civil-Military Relations in Iraq: The Quest for Legitimacy and Power," *Middle East Journal* 57, no. 1 (2003): 9–41.

3. This dataset is an extension and updated version of the dataset used in Erica De Bruin, "Preventing Coups d'État: How Counterbalancing Works," *Journal of Conflict Resolution* 62, no. 7 (2018): 1433–1458. The number of states included in the dataset expanded from 65 to 110. For a full description of the dataset, see Erica De Bruin, "Mapping Coercive Institutions: The State Security Forces Dataset, 1960–2010" (unpublished manuscript, October 17, 2019), https://papers.ssrn.com/sol3/papers.cfm?abstract_id=3317127.

4. E.g., James T. Quinlivan, "Coup-Proofing: Its Practice and Consequence in the Middle East," *International Security* 24, no. 2 (1999): 131–165; Aaron Belkin and Evan Schofer, "Toward a Structural Understanding of Coup Risk," *Journal of Conflict Resolution* 47, no. 5 (2003): 594–620; Aaron Belkin, *United We Stand? Divide-and-Conquer Politics and the Logic of International Hostility* (Albany: State University of New York Press, 2005); Ulrich Pilster and Tobias Böhmelt, "Coup-Proofing and Military Effectiveness in Interstate Wars, 1967–99," *Conflict Management and Peace Science* 28, no. 4 (2011): 331–350; Ulrich Pilster and Tobias Böhmelt, "Do Democracies Engage Less in Coup-Proofing? On the Relationship between Regime Type and Civil-Military Relations," *Foreign Policy Analysis* 8, no. 4 (2012): 355–372; Tobias Böhmelt and Ulrich Pilster, "The Impact of Institutional Coup-Proofing on Coup Attempts and Coup Outcomes," *International Interactions* 41, no. 1 (2015): 158–182; Jonathan Powell, "Determinants of the Attempting and Outcome of Coups d'État," *Journal of Conflict Resolution* 56, no. 6 (2012): 1017–1040; Cameron S. Brown, Christopher J. Fariss, and R. Blake McMahon, "Recouping after Coup-Proofing: Compromised Military Effectiveness and Strategic Substitution," *International Interactions* 42, no. 1 (2016): 1–30.

5. International Institute for Strategic Studies [IISS], *The Military Balance* (London: IISS, 2010), 8.

6. E.g., Belkin and Schofer, "Toward a Structural Understanding"; Pilster and Böhmelt, "Coup-Proofing and Military Effectiveness"; Pilster and Böhmelt, "Do Democracies Engage Less in Coup-Proofing?"; Powell, "Determinants of the Attempting and Outcome."

7. E.g., Clare Mundy and Dan Smith, "'Facts' about the Military," *Journal of Peace Research* 17, no. 3 (1980): 261–267; John T. Ostrich Jr. and William C. Green, "Methodological Problems Associated with the IISS Military Balance," *Comparative Strategy* 3, no. 2 (1981): 151–171; Milton Leitenberg, "The Numbers Game or 'Who's on First?,'" *Bulletin of the Atomic Scientists* 38, no. 6 (1982): 27–32; Jeff Colgan, "Venezuela and Military Expenditure Data," *Journal of Peace Research* 48, no. 4 (2011): 547–556.

8. I am grateful to Jonathan Powell for emphasizing this point.

9. Leitenberg, "The Numbers Game," 28. For a more recent, in-depth analysis of how these issues distort *Military Balance* data on expenditures and personnel in Venezuela, see Colgan, "Venezuela and Military Expenditure Data."

10. E.g., IISS, *Military Balance*, 6–7. Because prior editions are not updated when new information is available, this can result in large fluctuations in reported force size from year to year. In Egypt, for instance, *The Military Balance* estimates the size of the National Guard as 6,000 in 1974, 60,000 from 1975 to 1976, then back down to 6,000 in 1977.

11. World Bank, "Population Ranking," accessed October 27, 2017, https://data.worldbank.org. For more information on the data collection process, see De Bruin, "Mapping Coercive Institutions," and associated online appendix.

12. Dennis Deletant, "Ghosts from the Past: Successors to the Securitate in Post-Communist Romania," in *Post-Communist Romania: Coming to Terms with Transition*, ed. Duncan Light and David Phinnemore (London: Palgrave Macmillan, 2001), 35–58; George Cristian Maior, "Managing Change: The Romanian Intelligence Service in the 21st Century," *International Journal of Intelligence and CounterIntelligence* 25, no. 2 (2012): 217–239.

13. Carey, Mitchell, and Lowe have constructed a useful, and complementary, dataset that focuses on pro-government militia. See Sabine Carey, Neil Mitchell, and Will Lowe, "States, the Security Sector, and the Monopoly of Violence: A New Data-Base on Pro-Government Militias," *Journal of Peace Research* 50, no. 2 (2013): 249–258.

14. Federal police forces are included only if they have two or more of the following organizational indicators of militarization: command and control centers; the use of elite squads patterned after military special operations; barracked housing; and/or long-range deployment. For a discussion of these and other indicators of police militarization, see Oscar Rantatalo, "The Miscellany of Militaristic Policing: A Literature Review," *Journal of Policing, Intelligence, and Counter Terrorism* 7, no. 1 (2012): 51–65.

15. On this distinction, see David Pion-Berlin, "Defense Organization and Civil-Military Relations," *Armed Forces and Society* 35, no. 3 (2009): 562–586.

16. Morris Janowitz, *Military Institutions and Coercion in the Developing Nations: The Military in the Political Development of New Nations* (Chicago: University of Chicago Press, 1988). Security forces are distinguished from units in the regular army on the basis of their names and qualitative accounts of how the forces operate. Companies, battalions, brigades, divisions, and other units of the regular army that are titled sequentially in line with other units (e.g., first armored division, second infantry battalion) are not included in the dataset unless they are described in qualitative, country-specific accounts as operating independently, or are found to report to the regime outside the military chain of command. Forces that are given distinct titles (President's Own Guard Regiment, Special Republican Guards, etc.) or which are described in qualitative accounts as distinct organizations are included in the dataset.

17. Donald Horowitz, *Ethnic Groups in Conflict* (Berkeley: University of California Press, 1985), 547.

18. Quinlivan, "Coup-Proofing," 141.

19. Edward Luttwak, *Coup d'État: A Practical Handbook* (Cambridge, MA: Harvard University Press, 1979); Naunihal Singh, *Seizing Power: The Strategic Logic of Military Coups* (Baltimore: Johns Hopkins University Press, 2014).

20. Janowitz, *Military Institutions and Coercion*, 7.

21. For a list of sources used and more information on the coding process, see De Bruin, "Mapping Coercive Institutions," online appendix.

22. Steven I. Wilkinson, *Army and Nation: The Military and Indian Democracy since Independence* (Cambridge, MA: Harvard University Press, 2015), 145.

23. Jan Teorell, Nicholas Charron, Marcus Samanni, Soren Holmberg, and Rothstein Bo, *The Quality of Government Dataset*, version April 6, 2011 (Gothenburg, Sweden: University of Gothenburg, 2011).

24. Bettina Renz, "Russia's 'Force Structures' and the Study of Civil-Military Relations," *Journal of Slavic Military Studies* 18, no. 4 (2005): 559–585.

25. These include forces supervised by the KGB (1985–1991), MVD (1985–2000), Border Guard Service (1992–2000), Civil Defense Troops (1992–2000), Federal Guard Service (1992–2000), Railway Troops (1999–2000), Presidential Security Service (1993–1996), Forces for the Protection of the Russian Federation (1996–2000), Federal Security Service (1997–2000), Federal Communications and Information Agency (1998–2000), and Federal Protection Service (2000).

26. Anatol Lieven, *Chechnya: Tombstone of Russian Power* (New Haven, CT: Yale University Press, 1999), 280.

27. Monty G. Marshall and Donna Ramsey Marshall, *Coup d'État Events, 1946–2015*, Center for Systemic Peace, 2016, http://www.systemicpeace.org/inscr/CSPCoupsCodebook2015.pdf.

28. Janowitz, *Military Institutions and Coercion*; Kristen A. Harkness, *When Soldiers Rebel: Ethnic Armies and Political Instability in Africa* (Cambridge: Cambridge University Press, 2018)

29. Holger Albrecht, "The Myth of Coup-Proofing: Risk and Instances of Military Coups d'État in the Middle East and North Africa, 1950–2013," *Armed Forces and Society* 41, no. 4 (2015): 659–687.

30. Marina Caparini and Otwin Marenin, eds., *Transforming Police in Central and Eastern Europe* (New Brunswick, NJ: Transaction Publishers, 2004).

31. Singh, *Seizing Power*, 9.

32. See Erica De Bruin, "Will There Be Blood? The Determinants of Violence during Coups d'État," *Journal of Peace Research* 56, no. 6 (2019): 797–811, and the online appendix.

33. Singh, *Seizing Power*, 35.

34. I considered admirals, marshals, and commodores the equivalent rank of army generals, and captains and commanders the equivalent of army majors and colonels.

35. Curtis Bell, "Coup d'État and Democracy," *Comparative Political Studies* 49, no. 9 (2016): 1167–1200; Barbara Geddes, "How Autocrats Defend Themselves against Armed Rivals" (paper presented at the American Political Science Association Annual Meeting, Toronto, Canada, 2009).

36. Barbara Geddes, Joseph Wright, and Erica Frantz, "Autocratic Breakdown and Regime Transitions: A New Data Set," *Perspectives on Politics* 12, no. 2 (2014): 313–331; Barbara Geddes, "What Do We Know about Democratization after Twenty Years?," *Annual Review of Political Science* 2, no. 1 (1999): 115–144.

37. John B. Londregan and Keith T. Poole, "Poverty, the Coup Trap, and the Seizure of Executive Power," *World Politics* 42, no. 2 (1990): 151–183; Samuel E. Finer, *The Man on Horseback: The Role of the Military in Politics* (New York: Praeger, 2002).

38. Thomas H. Johnson, Robert O. Slater, and Pat McGowan, "Explaining African Military Coups d'État," *American Political Science Review* 78, no. 3 (1984): 622–640; Egil Fossum, "Factors Influencing the Occurrence of Military Coups d'État in Latin America," *Journal of Peace Research* 4, no. 3 (1967): 228–251; William R. Thompson, "Regime Vulnerability and the Military Coup," *Comparative Politics* 7, no. 4 (1975): 459–487.

39. Kristian Skrede Gleditsch, "Expanded Trade and GDP Data," *Journal of Conflict Resolution* 46, no. 5 (2002): 712–724.

40. Horowitz, *Ethnic Groups in Conflict*; Bruce W. Farcau, *The Coup: Tactics in the Seizure of Power* (Westport, CT: Praeger, 1994).

41. Jeff Colgan, "Measuring Revolution," *Conflict Management and Peace Science* 29, no. 4 (2012): 444–467.

42. Clayton L. Thyne, "Supporter of Stability or Agent of Agitation? The Effect of US Foreign Policy on Coups in Latin America, 1960–99," *Journal of Peace Research* 47, no. 4 (2010): 449–461.

43. Nikolay Marinov and Hein Goemans, "Coups and Democracy," *British Journal of Political Science* 44, no. 4 (2014): 799–825.

44. Alberto Abadie, Susan Athey, Guido Imbens, and Jeffrey Wooldridge, "When Should You Adjust Standard Errors for Clustering?" NBER Working Paper No. 24003, November, 2017.

45. Luke Keele, Randolph T. Stevenson, and Felix Elbert, "The Causal Interpretation of Estimated Associations in Regression Models," *Political Science Research and Methods* 8, no. 1 (2020): 1–13; Daniel Westreich and Sander Greenland, "The Table 2 Fallacy: Presenting and Interpreting Confounder and Modifier Coefficients," *American Journal of Epidemiology* 177, no. 4 (2013): 292–298.

46. Geddes, Wright, and Frantz, "Autocratic Breakdown and Regime Transitions."

47. Jessica L. Weeks, "Strongmen and Straw Men: Authoritarian Regimes and the Initiation of International Conflict," *American Political Science Review* 106, no. 2 (2012): 326–347.

48. Peter B. White, "Crises and Crisis Generations: The Long-Term Impact of International Crises on Military Political Participation," *Security Studies* 26, no. 4 (2017): 575–605.

49. James J. Heckman, "Sample Selection Bias as a Specification Error," *Econometrica: Journal of the Econometric Society* 47, no. 1 (1979): 153–161; Wynand P. M. M. Van de Ven and Bernard M. S. Van Praag, "The Demand for Deductibles in Private Health Insurance: A Probit Model with Sample Selection," *Journal of Econometrics* 17 (1981): 229–252.

50. Jonathan M. Powell and Clayton L. Thyne, "Global Instances of Coups from 1950 to 2010: A New Dataset," *Journal of Peace Research* 48, no. 2 (2011): 249–259.

3. HOW COUNTERBALANCING WORKS

1. The cases were selected from among 148 known cases of coup attempts preceded by counterbalancing between 1960 and 2010. The full list of coup attempts can be found in the appendix.

2. Quoted in Norman Miller and Rodger Yeager, *Kenya: The Quest for Prosperity*, 2nd ed. (Boulder, CO: Westview Press, 1994), 101.

3. The National Archives of the United Kingdom (TNA), Foreign and Commonwealth Office (FCO) 31/3566 2, Telegram from Sir John Williams, High Commissioner of the United Kingdom, to Kenya, August 1, 1982.

4. "Minorities at Risk Dataset," Minorities at Risk Project (College Park, MD: Center for International Development and Conflict Management), accessed September 7, 2018, http://www.mar.umd.edu.

5. Jendayi Elizabeth J. Frazer, "Sustaining Civilian Control: Armed Counterweights in Regime Stability in Africa" (PhD diss., Stanford University, 1994), 255; TNA FCO 31/3556 39, "Situation in Kenya," Telegram No. 769, August 8, 1982; Miller and Yeager, *Kenya*, 98–100.

6. Alan Cowell, "Kenya Regime Seeks One-Party Law to Subdue Opposition," *International Herald Tribune*, May 31, 1982; Miller and Yeager, *Kenya*, 101.

7. Boubacar N'Diaye, "How Not to Institutionalize Civilian Control: Kenya's Coup Prevention Strategies, 1964–1997," *Armed Forces and Society* 28, no. 4 (2002): 629.

8. Daniel Branch, *Kenya: Between Hope and Despair, 1963–2011* (New Haven, CT: Yale University Press, 2011), 155.

9. Miller and Yeager, *Kenya*, 103.

10. N'Diaye, "How Not to Institutionalize Civilian Control," 629.

11. James Dianga, *Kenya 1982, the Attempted Coup: The Consequence of a One Party Dictatorship* (London: Pen Press, 2002).

12. Kate Currie and Larry Ray, "The Pambana of August 1—Kenya's Abortive Coup," *Political Quarterly* 57 (1986): 52; Charles Hornsbsy, *Kenya: A History since Independence* (London: I. B. Tauris, 2013), 376.

13. TNA FCO 31/3556 32, "Coup Attempt," Telegram No. 381, August 4, 1982; TNA FCO 31/3556 13, "Attempted Coup," Telegram No. 375 from Sir John Williams, High Commissioner of the United Kingdom, to Kenya, August 2, 1982; Samuel Decalo, *The Stable Minority: Civilian Rule in Africa* (Gainesville, FL: Florida Academic Press, 1998), 243.

14. Frazer, "Sustaining Civilian Control," 258; Edwin A. Gimode, "The Role of the Police in Kenya's Democratisation Process," in *Kenya: The Struggle for Democracy*, ed. Godwin R. Murunga and Shadrack Wanjala Nasong'o (Dakar: Codesria Books, 2007), 242.

15. *Africa Research Bulletin* 19 (1982): 6559.

16. Currie and Ray, "The Pambana of August 1," 53.

17. Mordechai Tamarkin, "The Roots of Political Stability in Kenya," *African Affairs* 77, no. 308 (1978): 301; William Robert Foran, *The Kenya Police: 1887–1960* (London: Hale, 1962), 190–191.

18. N'Diaye, "How Not to Institutionalize Civilian Control," 624–627; Decalo, *The Stable Minority*, 237; Branch, *Kenya*, 157.

19. U.S. National Archives II (USNA), Department of State Central Files, Record Group (RG) 59, Central Foreign Policy File, 1979, "Moi Rejects Criticism of GSU Abuses," Airgram from Nairobi to Washington, DC, November 7, 1979; Alice Hills, "Policing in Kenya: A Selective Service," in *Policing Developing Democracies*, ed. Mercedes S. Hinton and Tim Newurn (London: Routledge, 2009).

20. Ryan Shaffer, "Following in Footsteps: The Transformation of Kenya's Intelligence Services since the Colonial Era," *Studies in Intelligence* 63, no. 1 (2019): 27; Branch, *Kenya*, 102; Kama Ngotho, "Tough Call for Kanyotu in the Kenyatta Succession Saga," *Daily Nation*, May 29, 2008, https://allafrica.com/stories/200805290107.html.

21. Miller and Yeager, *Kenya*, 101; Colin Legum, ed., *Africa Contemporary Record* [hereafter *ACR*], *1980–1981* (New York: Africana Publishing, 1981), B215.

22. There may have been some lingering tensions between Moi and the Special Branch. In the months prior to the coup, the operational head of the Special Branch, Stephen Muriithi, was detained without trial for challenging Moi's authority to make personnel changes; see Hornsby, *Kenya*, 374–379; Decalo, *The Stable Minority*, 242.

23. *Africa Research Bulletin*, 1982, 6560; Decalo, *The Stable Minority*, 243; Hornsby, *Kenya*, 376; TNA FCO 31/3556 13, "Attempted Coup," Telegram No. 375 from Sir John Williams, High Commissioner of the United Kingdom to Kenya, August 2, 1982; Decalo, *The Stable Minority*, 20.

24. TNA FCO 31/3556 9, "Kenya-Situation," August 2, 1982.

25. TNA FCO 31/3556 5, Telegram from Sir John Williams, High Commissioner of the United Kingdom to Kenya, August 2, 1982; TNA FCO 31/3556 10, "Coup Attempt," Telegram No. 370, August 6, 1982; Branch, *Kenya*, 156.

26. Miller and Yeager, *Kenya*, 101–2; Branch, *Kenya*, 157.

27. Frazer, "Sustaining Civilian Control," 259.

28. John L. Hess, "King Hassan Says Rebels' Leaders Will Be Executed," *New York Times*, July 12, 1971; John L. Hess, "A Bit of Disloyalty among all the King's Men," *New York Times*, July 18, 1971; U.S. National Archives II (USNA), Department of State Central Files, Record Group (RG) 59, Central Files 1970–73, POL 23-9 MOR, "The Moroccan Coup Attempt of July 10, 1971," July 17, 1971.

29. John Waterbury, "The Coup Manqué," in *Arabs and Berbers: From Tribe to Nation in North Africa*, ed. Ernest Gellner and Charles Micaud (Lexington, MA: Lexington Books, 1973), 398.

30. Stephen O. Hughes, *Morocco under King Hassan* (Reading, UK: Ithaca Press, 2001), 160; "Soldiers Attack Moroccan Palace; King Keeps Power," *New York Times*, July 11, 1971, 15.

31. Frank H. Braun, "Morocco: Anatomy of a Palace Revolution That Failed," *International Journal of Middle East Studies* 9, no. 1 (1978): 65, 67.

32. Susan Gibson Miller, *A History of Modern Morocco* (New York: Cambridge University Press, 2013); Colin Legum, ed., *ACR: Annual Survey and Documents, 1970–71* (London: Rex Collings, 1971B31.

33. One, Mehdi Ben Barka, was kidnapped in Paris and not seen again. Stuart Schaar, "L'affaire Ben Barka: The Kidnaping Casts Its Shadow," *Africa Report* 11, no. 3 (1966): 37.

34. TNA FCO 160/116 23, "Morocco: New Constitution," August 24, 1970; Waterbury, "The Coup Manqué," 399.

35. USNA, RG 59, Central Files 1970–73, POL 23-9 MOR, "Morocco: King Hassan, His Army, and His Future," July 15, 1971; TNA FCO 160/128 47, "Coup in Morocco," July 21, 1971; Telegram 3745 from the Embassy in Morocco to the Department of State, July 23, 1971, 1115Z, "Future of the Regime," *Foreign Relations of the United States* [hereafter *FRUS*], *1969–1976*, vol. E-5, pt. 2, *Documents on North Africa, 1969–1972*, ed. Monica L. Belmonte (Washington, DC: Government Printing Office, 2007), Document 119; Miller, *Modern Morocco*, 175; Aomar Boum and Thomas K. Park, *Historical Dictionary of Morocco*, 3rd ed. (Lanham, MD: Rowman and Littlefield, 2016), 317.

36. Hughes, *Morocco under King Hassan*, 159.

37. TNA FCO 160/128 42; Legum, *ACR: Annual Survey and Documents, 1970–71*, B55.

38. Colin Legum, ed., *ACR: Annual Survey and Documents, 1971–1972*, (London: Rex Collings, 1972), B55; TNA FCO 160/128 42, "Events of 10 July in Morocco," Diplomatic Report No. 370/71, July 16, 1971.

39. Braun, "Morocco," 70; USNA, RG 59, Central Files 1970–73, POL 23-9 MOR, "Coup Attempt: Where Did the King Hide?," July 31, 1971; Michael J. Willis, *Politics and Power in the Maghreb: Algeria, Tunisia and Morocco from Independence to the Arab Spring* (New York: Columbia University Press, 2012), 91; Willis, *Politics and Power in the Maghreb*, 91; Legum, *ACR: Annual Survey and Documents, 1971–1972*, B54–57.

40. Waterbury, "The Coup Manqué," 411.

41. Braun, "Morocco," 66.

42. Remy Leveau, "The Moroccan Monarchy: A Political System in Quest of a New Equilibrium," in *Middle East Monarchies: The Challenge of Modernity*, ed. Joseph Kostiner (Boulder, CO: Lynne Rienner, 2000), 120; Braun, "Morocco," 64–66; National Intelligence Estimate 61–72, Washington, June 15, 1972, *FRUS, 1969–1976*, vol. E-5, pt. 2, *Documents on North Africa, 1969–1972*, Document 125.

43. Braun, "Morocco," 68.

44. Special National Intelligence Estimate, 61-1-72, September 14, 1972, "Prospects for the Moroccan Monarchy," *FRUS, 1969–1976*, vol. E-5, pt. 2, *Documents on North Africa, 1969–1972*, Document 131; Legum, *ACR: Annual Survey and Documents, 1971–1972*, B59.

45. "Soldiers Attack Moroccan Palace," 15; Waterbury, "The Coup Manqué," 405.

46. Waterbury, "The Coup Manqué," 411; Braun, "Morocco," 69–71.

47. USNA, RG 59, Central Files 1970–73, POL 23-9 MOR, "Morocco: King Hassan, His Army, and His Future," July 15, 1971; Legum, *ACR: Annual Survey and Documents, 1971–1972*, B55–56; Hess, "King Hassan Says Rebels' Leaders," 5.

48. Memorandum from the President's Deputy Assistant for National Security Affairs (Haig) to President Nixon, Washington, July 11, 1971, "Coup Attempt in Morocco," *FRUS 1969–1976*, vol. E-5, pt. 2, *Documents on North Africa, 1969–1972*, Document 117.

49. TNA FCO 39/884 7, "Internal Security of Morocco: Attempted Coup d'État in July 1971," July 12, 1971; USNA, RG 59, Central Files 1970–73, POL 23-9 MOR, "The Moroccan Coup Attempt of July 10, 1971," July 17, 1971.

50. USNA, RG 59, Central Files 1970–73, POL 23-9 MOR, "Morocco: King Hassan, His Army, and His Future," July 15, 1971; see also Special National Intelligence Estimate 61-1-72, September 14, 1972, "Prospects for the Moroccan Monarchy," *FRUS, 1969–1976*, vol. E-5, pt. 2, *Documents on North Africa, 1969–1972*, Document 131.

51. Steve C. Ropp, "Explaining the Long-Term Maintenance of a Military Regime: Panama before the US Invasion," *World Politics* 44, no. 2 (1992): 210–234; Sharon Erickson Nepstad, *Nonviolent Revolutions: Civil Resistance in the Late 20th Century* (New York: Oxford University Press, 2011).

52. Robert C. Harding, *Military Foundations of Panamanian Politics* (New Brunswick, NJ: Transaction, 2001), 167–172; Richard H. Cole, *Operation Just Cause: The Planning and Execution of Joint Operations in Panama, February 1988–January 1990* (Washington, DC: Joint History Office, Office of the Chairman of the Joint Chiefs of Staff, 1995).

53. James A. Baker III, *The Politics of Diplomacy: Revolution, War, and Peace, 1989–1992* (New York: G. P. Putnam's Sons, 1995), 185.

54. Baker, 179.

55. Julia Preston, "Panama's New President Faces a Tough Task," *Washington Post*, December 21, 1989; Corinne Caumartin, "'Depoliticization' in the Reform of the Panamanian Security Apparatus," *Journal of Latin American Studies* 39, no. 1 (2007): 110; Keven Buckley, *Panama: The Whole Story* (New York: Simon and Schuster, 1991), 196.

56. Thomas L. Pearcy, "Manuel Antonio Noriega Moreno," in *Encyclopedia of U.S.-Latin American Relations*, ed. Thomas M. Leonard (Washington, DC: Sage, 2012), 661–662.

57. Gordon L. Rottman, *Panama, 1989–90* (Oxford: Osprey Publishing, 1991); Thomas M. Leonard, *Historical Dictionary of Panama* (Lanham, MD: Rowman and Littlefield, 2015), 16; Margaret E. Scranton, *The Noriega Years: U.S.-Panamanian Relations, 1981–1990* (Boulder, CO: Lynne Rienner, 1991), 24.

58. Arthur Davis, interview by Charles Stuart Kennedy, May 24, 1991, Association for Diplomatic Studies and Training Foreign Affairs Oral History Project, 54.

59. Andrew Rosenthal and Michael E. Gordon, "A Failed Coup: The Bush Team and Noriega," *New York Times*, Special Report, October 8, 1989; Lawrence A. Yates, *The U.S. Military Intervention in Panama: Origins, Planning, and Crisis Management, June 1987–December 1989* (Washington, DC: Center of Military History, United States Army), 249; Cole, *Operation Just Cause*, 14–16.

60. Buckley, *Panama: The Whole Story*.

61. The White House, National Security Directive 21, "U.S. Policy towards Panama under Noriega after September 1, 1989," September 1, 1989; Yates, *U.S. Military Intervention in Panama*, 249–260.

62. Quoted in Giancarlo Soler Torrijos, *In the Shadow of the United States: Democracy and Regional Order in the Latin Caribbean* (Boca Raton, FL: Brown Walker Press, 2008), 257; Bob Woodward, *The Commanders* (New York: Simon and Schuster, 1991), 121.

63. Robert C. Harding, *The History of Panama* (Westport, CT: Greenwood Press, 2006), 113; Linda Robinson, "Dwindling Options in Panama," *Foreign Affairs* 68, no. 5 (1989):

202; David E. Pitt, "Widow of Panama Coup Leader Says Fellow Plotter Betrayed Him," *New York Times*, October 12, 1989.

64. Don Podesta, "Coup Attempt against Noriega by Rebel Troops Fails in Panama," *Washington Post*, October 4, 1989, 1.

65. William Branigin, "Rebel Ignored Plea to Delay Coup," *Washington Post*, October 14, 1989.

66. Mark A. Uhlig, "Some of Noriega's Top Advisors are Seen Among Coup's Plotters," *New York Times*, October 6, 1989; Joe Pichirallo and Molly Moore, "Coup Leader Barred Giving U.S. Noriega," *Washington Post*, October 11, 1989; David E. Pitt, "Panamanian Tells of Goal of Rebels," *New York Times*, October 13, 1989.

67. Branigin, "Rebel Ignored Plea."

68. Frederick Kempe, *Divorcing the Dictator: America's Bungled Affair with Noriega* (I. B. Tauris, 1990), 385.

69. Pitt, "Widow of Panama Coup Leader"; R. Cody Phillips, *Operation Just Cause: The Incursion into Panama* (Washington, DC: U.S. Army Center of Military History, 2004), 35.

70. Yates, *U.S. Military Intervention in Panama*, 256.

71. Peter Eisner, "Noriega Psyched Out Rebels, Friend Says," *Newsday*, October 7, 1989; Podesta, "Coup Attempt against Noriega."

72. Pitt, "Panamanian Tells of Goal of Rebels"; Kenneth J. Jones, *The Enemy Within: Casting Out Panama's Demon* (El Dorado, Panama: Focus Publishing), 49, 71; Nepstad, *Nonviolent Revolutions*, 69–71; Yates, *U.S. Military Intervention in Panama*, 256.

73. Kempe, *Divorcing the Dictator*, 391.

74. Yates, *U.S. Military Intervention in Panama*, 259–260; also see Kempe, *Divorcing the Dictator*, 392; Baker, *Politics of Diplomacy*, 186.

75. Harding, *History of Panama*, 133.

76. Torrijos, *In the Shadow of the United States*, 157; Preston, "Panama's New President Faces a Tough Task."

77. Julia Preston, "Haitian Government Announces Defeat of Mutinous Soldiers," *Washington Post*, April 9, 1989. See the appendix for further information on this and other coups discussed only briefly in the main text.

78. Stephen L. Rozman, "The Evolution of the Political Role of the Peruvian Military," *Journal of Interamerican Studies and World Affairs* 12, no. 4 (1970): 539–564; Joanne Omang, "President of Peru Ousted by Premier," *Washington Post*, August 30, 1975, A8.

79. Francis X. Clines, "Gorbachev Is Ousted in Apparent Coup by Soviet Armed Forces and Hard-Liners," *New York Times*, August 19, 1991.

80. Brian D. Taylor, *Politics and the Russian Army: Civil-Military Relations, 1689–2000* (Cambridge: Cambridge University Press, 2003).

81. Louise I. Shelley, *Policing Soviet Society: The Evolution of State Control* (London: Routledge, 2005); G. H. Turbiville Jr., "Soviet Security Forces and the Army: Hidden Dimensions of Interaction, Subordination, and Control," *Journal of Slavic Military Studies* 4, no. 2 (1991): 278–298.

82. William E. Odom, *The Collapse of the Soviet Military* (New Haven, CT: Yale University Press, 1998), 311–312; Naunihal Singh, *Seizing Power: The Strategic Logic of Military Coups* (Baltimore: Johns Hopkins University Press, 2014), 199–202; Taylor, *Politics and the Russian Army*, 235.

83. Odom, *Collapse of the Soviet Military*, 311–312, 319.

84. Singh, *Seizing Power*, 203.

85. Bill Kellers, "Sporadic Mutinies Rack Soviet Army," *New York Times*, August 21, 1991.

86. Michael McFaul, *Russia's Unfinished Revolution: Political Change from Gorbachev to Putin* (Ithaca, NY: Cornell University Press, 2001).

87. John F. Burns, "In Power Still, Afghan Can Thank His 4-Star Aide," *New York Times*, May 10, 1990.

88. Abraham F. Lowenthal, *The Dominican Intervention* (Cambridge, MA: Harvard University Press, 1972).

89. Ibrahim Al-Marashi and Sammy Salama, *Iraq's Armed Forces: An Analytical History* (London: Routledge, 2008), 188; Agence France-Presse (AFP), "Ba'th Party Official Notes Situation 'under Control,'" in Foreign Broadcast Information Service (FBIS), Daily Report: Middle East and North Africa, FBIS-NES-95-116, 1995: 35; AFP, "Saddam's Forces Siege al-Rairamadi; Supplies Cut," in FBIS, Daily Report, Middle East and North Africa, FBIS-NES-95-118, June 18, 1995: 33; Youssef M. Ibrahim, "Iraq Reportedly Cracks Down on Clan That Tried a Coup," *New York Times*, June 20, 1995, A6; Sharon Otterman, "Iraq: What Is the Fedayeen Saddam?," *Council on Foreign Relations Backgrounder*, February 3, 2005, https://www.cfr.org/backgrounder/iraq-what-fedayeen-saddam.

90. Guy Arnold, *The Maverick State: Gaddafi and the New World Order* (London: Cassell, 1996), 38; John Oakes, *Libya: The History of Gaddafi's Pariah State* (Stroud, UK: History Press, 2011), 135.

91. Simon J. Baynham, "Soldier and State in Ghana," *Armed Forces and Society* 5, no. 1 (1978): 155–168; Akwasi Amankwaa Afrifa, *The Ghana Coup: 24th February 1966* (London: Frank Cass, 1967).

92. Victoria Clark, *Yemen: Dancing on the Heads of Snakes* (New Haven, CT: Yale University Press, 2010); Edgar O'Ballance, *The War in the Yemen* (Hamden, CT: Shoe String Press, 1971).

93. The coups in Afghanistan, Peru, Morocco, and Russia were staged from the top of the military hierarchy; as such they are the only ones examined in which coup plotters might have attempted to stage a coup during a face-to-face meeting with other high-ranking officers. The fact that half of the coups staged from the higher ranks—those in Peru and Russia—were able to use meetings or joint proclamations, which included counterweights, suggests that counterbalancing does not create insurmountable obstacles to these forms of coordination.

94. William Borders, "Mujib Reported Overthrown and Killed in a Coup by the Bangladesh Military," *New York Times*, August 15, 1975.

95. Alan Lindquist, "Military and Development in Bangladesh," *IDS Bulletin* 9, no. 1 (1977): 10–18.

96. Z. R. Khan, "Politicization of the Bangladesh Military: A Response to Perceived Shortcomings of Civilian Government," *Asian Survey* 21, no. 5 (1981): 551–564.

97. Anthony Mascarenhas, *Bangladesh: A Legacy of Blood* (London: Hodder and Stoughton Sevenoaks, 1986).

98. These ties were not universally welcomed; there was some resentment about the perception that Indian troops stayed too long after the war of independence (they did not depart until March 1972).

99. James Heitzman and Robert L. Worden, *Bangladesh: A Country Study* (Washington, DC: Library of Congress, 1989). There was less disagreement about the former East Bangladesh Rifles, which were reconstituted as the Bangladesh Rifles shortly after independence, as the utility of monitoring the border seemed clear.

100. Emajuddin Ahamed, "The Military and Democracy in Bangladesh," in *The Military and Democracy in Asia and the Pacific*, ed. Ron May and Viberto Selochan (Canberra: Australian National University Press, 2004); Khan, "Politicization of the Bangladesh Military," 533.

101. Khan, "Politicization of the Bangladesh Military," 554. See also P. B. Sinha, *Armed Forces of Bangladesh*, Occasional Paper No. 1 (New Delhi: Institute for Defence Studies and

Analysis, 1979); Md Ataur Rahman, "Bangladesh in 1983: A Turning Point for the Military," *Asian Survey* 24, no. 2 (1984): 240–249; Heitzman and Worden, *Bangladesh*.

102. Rahman, 161.

103. Lindquist, "Military and Development in Bangladesh," 13.

104. Dina Mahnaz Siddiqi, "Political Culture in Contemporary Bangladesh: Histories, Ruptures, and Contradictions," in *Political Islam and Governance in Bangladesh*, ed. Ali Riaz and Christine Fair (London: Routledge, 2011), 10; Rounaq Jahan, *Bangladesh Politics: Problems and Issues* (Dhaka: University Press, 1980), 84, 112, 132; Asish Kuma Roy, *Praetorian Politics in Bangladesh: 1975–1981* (Kolkata: Progressive Publishers, 2002); Lawrence Ziring, *Bangladesh: From Mujib to Ershad; An Interpretive Study* (Karachi: Oxford University Press, 1992), 97–103.

105. U.S. Embassy in Dacca to Secretary of State in Washington, "Conversation with President Mujibur Rahman," February 24, 1975 (declassified under the Freedom of Information Act [FOIA]).

106. Heitzman and Worden, *Bangladesh*.

107. Mascarenhas, *Bangladesh*, 69.

108. Mascarenhas, 70–75; William Borders, "Leaders of Coup Move to Solidify Bangladesh Rule," *New York Times*, August 16, 1975.

109. William Borders, "Curfew Is Eased by Dacca Regime," *New York Times*, August 18, 1975; Jatiya Rakkhi Bahini (Absorption in the Army) Ordinance, October 9, 1975.

110. Rozman, "Evolution of the Political Role of the Peruvian Military."

111. Paul Hofmann, "President of Peru Ousted in Coup Led by the Military," *New York Times*, August 29, 1975, 6; Omang, "President of Peru Ousted," A8; Peter S. Cleaves and Henry Pease García, "State Autonomy and Military Policy Making," in *The Peruvian Experiment Reconsidered*, ed. Cynthia McClintock and Abraham F. Lowenthal (Princeton, NJ: Princeton University Press, 1983), 240; David P. Werlich, *Peru: A Short History* (Carbondale, IL: Southern Illinois University Press, 1978), 364.

112. Rozman, "Evolution of the Political Role of the Peruvian Military," 529; Daniel M. Masterson, *Militarism and Politics in Latin America: Peru from Sanchez Cerro to Sendero Luminoso* (Westport, CT: Greenwood Press, 1991), 31–32.

113. Elisabeth Acha, "Police Reform and Police Organizational Culture in Peru" (paper presented at the Annual Meeting of the Latin American Studies Association, Las Vegas, Nevada, October 7–9, 2004), 2.

114. Gustavo Gorriti Ellenbogen, *The Shining Path: A History of the Millenarian War in Peru* (Chapel Hill: University of North Carolina Press, 1999), 42; Rex A. Hudson, ed., *Peru: A Country Study* (Washington, DC: Library of Congress, 1992), 300.

115. Jonathan Kandell, "Peruvian Police Strike over Pay," *New York Times*, February 4, 1975.

116. Kandell, "Peruvian Police Strike over Pay;" Omang, "President of Peru Ousted," A8; Hudson, *Peru*.

117. Hofmann, "President of Peru Ousted," 6.

118. Omang, "President of Peru Ousted," A1; Werlich, *Peru*, 364.

4. AN EFFECTIVE DETERRENT?

1. John Roosa, *Pretext for Mass Murder: The September 30th Movement and Suharto's Coup d'État in Indonesia* (Madison: University of Wisconsin Press, 2006), 205.

2. Within the presidential guard, a smaller unit, called the Detaemen Kawal Pribadi Presiden (DPK), protected Sukarno. See Roosa, 271.

3. Robert H. Bruce, "Keeping the Military at Bay with Countervailing Force: The Utility of Indonesian Civilian Leaders' Use of Paramilitary Police," Indian Ocean Centre for

Peace Studies Occasional Paper No. 20 (Nedlands, Western Australia: Indian Ocean Centre for Peace Studies, 1992).

4. Harold Crouch, *Army and Politics in Indonesia* (Ithaca, NY: Cornell University Press, 1978), 198.

5. Roosa, *Pretext for Mass Murder*, 209.

6. Seth S. King, "Indonesian Coup Still a Mystery," *New York Times*, October 17, 1965.

7. Roosa, *Pretext for Mass Murder*, 4.

8. Monty G. Marshall and Donna Ramsey Marshall, *Coup d'État Events, 1946–2015*, Center for Systemic Peace, 2016, http://www.systemicpeace.org/inscr/CSPCoupsCodebook2015.pdf.

9. This is also the approach taken to modeling coups in Varun Piplani and Caitlin Talmadge, "When War Helps Civil-Military Relations: Prolonged Interstate Conflict and the Reduced Risk of Coups," *Journal of Conflict Resolution* 60, no. 8 (2015): 1368–1394; Leonardo R. Arriola, "Patronage and Political Stability in Africa," *Comparative Political Studies* 42, no. 10 (2009): 1339–1362; and Clayton L. Thyne, "Supporter of Stability or Agent of Agitation? The Effect of US Foreign Policy on Coups in Latin America, 1960–99," *Journal of Peace Research* 47, no. 4 (2010): 449–461.

10. Barbara Geddes, Joseph Wright, and Erica Frantz, "Autocratic Breakdown and Regime Transitions: A New Data Set," *Perspectives on Politics* 12, no. 2 (2014): 313–331; Barbara Geddes, "What Do We Know About Democratization after Twenty Years?" *Annual Review of Political Science* 2: 115–144; Thyne, "Supporter of Stability or Agent of Agitation?"; Staffan I. Lindberg And and John F. Clark, "Does Democratization Reduce the Risk of Military Interventions in Politics in Africa?" *Democratization* 15, no. 1 (2008): 86–105.

11. Paul Collier and Anke Hoeffler, "Military Spending and the Risks of Coups d'État" (working paper, Centre for the Study of African Economies, Oxford University, 2007); William R. Thompson, "Regime Vulnerability and the Military Coup," *Comparative Politics* 7, no. 4 (1975): 459–487; Eric A. Nordlinger, *Soldiers in Politics: Military Coups and Governments* (Englewood Cliffs, NJ: Prentice-Hall, 1977); Gabriel Leon, "Military Loyalty for Sale? Military Spending and Coups d'État," *Public Choice* 159, no. 3–4 (2014): 363–383.

12. Holger Albrecht and Ferdinand Eibl, "How to Keep Officers in the Barracks: Causes, Agents, and Types of Military Coups," *International Studies Quarterly* 62, no. 2 (2018): 319.

13. J. David Singer, Stuart Bremer, and John Stuckey, "Capability Distribution, Uncertainty, and War, 1820–1965," in *Peace, War, and Numbers*, ed. Bruce Russett (Beverly Hills, CA: Sage, 1972), 19–48.

14. Henry Bienen, "Foreign Policy, the Military, and Development: Military Assistance and Political Change in Africa," in *Foreign Policy and the Developing Nations*, ed. R. Butwell (Lexington: University Press of Kentucky, 1969), 67–111; Jonathan Powell, "Determinants of the Attempting and Outcome of Coups d'État," *Journal of Conflict Resolution* 56, no. 6 (2012): 1017–1040.

15. Rosemary H. T. O'Kane, "A Probabilistic Approach to the Causes of Coups d'État," *British Journal of Political Science* 11, no. 3 (1981): 287–308; John B. Londregan and Keith T. Poole, "Poverty, the Coup Trap, and the Seizure of Executive Power," *World Politics* 42, no. 2 (1990): 151–183; Collier and Hoeffler, "Military Spending and the Risk of Coups."

16. Alexander Galetovic and Ricardo Sanhueza, "Citizens, Autocrats, and Plotters: A Model and New Evidence on Coups d'État," *Economics and Politics* 12, no. 2 (2000): 183–204.

17. The measures come from Kristian Skrede Gleditsch, "Expanded Trade and GDP Data," *Journal of Conflict Resolution* 46, no. 5 (2002): 712–724.

18. Edward Luttwak, *Coup d'État: A Practical Handbook* (Cambridge, MA: Harvard University Press, 1979); Samuel E. Finer, *The Man on Horseback: The Role of the Military in*

Politics (New York: Praeger, 2002). The data on instability comes from Arthur Banks, Cross-National Time-Series Data Archive (Binghamton, NY: Computer Systems Unlimited, 2001).

19. Jeff Colgan, "Measuring Revolution," *Conflict Management and Peace Science* 29, no. 4 (2012): 444–467.

20. E.g., Londregan and Poole, "Poverty, the Coup Trap"; Aaron Belkin and Evan Schofer, "Toward a Structural Understanding of Coup Risk," *Journal of Conflict Resolution* 47, no. 5 (2003): 594–620; Powell, "Determinants of the Attempting and Outcome"; Collier and Hoeffler, "Military Spending and the Risk of Coup."

21. Nathaniel Beck, Jonathan Katz, and Richard Tucker, "Beyond Ordinary Logit: Taking Time Seriously in Binary-Time-Series-Cross-Section Models," *American Journal of Political Science* 42, no. 2 (1998): 1260–1288.

22. Janet M. Box-Steffensmeier and Bradford S. Jones, "Time Is of the Essence: Event History Models in Political Science," *American Journal of Political Science* 41, no. 4 (1997): 1414–1461; Janet M. Box-Steffensmeier and Bradford S. Jones, *Event History Modeling: A Guide for Social Scientists* (Cambridge: Cambridge University Press, 2004).

23. Box-Steffensmeier and Jones, *Event History Modeling*.

24. Aaron Belkin and Evan Schofer, "Coup Risk, Counterbalancing, and International Conflict," *Security Studies* 14, no. 1 (2005): 144.

25. Aaron Belkin, *United We Stand? Divide-and-Conquer Politics and the Logic of International Hostility* (Albany: State University of New York Press, 2005), 76.

26. Ulrich Pilster and Tobias Böhmelt, "Do Democracies Engage Less in Coup-Proofing? On the Relationship between Regime Type and Civil-Military Relations," *Foreign Policy Analysis* 8, no. 4 (2012): 355–372.

27. Jun Koga Sudduth, "Coup Risk, Coup-Proofing, and Leader Survival," *Journal of Peace Research* 54, no. 1 (2017): 6; Jun Koga Sudduth, "Strategic Logic of Elite Purges in Dictatorships," *Comparative Political Studies* 50, no. 13 (2017): 1768–1801.

28. In particular, Jendayi Elizabeth Frazer argues, in "Sustaining Civilian Control: Armed Counterweights in Regime Stability in Africa" (PhD diss., Stanford University, 1994), that the period following a successful armed struggle for independence is one in which rulers can remake the military and other coercive institutions without opposition. Similarly, Bruce W. Farcau, in *The Coup: Tactics in the Seizure of Power* (Westport, CT: Praeger, 1994), points to the years following a successful revolution as ones in which new counterweights might be created.

29. The data on regime type comes from Geddes, Wright, and Frantz, "Autocratic Breakdown."

30. Gregory Bart Weeks, *The Military and Politics in Postauthoritarian Chile* (Tuscaloosa: University of Alabama Press, 2003).

31. Donald Horowitz, *Ethnic Groups in Conflict* (Berkeley: University of California Press, 1985); Hillel Frisch, "Explaining Third World Security Structures," *Journal of Strategic Studies* 25, no. 3 (2002): 161–190.

32. Milan Svolik, "Contracting on Violence: The Moral Hazard in Authoritarian Repression and Military Intervention in Politics," *Journal of Conflict Resolution* 57, no. 5 (2013): 765–794.

33. The indicator for civil conflict is a binary variable equal to 1 where a civil conflict results in at least twenty-five fatalities in a given year; it comes from Nils Petter Gleditsch, Peter Wallensteen, Mikael Eriksson, Margareta Sollenberg, and Håvard Strand, "Armed Conflict 1946–2001: A New Dataset," *Journal of Peace Research* 39, no. 5 (2002): 615–637. Interstate conflict is a binary indicator for whether a fatal Militarized Interstate Dispute (MID) is ongoing; from Glenn Palmer, Vito d'Orazio, Michael Kenwick, and Matthew

Lane, "The MID4 Dataset, 2002–2010: Procedures, Coding Rules and Description," *Conflict Management and Peace Science* 32, no. 2 (2015): 222–242.

5. CHALLENGES TO BUILDING COERCIVE INSTITUTIONS

1. Bruce W. Farcau, *The Coup: Tactics in the Seizure of Power* (Westport, CT: Praeger, 1994), 192–193; Jendayi Elizabeth J. Frazer, "Sustaining Civilian Control: Armed Counterweights in Regime Stability in Africa" (PhD diss., Stanford University, 1994). Specifically, Farcau contends that militia formation will be easier in the wake of a revolution.

2. Claude Welch, *Civilian Control of the Military: Theory and Cases from Developing Countries* (Albany: State University of New York Press, 1976); Simon J. Baynham, "Soldier and State in Ghana," *Armed Forces and Society* 5, no. 1 (1978): 155–168.

3. Beth S. Rabinowitz, *Coups, Rivals, and the Modern State: Why Rural Coalitions Matter in Sub-Saharan Africa* (Cambridge: Cambridge University Press, 2018), 120–129.

4. Jon Kraus, "Arms and Politics in Ghana," in *Soldier and State in Africa: A Comparative Analysis of Military Intervention and Political Change*, ed. Claude E. Welch Jr. (Evanston, IL: Northwestern University Press, 1970), 180.

5. Kraus, 180.

6. Quoted in Simon J. Baynham, *The Military and Politics in Nkrumah's Ghana* (Boulder, CO: Westview Press, 1988), 131.

7. Simon Baynham, "Quis Custodiet Ipsos Custodes? The Case of Nkrumah's National Security Service," *Journal of Modern African Studies* 23, no. 1 (1985): 91; Baynham, *The Military and Politics*, 128–129; Rabinowitz, *Coups, Rivals, and the Modern State*, 135; U.S. National Archives II (USNA), Department of State Central Files, Record Group (RG) 59, Central Foreign Policy File, 1963, POL 15-1 Ghana, "Ghana Assassination Rumor," April 5, 1963.

8. Baynham, "Quis Custodiet Ipsos Custodes?," 87–103; Ama Barbara Biney, "Kwame Nkrumah: An Intellectual Biography" (PhD diss., University of London, 2007), 176; Naomi Chazan, "Ethnicity and Politics in Ghana," *Political Science Quarterly* 97, no. 3 (1982): 461.

9. USNA, RG 59, Central Foreign Policy Files, 1964–1966, POL 15-1 Ghana, "Is Nkrumah Attempting to Buy the Presidential Guard's Loyalty?," February 27, 1964.

10. Seth Anthony, "The State of Ghana," *African Affairs* 68, no. 273 (1969): 337–339.

11. Akwasi Amankwaa Afrifa, *The Ghana Coup: 24th February 1966* (London: Frank Cass, 1967), 99.

12. Henry L. Bretton, *The Rise and Fall of Kwame Nkrumah* (New York: Praeger, 1966), 104.

13. Afrifa, *The Ghana Coup*, 100.

14. Albert Kwesi Ocran, *A Myth Is Broken: An Account of the Ghana Coup d'État of 24 February 1966* (London: Longmans, 1968), 37.

15. Baynham, *The Military and Politics*, 197.

16. Kraus, "Arms and Politics," 185.

17. Kwame Nkrumah, *Dark Days in Ghana* (New York: International, 1968), 39.

18. Baynham, *The Military and Politics*, 198; Bretton, *The Rise and Fall*, 63.

19. USNA, RG 59, Central Foreign Policy Files, 1964–1966, POL 23-9 Ghana, Telegram from Accra to Department of State, July 12, 1965; Baynham, *The Military and Politics*, 137–138; Rabinowitz, *Coups, Rivals, and the Modern State*, 132.

20. Baynham, *The Military and Politics*, 138.

21. Ocran, *A Myth Is Broken*, 30, 33.

22. Baynham, *The Military and Politics*, 142; Afrifa, *The Ghana Coup*, 86.

23. Lloyd Garrison, "Coup in Ghana: Elaborately Organized Upheaval," *New York Times*, March 5, 1966; Nkrumah, *Dark Days in Ghana*, 47.

24. Henry L. Bretton, "The Overthrow of Kwame Nkrumah," in *Problems in International Relations*, 3rd ed., ed. Andrew George, Hubert S. Gibbs, and Robert S. Jordan (Englewood Cliffs, NJ: Prentice-Hall, 1970), 289.

25. Baynham, *The Military and Politics*, 181–185; Chazan, "Ethnicity and Politics in Ghana," 461; Garrison, "Coup in Ghana," 2; Kraus, "Arms and Politics," 154.

26. USNA, RG 59, Central Foreign Policy Files, 1964–1966, POL 15-1 Ghana, Telegram from Accra to the Department of State, February 28, 1966; National Liberation Council, *The Rebirth of Ghana, the End of Tyranny* (Accra: Ministry of Information and Broadcasting, 1966), 25.

27. USNA, RG 59, Central Foreign Policy Files, 1964–1966, POL 15 Ghana, Telegram from Accra to Department of State, March 11, 1966.

28. Kwame Nkrumah, interview by Douglas Rogers, April 12, 1966, transcript, Moorland-Spingarn Research Center, Howard University, Washington, DC; Nkrumah, *Dark Days in Ghana*, 44.

29. Afrifa, *The Ghana Coup*, 33; Lloyd Garrison, "Army in Control after Ghana Coup Topples Nkrumah," *New York Times*, February 25, 1966; Kwame Nkrumah, "Second Address to the People of Ghana," March 13, 1966, Moorland-Spingarn Research Center, Howard University, Washington, DC.

30. USNA, RG 59, Central Foreign Policy Files, 1964–1967, Telegram from Accra to Department of State, February 25, 1966.

31. Baynham, *The Military and Politics*, 183; Garrison, "Army in Control," 1; Bob Fitch and Mary Oppenheimer, *Ghana: End of an Illusion* (New York: Monthly Review Press, 1966), 2.

32. Baynham, 148. Similarly, Kraus concludes, "Based on the coup leaders' comments, it is difficult to resist the thought that the most important reason for the coup was the army's fear that it was gradually being opposed and replaced by the POGR" (see Kraus, "Arms and Politics," 185).

33. Quoted in Nkrumah, *Dark Days in Ghana*, 47.

34. Walter Barrows, *Grassroots Politics in an African State: Integration and Development in Sierra Leone* (New York: Africana/Holmes, 1976); David Keen, *Conflict and Collusion in Sierra Leone* (Martlesham, UK: James Currey, 2005); Anton Bebler, *Military Rule in Africa: Dahomey, Ghana, Sierra Leone, and Mali* (New York: Praeger, 1973), 64.

35. Jimmy D. Kandeh, "Politicization of Ethnic Identities in Sierra Leone," *African Studies Review* 35, no. 1 (1992): 81–99; Kristen A. Harkness, *When Soldiers Rebel: Ethnic Armies and Political Instability in Africa* (Cambridge: Cambridge University Press, 2018).

36. E. D. A. Turay and A. Abraham, *The Sierra Leone Army: A Century of History* (London: Macmillan, 1987), 103.

37. Quoted in Turay and Abraham, *The Sierra Leone Army*, 107.

38. Bebler, *Military Rule in Africa*, 67, 68–71.

39. Quoted in Humphrey J. Fisher, "Elections and Coups in Sierra Leone, 1967," *Journal of Modern African Studies* 7, no. 4 (1969): 631; TNA FCO 38/33 17, Telegram from Freetown to Commonwealth Office, March 24, 1967.

40. Turay and Abraham, *The Sierra Leone Army*, 133; Thomas S. Cox, *Civil-Military Relations in Sierra Leone: A Case Study of African Soldiers in Politics* (Cambridge, MA: Harvard University Press, 1976), 198.

41. C. Magbaily Fyle, *Historical Dictionary of Sierra Leone* (Lanham, MD: Scarecrow Press, 2006), xli; Fisher, "Elections and Coups"; TNA FCO 38/44 106, Sierra Leone: The Army Mutiny and Its Aftermath, July 8, 1968.

42. Quoted in *Daily Mail*, April 19, 1968, 1.

43. U.S. National Archives II (USNA), Department of State Central Files, Record Group (RG) 59, Central Foreign Policy Files, 1967–1969, POL 23-9 S Leone, "Private Morlai Ka-

mara and the Coup in Sierra Leone," May 1, 1968; USNA, RG 59, Central Foreign Policy Files, 1967–1969, POL 23-9 S Leone, "Sierra Leone: The Sergeants' Putsch," Intelligence Note, April 18, 1968.

44. John R. Cartwright, *Politics in Sierra Leone, 1947–1967* (Toronto: University of Toronto Press, 1970).

45. David Harris, *Sierra Leone: A Political History* (New York: Oxford University Press, 2014), 63.

46. Fyle, *Historical Dictionary of Sierra Leone*, xli; Harris, *Sierra Leone*, 64; Cox, *Civil-Military Relations in Sierra Leone*, 210–211.

47. TNA FCO 38/46 63, Sierra Leone, August 6, 1968.

48. Harkness, *When Soldiers Rebel*, 98–99.

49. Cox, *Civil-Military Relations in Sierra Leone*, 209.

50. TNA FCO 38/46 65, Round-Up from High Commission to Sierra Leone, August 9, 1968; TNA FCO 38/46 66, Round-Up from High Commission to Sierra Leone, August 16, 1968; Kandeh, "Politicization of Ethnic Identities"; Keen, *Conflict and Collusion*.

51. Mac Dixon-Fyle, "Reflections on the Role of the Military in Civilian Politics: The Case of Sierra Leone," *Australian Journal of Politics and History* 35, no. 2 (1989): 214.

52. USNA, RG 59, Central Foreign Policy Files, 1970–1973, POL 2 S Leone, Airgram from Robert Graham Miner, Ambassador to Sierra Leone, to Secretary of State, "The Uncertain Present," February 18, 1971.

53. USNA, RG 59, Central Foreign Policy Files, 1970–1973, POL 2 S Leone, Telegram from Robert Graham Miner, Ambassador to Sierra Leone, to Department of State, "Recent Developments," January 28, 1971.

54. USNA, RG 59, Central Foreign Policy Files, 1970–1973, POL 23-9 S Leone, "Sierra Leone: Guinean Involvement and Accusations of US," Intelligence Note, April 5, 1971; Cox, *Civil-Military Relations in Sierra Leone*, 213–214. There was some debate as to whether the coup itself was timed when it was because of reports that Guinean troops were arriving; this prospect was based on the inauspicious date—the fourth anniversary of a very unpopular coup of 1968 and, as a result, as the American Ambassador to Sierra Leone noted, the "last date anyone in his right mind would have chosen for another military putsch." See USNA, RG 59, Central Foreign Policy Files, 1970–1973, POL 23-9 S Leone, Telegram from Robert Graham Miner, Ambassador to Sierra Leone, to Secretary of State, March 30, 1971.

55. Quoted in *Africa Contemporary Record (ACR), 1971–1972* (New York: Africana Publishing, 1981), B681.

56. Harkness, *When Soldiers Rebel*, 99–101; Turay and Abraham, *The Sierra Leone Army*, 136–139.

57. Keen, *Conflict and Collusion*, 16, 17; Herbert M. Howe, *Ambiguous Order: Military Forces in African States* (Boulder, CO: Lynne Rienner, 2001), 44.

58. Truth and Reconciliation Commission [TRC], Sierra Leone, *Witness to Truth*, vol. 3A (Accra: Graphic Packaging, 2004), 76.

59. Quoted in TRC, *Witness to Truth*, 26.

60. C. Magbaily Fyle, "The Military and Civil Society in Sierra Leone: The 1992 Military Coup d'État," *African Development* 19, no. 2 (1994): 129; USNA, RG 59, Central Foreign Policy Files, 1970–1973, POL 2 S Leone, Telegram from Robert Graham Miner, Ambassador to Sierra Leone, to Department of State, "Assessment of Political Situation in Sierra Leone," August 6, 1971; TRC, *Witness to Truth*, 26; Erland Grøner Krogstad, "Security, Development, and Force: Revisiting Police Reform in Sierra Leone," *African Affairs* 111, no. 443 (2012): 274; Cox, *Civil-Military Relations in Sierra Leone*, 216.

61. USNA, RG 59, Central Foreign Policy Files, 1970–1973, POL 23 S Leone, Telegram from US Embassy Freetown to Department of State, "GOSL Security Forces—Recent

Developments," January 2, 1973; Turay and Abraham, *The Sierra Leone Army*, 154–155; Dixon-Fyle, "Role of the Military," 214.

62. USNA, RG 59, Central Foreign Policy Files, 1970–1973, POL 23 S Leone, Telegram from US Embassy Freetown to Department of State, "GOSL Security Forces," December 5, 1972; David Fasholé Luke, "Continuity in Sierra Leone: From Stevens to Momoh," *Third World Quarterly* 10, no. 1 (1988): 71; Fyle, *Historical Dictionary of Sierra Leone*, 5.

63. Dixon-Fyle, "Role of the Military," 215.

64. Turay and Abraham, *The Sierra Leone Army*, 155; Fyle, "The Military and Civil Society," 129.

65. Keen, *Conflict and Collusion*, 22.

66. Fyle, "The Military and Civil Society," 129.

67. Luke, "Continuity in Sierra Leone," 71.

68. Dixon-Fyle, "Role of the Military," 215.

69. Farcau, *The Coup*, 193.

70. Richard Vengroff and Moctar Kone, "Mali: Democracy and Political Change," in *Democracy and Political Change in Sub-Saharan Africa*, ed. John A. Wiseman (London: Routledge, 1995), 45.

71. Anatole Ayissi and Nouhoum Sangare, "Mali," in *Budgeting for the Military Sector in Africa: The Process and Mechanisms of Control*, ed. Wuyi Omitoogun and Eboe Hutchful (New York: Oxford University Press, 2006), 123.

72. USNA, RG 59, Central Foreign Policy Files, 1967–1969, DEF 6 Mali, "Security Forces of the Republic of Mali," March 13, 1967; Bret L. Billet, "The Precipitants of African Coups d'État: A Case Study of the 1968 Malian Coup" (paper presented at the International Studies Association Annual Convention, St. Louis, Missouri, March 29–April 2, 1988); Gregory Mann, "Violence, Dignity, and Mali's New Model Army, 1960–68," *Mande Studies* 5 (2003): 74.

73. Pascal James Imperato, *Mali: A Search for Direction* (Boulder, CO: Westview Press, 1989), 61; Vengroff and Kone, "Mali," 45–46; Billet, "The Precipitants of African Coups."

74. USNA, RG 59, Central Foreign Policy Files, 1967–1969, POL 1 Mali-US, "Political-Economic Policy Assessment for Mali," March 6, 1967.

75. Vengroff and Kone, "Mali," 46.

76. Mann, "Violence, Dignity, and Mali's New Model Army," 66.

77. Bebler, *Military Rule in Africa*, 82; Pascal James Imperato and Gavin H. Imperato, *Historical Dictionary of Mali*, 4th ed. (Lanham, MD: Scarecrow Press, 2008), 74.

78. Billet, "The Precipitants of African Coups," 15, 16.

79. Mann, "Violence, Dignity, and Mali's New Model Army," 69

80. USNA, RG 59, Central Foreign Policy Files, 1967–1969, POL 23-9 Mali, "Mali: The Military Takes Over," Intelligence Note, November 20, 1968.

81. USNA, RG 59, Central Foreign Policy Files, 1967–1969, DEF 6 Mali, "Security Forces of the Republic of Mali," March 13, 1967; Bebler, *Military Rule in Africa*, 85; Miles D. Wolpin, "Dependency and Conservative Militarism in Mali," *Journal of Modern African Studies* 13, no. 4 (1975): 601; Imperato and Imperato, *Historical Dictionary of Mali*, 170.

82. Michael G. Schatzberg, "The Coup and After: Continuity or Change in Malian Politics?," Occasional Paper No. 5, African Studies Program (Madison: University of Wisconsin, 1972), 3.

83. Francis Gregory Snyder, "The Keita Decade 1: An Era Ends in Mali," *Africa Report* 14, no. 3 (1969): 16–22; Imperato, *Mali*, 62; Billet, "The Precipitants of African Coups," 15.

84. Quoted in Mann, "Violence, Dignity, and Mali's New Model Army," 69.

85. Schatzberg, "The Coup and After," 3.

86. Wolpin, "Dependency and Conservative Militarism in Mali," 610.

87. Imperato, *Mali*, 62; see also Billet, "The Precipitants of African Coups," 17; Victor T. Le Vine, *Politics in Francophone Africa* (Boulder, CO: Lynne Rienner, 2004), 236; Imperato and Imperato, *Historical Dictionary of Mali*, 70.

88. Bebler, *Military Rule in Africa*, 88. Similarly, Wolpin, "Dependency and Conservative Militarism in Mali," 616, argues, "To junior officers with insecure careers due to counterrevolutionary sentiments, and/or a desire to be able to overthrow the civilian government in the future, the Milice populaire certainly did constitute a genuine long-term threat."

89. USNA, RG 59, Central Foreign Policy Files, 1967–1969, POL 23-9 Mali, "Mali: The Military Takes Over," Intelligence Note, November 20, 1968.

90. USNA, RG 59, Central Foreign Policy Files, 1967–1969, POL 23-9 Mali, Telegram from Bamako to the Department of State, November 20, 1968.

91. Quoted in Imperato, *Mali*, 63; Wolpin, "Dependency and Conservative Militarism in Mali," 611; Valerie Plave Bennett, "Military Government in Mali," *Journal of Modern African Studies* 13, no. 2 (1975): 252; Robert Legvold, *Soviet Policy in West Africa* (Cambridge, MA: Harvard University Press, 1970), 299.

92. Bebler, *Military Rule in Africa*, 81.

93. Hugh Thomas, *The Cuban Revolution* (New York: Harper and Row, 1977), 215.

94. Michael Mazarr, "The Cuban Security Apparatus," in *Cuba: The International Dimension*, ed. Georges Fauriol and Eva Loser (New Brunswick, NJ: Transaction, 1990), 261; Defense Intelligence Agency, *Handbook on the Cuban Armed Forces* (Washington, DC: Defense Intelligence Agency, 1979).

95. These included Castro's 26 July Movement along with competing groups such as the Revolutionary Directorate, the Cuban Communist Party, and Organizacion Autentica. See Mazarr, "The Cuban Security Apparatus," 261; Rafael Fermoselle, *The Evolution of the Cuban Military: 1492–1986* (Miami: Ediciones Universal, 1987), 266–267.

96. Mazarr, "The Cuban Security Apparatus," 262–263.

97. Frank O. Mora, "Cuba's Ministry of Interior: The FAR's Fifth Army," *Bulletin of Latin American Research* 26, no. 2 (2007): 224.

98. Thomas, *The Cuban Revolution*, 543; Memorandum from Benjamin Stephansky of the Office of Inter-American Regional Political Affairs to the Deputy Assistant Secretary of State for Inter-American Affairs (Snow), April 30, 1959, in *Foreign Relations of the United States* [hereafter *FRUS*], *1958–1960, Cuba*, vol. 6, ed. John P. Glennon (Washington, DC: Government Printing Office, 1991), Document 299.

99. Report Prepared by a Combined Working Group from the Bureau of Intelligence and Research of the Department of State and the Office of National Estimates of the Central Intelligence Agency, May 2, 1961, in *FRUS, 1961–1963*, vol. 10, *Cuba, January 1961–September 1962*, ed. Louis J. Smith (Washington, DC: Government Printing Office, 1997), Document 194.

100. USNA, RG 59, Central Decimal File, 1960–63, 737.554, "Militias Organized on National Basis," January 29, 1960; Mazarr, "The Cuban Security Apparatus," 262.

101. Phyllis Greene Walker, "Political-Military Relations since 1959," in *Conflict and Change in Cuba*, ed. Enrique A. Baloyra and James A. Morris (Albuquerque: University of New Mexico Press, 1993), 117.

102. Quoted in Thomas, *The Cuban Revolution*, 466.

103. Walker, "Political-Military Relations," 117; Thomas, *The Cuban Revolution*, 478.

104. William M. LeoGrande, "The Politics of Revolutionary Development: Civil-Military Relations in Cuba, 1959–1976," *Journal of Strategic Studies* 1, no. 3 (1978): 260–294.

105. Jack B. Pfeiffer, *The Official History of the Bay of Pigs Operation, vol. 3: Evolution of CIA's Anti-Castro Policies, 1951–January 1961* (Langley, VA: Central Intelligence Agency,

1979), 25; *Alleged Assassination Plots Involving Foreign Leaders,* Interim Report of the Select Committee to Study Governmental Operations with Respect to Intelligence Activities, United States Senate, Church Committee (Washington, DC: U.S. Government Printing Office, 1975), 116.

106. "Cuba and Communism in the Hemisphere," Paper Prepared for the National Security Council by an Interagency Task Force on Cuba, May 4, 1961, in *FRUS, 1961–1963,* vol. 10, *Cuba, January 1961–September 1962,* Document 202.

107. Walker, "Political-Military Relations," 199.

108. Mazarr, "The Cuban Security Apparatus," 266.

109. Mazarr, "The Cuban Security Apparatus," 264.

110. Walker, "Political-Military Relations," 120.

111. Mora, "Cuba's Ministry of Interior," 225.

112. Mora, 227.

113. Mora, 222.

114. Defense Intelligence Agency, *Handbook on the Cuban Armed Forces,* 3-14; Eugene Rothman, *Securing the Future: A Blueprint for the Reconstruction of the Cuban Security Sector* (Miami: Cuba Transitions Project, 2003), 9.

115. Rothman, *Securing the Future,* 9.

116. Defense Intelligence Agency, *Handbook on the Cuban Armed Forces,* 3-14; also see Fermoselle, *Evolution of the Cuban Military,* 332.

117. Defense Intelligence Agency, *Handbook on the Cuban Armed Forces,* 2-45.

118. Walker, "Political-Military Relations," 118.

6. HOW COUPS D'ÉTAT ESCALATE TO CIVIL WAR

1. Samuel E. Finer, *The Man on Horseback: The Role of the Military in Politics* (New York: Praeger, 2002), 154.

2. Edward Luttwak, *Coup d'État: A Practical Handbook* (Cambridge, MA: Harvard University Press, 1979), 158.

3. Naunihal Singh, *Seizing Power: The Strategic Logic of Military Coups* (Baltimore: Johns Hopkins University Press, 2014), 34.

4. Luttwak, *Coup d'État;* Barbara Geddes, "What Do We Know about Democratization after Twenty Years?," *Annual Review of Political Science* 2, no. 1 (1999): 115–144; Barbara Geddes, "Authoritarian Breakdown" (unpublished manuscript, January 2004), PDF file, http://pages.ucsd.edu/~mnaoi/page4/POLI227/files/page1_11.pdf

5. Fred Halliday, *Arabia without Sultans* (London: Penguin, 1974), 118. Throughout, I refer to the territory in which the 1962 coup and initial stages of the civil war occurred as "Yemen." The coup plotters who seized power renamed it the "Yemen Arab Republic," and it eventually also became known as "North Yemen." I use "Yemen" because that is what the territory was called in 1962.

6. Quoted in Stephen G. Rabe, "The Caribbean Triangle: Betancourt, Castro, and Trujillo and US Foreign Policy, 1958–1963," *Diplomatic History* 20, no. 1 (1996): 58.

7. José A. Moreno, *Barrios in Arms: Revolution in Santo Domingo* (Pittsburgh: University of Pittsburgh Press, 1970); G. Pope Atkins and Larman Curtis Wilson, *The Dominican Republic and the United States: From Imperialism to Transnationalism* (Athens: University of Georgia Press, 1998).

8. U.S. National Archives II (USNA), Department of State Central Files, Record Group (RG) 59, Decimal File, 1960–6, 739.00/1-1262, Telegram from the Department of State to the American Consul in Santo Domingo, January 12, 1962.

9. Norman Gall, "Anatomy of a Coup: The Fall of Juan Bosch," *The Nation* 26 (October 26, 1963): 255.

10. USNA, RG 59, Decimal File, 1960–196, 739.00/12-2262, Telegram from the Navy Attaché in Santo Domingo, December 22, 1962.

11. Theodore Draper, *The Dominican Revolt: A Case Study in American Policy* (New York: Commentary, 1968); Richard A. Haggerty, ed., *Dominican Republic: A Country Study* (Washington, DC: Federal Research Division, Library of Congress, 1989).

12. Memorandum Prepared in the Central Intelligence Agency, President Bosch and Internal Security in the Dominican Republic, June 14, 1963, *Foreign Relations of the United States* [hereafter *FRUS*], *1961–1963*, vol. 12, *American Republics*, ed. Edward C. Keefer, Harriet Dashiell Schwar, and W. Taylor Fain III (Washington, DC: Government Printing Office, 1996), Document 356.

13. Atkins and Wilson, *The Dominican Republic*, 136.

14. Giancarlo Soler Torrijos, *In the Shadow of the United States: Democracy and Regional Order in the Latin Caribbean* (Boca Raton, FL: Brown Walker Press, 2008), 60.

15. *FRUS, 1961–1963*, vol. 12, *American Republics*, Document 356.

16. Abraham F. Lowenthal, *The Dominican Intervention* (Baltimore: Johns Hopkins University Press, 1995); Dan Kurzman, "Service Rivalries Peril Dominican Junta Rule," *Washington Post*, October 25, 1963.

17. Draper, *The Dominican Revolt*, 3; Rabe, "The Caribbean Triangle," 65.

18. Howard J. Wiarda, "The Politics of Civil-Military Relations in the Dominican Republic," *Journal of Inter-American Studies* 7, no. 4 (1965): 480.

19. Atkins and Wilson, *The Dominican Republic*, 136; Edwin Lieuwen, *Generals vs. Presidents: Neomilitarism in Latin America* (New York: Praeger, 1964), 61, also notes concern among some soldiers that urban and rural labor organizations Bosch supported could grow to serve as unarmed "counterpoises" to the military.

20. Testimony of Brigadier General Elías Wessin y Wessin, *Hearing before the Subcommittee to Investigate the Administration of the Internal Security Act and Other Internal Security Laws of the Committee on the Judiciary, United States Senate*, 89th Congress, First Session, October 1, 1965 (Washington, DC: Government Printing Office, 1965), 122.

21. Henry Raymont, "Clashes of Personality Evident behind the Ouster of Bosch," *New York Times*, September 26, 1963.

22. Quoted in Draper, *The Dominican Revolt*, 5.

23. Gall, "Anatomy of a Coup," 255.

24. Jerome Slater, "The United States, the Organization of American States, and the Dominican Republic, 1961–1963," *International Organization* 18, no. 2 (1964): 268–291.

25. Airgram from the Embassy in the Dominican Republic to the Department of State, September 22, 1963, "Six Months in a Quandary," *FRUS, 1961–1963*, vol. 12, *American Republics*, Document 357.

26. Raymont, "Clashes of Personality"; Lieuwen, *Generals vs. Presidents*; Atkins and Wilson, *The Dominican Republic*; Abraham F. Lowenthal, "The Political Role of the Dominican Armed Forces: A Note on the 1963 Overthrow of Juan Bosch and on the 1965 Dominican 'Revolution,'" *Journal of Interamerican Studies and World Affairs* 15, no. 3 (1973): 356; "Bosch Is Ousted in Coup," *Washington Post*, September 26, 1963.

27. Lieuwen, *Generals vs. Presidents*, 53–54.

28. "Military Seizes Dominican Rule; Bosch Is Deposed," *New York Times*, September 26, 1963.

29. Lowenthal, "Political Role of the Dominican Armed Forces," 359–360.

30. Telegram from John Marlow Martin to the Secretary of State, No. 245, September 26, 1963, Papers of John F. Kennedy, Presidential Papers, National Security Files, Countries, Dominican Republic: Cables, September 1963: 26–27, JFKNSF-067-013, John F. Kennedy Presidential Library and Museum.

31. Piero Gleijeses, *The Dominican Crisis: The Constitutionalist Revolt and American Intervention*, trans. Lawrence Lipson (Baltimore: Johns Hopkins University Press, 1978), 103.

32. Central Intelligence Agency, Special National Intelligence Estimate, January 17, 1964, "Instability and the Insurgency Threat in the Dominican Republic," *FRUS, 1964–1968*, vol. 32, *Dominican Republic, Cuba, Haiti, Guyana*, ed. Daniel Lawler and Carolyn Yee (Washington, DC: Government Printing Office, 2005), Document 1.

33. Henry Raymont, "Dominican Junta Sworn as Police Battle Students," *New York Times*, September 27, 1963; "Dominican 3-Man Rule Is Installed," *Washington Post*, September 27, 1963; "Bosch Is Ousted in Coup; U.S. Halts Dominican Aid," *Washington Post*, September 26, 1963.

34. Gall, "Anatomy of a Coup," 255.

35. Bosch had been alerted to the coup the night before when he received a phone call from the editor of *El Caribe*, an anti-Bosch newspaper in Santo Domingo, asking him to comment on a leaked statement from coup plotters. See Draper, *The Dominican Revolt*, 9.

36. Memorandum from President Kennedy to Secretary of Defense McNamara, October 4, 1963, *FRUS, 1961–1963*, vol. 12, *American Republics*, Document 358; Martin C. Needler, "Political Development and Military Intervention in Latin America," *American Political Science Review* 60, no. 3 (1966): 624; Slater, "United States, the Organization of American States, and the Dominican Republic," 284.

37. "Bosch Is Ousted in Coup"; Raymont, "Dominican Junta Sworn"; R. Hart Phillips, "Softness on Reds Denied by Bosch: He Says Personal Ambition of Foes Caused His Ouster," *New York Times*, October 3, 1963; Slater, "United States, the Organization of American States, and the Dominican Republic," 284.

38. Harry Kantor, "The Dominican Crisis," in *The Lingering Crisis: A Case Study of the Dominican Republic*, ed. Eugenio Chang-Rodriguez (New York: Las Americas Publishing, 1969); Lowenthal, *The Dominican Intervention*.

39. Gleijeses, *The Dominican Crisis*, 129.

40. Telegram from the Joint Army/Navy/Air Force Attachés to the Chief of Naval Operations (McDonald), August 26, 1964, "Appraisal Current Political/Military Situation," *FRUS, 1964–1968*, vol. 32, *Dominican Republic, Cuba, Haiti, Guyana*, Document 13.

41. Airgram from the Embassy in the Dominican Republic to the Department of State, February 19, 1964, "Conversation with Donald Reid," *FRUS, 1964–1968*, vol. 32, *Dominican Republic, Cuba, Haiti, Guyana*, Document 4.

42. USNA, RG 59, Central Foreign Policy Files, 1964–1966, POL 1 DOM REP, "Dominican Political Situation," August 21, 1964.

43. Gleijeses, *The Dominican Crisis*, 126.

44. Quoted in Jan Lundius and Mats Lundahl, *Peasants and Religion: A Socioeconomic Study of Dios Olivorio and the Palma Sola Movement in the Dominican Republic* (London: Routledge, 2000), 692, 693.

45. Wiarda, "Politics of Civil-Military Relations," 477.

46. Memorandum of Conversation, Communists in the Dominican Republic, September 1, 1965, *FRUS, 1964–1968*, vol. 32, *Dominican Republic, Cuba, Haiti, Guyana*, Document 129.

47. Brian J. Bosch, *Balaguer and the Dominican Military: Presidential Control of the Factional Officer Corps in the 1960s and 1970s* (Jefferson, NC: McFarland, 2007), 56.

48. Jerome Slater, *Intervention and Negotiation: The United States and the Dominican Revolution* (New York: Harper and Row, 1970), 19; Moreno, *Barrios in Arms*, 26.

49. Leaders of the coup had planned the intervention for two days later. However, on April 24, the chief of army staff jailed six high-ranking coup plotters. When that happened, the remaining conspirators decided to act. See Moreno, *Barrios in Arms*, 27.

50. Bryant Wedge, "The Case Study of Student Political Violence: Brazil, 1964, and Dominican Republic, 1965," *World Politics* 21, no. 2 (1969): 186.
51. Lowenthal, "Political Role of the Dominican Armed Forces," 357.
52. Lowenthal, *The Dominican Intervention*, 44; Moreno, *Barrios in Arms*.
53. Lowenthal, "Political Role of the Dominican Armed Forces," 357.
54. Gleijeses, *The Dominican Crisis*, 173.
55. John Bartlow Martin, *Overtaken by Events: The Dominican Crisis from the Fall of Trujillo to the Civil War* (Garden City, NY: Doubleday, 1966), 649.
56. Testimony of Brigadier General Elías Wessin y Wessin, 156.
57. Telegram from the White House Situation Room to President Johnson at Camp David, April 25, 1965, *FRUS, 1964–1968*, vol. 32, *Dominican Republic, Cuba, Haiti, Guyana*, Document 21.
58. Bosch, *Balaguer and the Dominican Military*.
59. Wiarda, "Politics of Civil-Military Relations."
60. Lowenthal, *The Dominican Intervention*, 65; Gleijeses, *The Dominican Crisis*, 161; Wedge, "Case Study of Student Political Violence," 205; Bosch, *Balaguer and the Dominican Military*.
61. USNA, RG59, Central Foreign Policy File, 1964–1966, POL 23-9 DOM REP, Telegram from the American Embassy in Santo Domingo to the Department of State, April 26, 1965, 7:59 a.m.
62. Telephone Conversation between Under Secretary of State for Economic Affairs (Mann) and President Johnson, April 26, 1965, *FRUS, 1964–1968*, vol. 32, *Dominican Republic, Cuba, Haiti, Guyana*, Document 22.
63. Gleijeses, *The Dominican Crisis*, 228.
64. Martin, *Overtaken by Events*, 647; Moreno, *Barrios in Arms*, 28–29.
65. Wedge, "Case Study of Student Political Violence," 205.
66. Testimony of Brigadier General Elías Wessin y Wessin, 160, 207–214.
67. Martin, *Overtaken by Events*, 647.
68. Philip Geyelin, *Lyndon Johnson and the World* (New York: Praeger, 1966), 249.
69. Gleijeses, *The Dominican Crisis*, 227.
70. *FRUS, 1964–1968*, vol. 32, *Dominican Republic; Cuba; Haiti; Guyana*, Document 22.
71. Bosch, *Balaguer and the Dominican Military*, 56.
72. Testimony of Juan Isidro Tapia Adames, *Hearing before the Subcommittee to Investigate the Administration of the Internal Security Act and Other Internal Security Laws of the Committee on the Judiciary, United States Senate*, 89th Congress, First Session, October 18, 1965 (Washington, DC: Government Printing Office, 1965), 17.
73. Gleijeses, *The Dominican Crisis*, 257–258.
74. Telegram from the Embassy in the Dominican Republic to the Director of the National Security Agency (Carter), April 28, 1965, *FRUS, 1964–1968*, vol. 32, *Dominican Republic, Cuba, Haiti, Guyana*, Document 32.
75. Mario Beras Mercedes, "Group Armed Themselves from the 'Cascos Blancos' Arsenal," *La Nacion*, May 11, 1965, in Testimony of Brigadier General Elías Wessin y Wessin, *Hearing before the Subcommittee to Investigate the Administration of the Internal Security Act and Other Internal Security Laws of the Committee on the Judiciary, United States Senate*, 89th Congress, First Session, October 1, 1965 (Washington, DC: Government Printing Office, 1965), 41; Charles Roberts, *LBJ's Inner Circle* (New York: Delacorte Press, 1965), 204.
76. U.S. Department of State, "Communist Efforts to Take Over the Revolt in the Dominican Republic," in Testimony of Brigadier General Elías Wessin y Wessin, *Hearing before the Subcommittee to Investigate the Administration of the Internal Security Act and Other Internal Security Laws of the Committee on the Judiciary, United States Senate*,

89th Congress, First Session, October 1, 1965 (Washington, DC: Government Printing Office, 1965), 212.

77. Quoted in Rowland Evans and Robert Novak, *Lyndon B. Johnson: The Exercise of Power* (New York: New American Library, 1966), 514.

78. For an excellent overview of American decision making, see Lindsey A. O'Rourke, *Covert Regime Change: America's Secret Cold War* (Ithaca, NY: Cornell University Press, 2018), 213–219.

79. Moreno, *Barrios in Arms*, 34.

80. Moreno, 29.

81. Lowenthal, "Political Role of the Dominican Armed Forces."

82. Singh, *Seizing Power*; Erica De Bruin, "Will There Be Blood? Explaining Violence During Coups d'État," *Journal of Peace Research* 56, no. 6 (2019): 797–811.

83. Wedge, "Case Study of Student Political Violence," 186.

84. Khaled Fattah, "A Political History of Civil-Military Relations in Yemen," *Alternative Politics*, Special Issue 1 (2010): 28.

85. Asher Aviad Orkaby, "The International History of the Yemen Civil War, 1962–1968" (PhD diss., Harvard University, 2014); Harold Ingrams, *The Yemen: Imams, Rulers, and Revolutions* (London: John Murray, 1963); Robin Bidwell, *The Two Yemens* (Boulder, CO: Westview Press, 1983).

86. USNA, RG 59, Central Decimal File, 1960–6, 786h.00/4-1761, "Reaction in Sana'a to Recent Attempt to Assassinate Imam," April 17, 1961; USNA, RG 59, Central Decimal File, 1960–6, 786h.00/11-1861, Telegram from Taiz to Department of State, November 18, 1961.

87. Zoltan Barany, *The Challenges of Building a National Army in Yemen* (Washington, DC: Center for Strategic and International Studies, 2016), 6–7; Memorandum of Conversation, President's Talk with Crown Prince Faysal, October 15, 1962, *FRUS, 1961–1963*, vol. 18, *Near East, 1962–1963*, ed. Nina J. Noring (Washington, DC: Government Printing Office, 1995), Document 71.

88. Victoria Clark, *Yemen: Dancing on the Heads of Snakes* (New Haven, CT: Yale University Press, 2010), 63; USNA, RG 59, Central Decimal File, 1960–6, 786h.00/10-1762, Airgram from American Legation, Taiz to Department of State, "Popular Participation in the Revolution," October 17, 1962.

89. J. E. Peterson, *Yemen: The Search for a Modern State* (New York: Routledge, 2016), 87.

90. Paper by the Officer in Charge of Arabian Peninsula Affairs (Seelye), "Death of Imam Ahmed Bin Yahya," *FRUS, 1961–1963*, vol. 18, *Near East, 1962–1963*, Document 51.

91. Robert W. Stookey, *Yemen: The Politics of the Yemen Arab Republic* (Boulder, CO: Westview Press, 1978); USNA, RG 59, Central Decimal File, 1960–6, 786H.00/10-162, Telegram from Jidda to Secretary of State, October 1, 1962.

92. Orkaby, "The International History," 43; *FRUS, 1961–1963*, vol. 18, *Near East, 1962–1963*, Document 51. The army itself had some nine thousand men at the time.

93. USNA, RG 59, Central Decimal File, 1960–6, 786h.00/10-1762, Airgram from American Legation, Taiz, to Department of State, "Popular Participation in the Revolution," October 17, 1962.

94. USNA, RG 59, Central Decimal File, 1960–6, 786h.00/9-2762, Telegram from Jidda to Department of State, September 27, 1962; Dana Adams Schmidt, *Yemen: The Unknown War* (London: Bodley Head, 1968), 28–29.

95. Clark, *Yemen*, 63. Edgar O'Ballance, *The War in the Yemen* (Hamden, CT: Shoe String Press, 1971), 67, noted, "One cannot be sure at that stage exactly what Sallal's plans were, but it is usually accepted that he hoped to kill the Imam, raise support for the absent, but very popular, Prince Hassan, and then take advantage of the situation to seize power himself."

96. O'Ballance, *The War in the Yemen*.
97. Clark, *Yemen*, 64–65.
98. USNA, RG 59, Central Decimal File, 1960–6, 786h.00/10-362, Telegram from Aden to Secretary of State, October 3, 1962.
99. Schmidt, *Yemen*, 30; USNA, RG 59, Central Decimal File, 1960–6, 786H.00/10-15662, Telegram from Cairo to Secretary of State, October 15, 1962.
100. O'Ballance, *The War in the Yemen*, 85.
101. USNA, RG 59, Central Decimal File, 1960–6, 786h.00/10-1762, Airgram from American Legation, Taiz, to Department of State, "Popular Participation in the Revolution," October 17, 1962.
102. Schmidt, *Yemen*, 29; O'Ballance, *The War in the Yemen*, 76.
103. O'Ballance, 69.
104. Clark describes the violence graphically: "Forty-six men, among them two of Badr's uncles and his entire council of ministers, were hauled to the main square and killed. Some were shot, some tied to army trucks by their feet and necks, some hacked to pieces with knives. Others were executed and their severed heads nailed to the city walls" (*Yemen*, 65).
105. TNA FCO 370/2859 5, The Yemen Conflict, 1962–1965, April 25, 1966.
106. Paul Dresch, *A History of Modern Yemen* (Cambridge: Cambridge University Press, 2000), 243–244.
107. TNA Prime Minister's Office (PREM) 11/3877 27, Telegram from Foreign Office to Washington, October 22, 1962; USNA, RG 59, Central Decimal File, 1960–6, 786H.00/10-762, Telegram from Taiz to Secretary of State, October 7, 1962.
108. USNA, RG 59, Central Decimal File, 1960–6, 786H.00/10-462, Telegram from Amman to Secretary of State, October 4, 1962; USNA, RG 59, Central Decimal File, 1960–6, 786H.00/10-462, Telegram from London to Secretary of State; October 4, 1962; USNA, RG 59, Central Decimal File, 1960–6, 786H.11/10-462, Telegram from Taiz to Secretary of State, October 4, 1962.
109. USNA, RG 59, Central Decimal File, 1960–6, 786H.00/10-2762, Response to Cable from Imam Muhammed, Memorandum for Mr. George Bundy, the White House, October 27, 1962.
110. Quoted in Schmidt, *Yemen*, 25.
111. Dresch, *A History of Modern Yemen*, 243.
112. Daniel Corstange, "Yemen (1962–1970)," in *Civil Wars of the World: Major Conflicts since World War II*, ed. Karl DeRouen and Uk Heo (Santa Barbara: ABC-CLIO, 2007), 809–827; USNA, RG 59, Central Decimal File, 1960–6, 786H.00/10-562, Implications of the Revolution in Yemen, Memorandum for Mr. McGeorge Bundy, The White House, October 5, 1962; USNA, RG 59, Central Decimal File, 1960–6, 786H.00/10-762, Telegram from Taiz to Secretary of State, October 7, 1962.
113. O'Ballance, *The War in the Yemen*, 80.
114. Schmidt, *Yemen*, 33.
115. O'Ballance, *The War in the Yemen*, 141–142; Corstange, "Yemen (1962–1970)," 811–812. Of course, for some, opportunism prevailed. An article in the *Times* (London) a few years into the war quoted soldiers in the royalist haven in Jizan, a small city just across the Yemeni-Saudi border, joking that they were "royalist by day, republican by night" (*Times*, February 16, 1966, 11).
116. Dresch, *A History of Modern Yemen*, 90; USNA, RG 59, Central Decimal File, 1960–6, 786h.00/10-1762, Airgram from American Legation, Taiz, to Department of State, Popular Participation in the Revolution, October 17, 1962.
117. TNA FCO 370/2859 5, The Yemen Conflict, 1962–1965, April 25, 1966.
118. USNA, RG 59, Central Decimal File, 1960–6, 786H.00/11-562, Telegram from Amman to Secretary of State, November 5, 1962; USNA, RG 59, Central Decimal File, 1960–6,

786H.00/11-762, Legation of the Mutawakelite Kingdom of Yemen to the Secretary of State, November 7, 1962.

119. Halliday, *Arabia without Sultans*, 108.

120. Robert D. Burrowes, *The Yemen Arab Republic: The Politics of Development, 1962–1986* (Boulder, CO: Westview Press, 1987), 23.

CONCLUSION

1. E.g., Juan José Linz and Alfred C. Stepan, eds., *The Breakdown of Democratic Regimes* (Baltimore: Johns Hopkins University Press, 1978); Larry Diamond and Marc F. Plattner, eds., *Civil-Military Relations and Democracy* (Baltimore: Johns Hopkins University Press, 1996); John Samuel Fitch, *The Armed Forces and Democracy in Latin America* (Baltimore: Johns Hopkins University Press, 1998); Eva Bellin, "The Robustness of Authoritarianism in the Middle East: Exceptionalism in Comparative Perspective," *Comparative Politics* 36, no. 2 (2004): 139–157.

2. Daron Acemoglu and James A. Robinson, *Economic Origins of Dictatorship and Democracy* (Cambridge: Cambridge University Press, 2005), 222.

3. E.g., Stephen Biddle and Robert Zirkle, "Technology, Civil-Military Relations, and Warfare in the Developing World," *Journal of Strategic Studies* 19, no. 2 (1996): 171–212; Ulrich Pilster and Tobias Böhmelt, "Coup-Proofing and Military Effectiveness in Interstate Wars, 1967–99," *Conflict Management and Peace Science* 28, no. 4 (2011): 331–350; Steffen Hertog, "Rentier Militaries in the Gulf States: The Price of Coup-Proofing," *International Journal of Middle East Studies* 43 (2011): 400–402; Risa Brooks, "Abandoned at the Palace: Why the Tunisian Military Defected from the Ben Ali Regime in January 2011," *Journal of Strategic Studies* 36, no. 2 (2013): 205–220; Zoltan Barany, "The Role of the Military," *Journal of Democracy* 22, no. 4 (2011): 24–35; Michael Makara, "Coup-Proofing, Military Defection, and the Arab Spring," *Democracy and Security* 9, no. 4 (2013): 334–359.

4. David E. Cunningham, "Veto Players and Civil War Duration," *American Journal of Political Science* 50, no. 4 (2006): 875–892; Kathleen Gallagher Cunningham, "Divide and Conquer or Divide and Concede: How Do States Respond to Internally Divided Separatists?," *American Political Science Review* 105, no. 2 (2011): 275–297; Kristin M. Bakke, Kathleen Gallagher Cunningham, and Lee J. M. Seymour, "A Plague of Initials: Fragmentation, Cohesion, and Infighting in Civil Wars," *Perspectives on Politics* 10, no. (2012): 265–283.

5. E.g., Corinna Jentzsch, Stathis N. Kalyvas, and Livia Isabella Schubiger, "Militias in Civil Wars," *Journal of Conflict Resolution* 59, no. 5 (2015): 755–769; Sabine Carey, Neil Mitchell, and Will Lowe, "States, the Security Sector, and the Monopoly of Violence: A New Data-Base on Pro-Government Militias," *Journal of Peace Research* 50, no. 2 (2013): 249–258.

6. E.g., Holger Albrecht and Ferdinand Eibl, "How to Keep Officers in the Barracks: Causes, Agents, and Types of Military Coups," *International Studies Quarterly* 62, no. 2 (2018): 315–328; Hicham Bou Nassif, "Generals and Autocrats: How Coup-Proofing Behavior Predetermined the Military Elite's Behavior in the Arab Spring," *Political Science Quarterly* 130, no. 2 (2015): 245–275; Peter B. White, "Crisis and Crisis Generations: The Long-Term Impact of International Crises on Military Political Participation," *Security Studies* 26, no. 4 (2017): 575–605; Sharan Grewal, "Military Defection during Localized Protests: The Case of Tatouine," *International Studies Quarterly* 63, no. 2 (2019): 259–269.

7. Andrew Hansen, "The French Military in Africa," Council on Foreign Relations Backgrounder, February 8, 2008, https://www.cfr.org/backgrounder/french-military-africa.

8. Risa A. Brooks, "Integrating the Civil-Military Relations Subfield," *Annual Review of Political Science* 22, no. 20 (2019): 14–15.

9. E.g., Sheena Greitens, *Dictators and Their Secret Police: Coercive Institutions and State Violence* (New York: Oxford University Press, 2018); Caitlin Talmadge, *The Dictator's Army: Battlefield Effectiveness in Authoritarian Regimes* (Ithaca, NY: Cornell University Press, 2015); Ariel I. Ahram, *Proxy Warriors: The Rise and Fall of State-Sponsored Militias* (Stanford, CA: Stanford University Press, 2011).

10. Ernesto Londoño and Nicholas Casey, "Trump Administration Discussed Coup Plans with Rebel Venezuela Officers," *New York Times*, September 8, 2018; Mark Landler and Julian E. Barnes, "With Maduro Still in Power, Questions about the U.S. Role in Venezuela," *New York Times*, May 1, 2019; Anne Gearan, Josh Dawsey, John Hudson, and Seung Min Kim, "A Frustrated Trump Questions His Administration's Venezuela Strategy," *New York Times*, May 8, 2019.

11. Erica De Bruin, "Trump Wants Venezuela's Military to Remove Its President. But Maduro Has Made That Difficult," *Washington Post*, Monkey Cage, May 2, 2019, https://www.washingtonpost.com/politics/2019/05/02/trump-wants-venezuelas-military-remove-its-president-maduro-has-made-that-difficult/.

12. E.g., Biddle and Zirkle, "Technology, Civil-Military Relations, and Warfare"; Talmadge, *The Dictator's Army*.

13. *Economist* Intelligence Unit [EIU], *Sudan: Country Profile, 1998/1999* (London: EIU, 1999), 11.

14. Thomas Bruneau and Harold Trinkunas, "Democratization as a Global Phenomenon and Its Impact on Civil-Military Relations," *Democratization* 13, no. 5 (2006): 784.

15. Jesse Dillon Savage and Jonathan D. Caverley, "When Human Capital Threatens the Capitol: Foreign Aid in the Form of Military Training and Coups," *Journal of Peace Research* 54, no. 4 (2017): 542–557.

APPENDIX

1. Andrew Rosenthal, "Afghans Report Crushing Official's Coup Attempt," *New York Times*, May 7, 1990; Astri Suhrke, "Afghanistan: Retribalization of the War," *Journal of Peace Research* 27, no. 2 (1990): 241–246.

2. Steve Coll, "Afghan Leader Says He Crushes Coup Bid," *Washington Post*, March 7, 1990; Steve Coll, "Afghan Plot Leader Flies to Pakistan; Coup Said to Fizzle," *Washington Post*, March 8, 1990.

3. John F. Burns, "In Power Still, Afghan Can Thank His 4-Star Aide," *New York Times*, May 10, 1990; Fred Halliday and Zahir Tanin, "The Communist Regime in Afghanistan: Institutions and Conflicts," *Europe-Asia Studies* 50, no. 8 (1998): 1357–1380; Diego Cordovez and Selig S. Harrison, *Out of Afghanistan: The Inside Story of the Soviet Withdrawal* (New York: Oxford University Press, 1995).

4. Mark Fineman, "Afghanistan Army Units Attempt Coup; President Najibullah Declares Rebellion Was Crushed by Loyal Forces," *New York Times*, March 7, 1990.

5. Arnhild Arnsten, "The Continuity of Neo-Colonial Practices in a New Context: French Use of Military Means to Promote National Interests in Chad from 2006 until Today" (master's thesis, University of Oslo, 2001); Marc Lacey, "Chadian Forces Repel Rebel Attack on Capital in Intense Combat," *New York Times*, April 14, 2006.

6. "Chad: Deby Hangs On," *Africa Confidential* 47, no. 9 (2006): 5.

7. Marc Lacey, "Family Feud Complicates Revolt over Chad's Leader," *New York Times*, April 21, 2006.

8. Günter Pamminger, "State-Internal Actors in the Armed Conflict in Chad," in *EUFOR Tchad/RCA Revisited*, ed. Walter Feichtinger and Gerald Hainzl (Vienna: National Defense Academy, 2011), 59–84; International Crisis Group, "Chad: Powder Keg in the East," Africa Report No. 149, Nairobi/Brussels, April 15, 2009.

9. Hans Van Dijk, "Political Deadlock in Chad," *African Affairs* 106, no. 425 (2007): 679.

10. John Prendergast, "Sudan, Chad, and the Central African Republic: The Regional Impact of the Darfur Crisis," statement before the U.S. House of Representatives Subcommittee on African Affairs, March 20, 2007, http://www.iccnow.org/documents/Sudan,_Chad,_and_the_Central_African_Republic_The_Regional_Impact_of_the_Darfur_Crisis.pdf; Emily Wax, "Rebels Fight Troops in Chad Capital; Analysts See No Fast Resolution to Crisis," *Washington Post*, April 14, 2006.

11. Arnsten, "Continuity of Neo-Colonial Practices," 50–51; "Chad: Deby Hangs On," 5; Emily Wax, "Chad Cuts Ties to Sudan, Saying It Backed Assault," *Washington Post*, April 15, 2006.

12. Robert I. Rotberg, *Haiti: The Politics of Squalor* (Boston: Houghton Mifflin, 1971); Michel S. Laguerre, *The Military and Society in Haiti* (Basingstoke, Hampshire: Macmillan, 2003).

13. Julia Preston, "Anti-Duvalierism Said to Gain in Haiti," *Washington Post*, April 17, 1989.

14. Joseph H. Treaster, "Rebellious Troops in Haiti Say They Are Ready to Negotiate," *New York Times*, April 10, 1989.

15. John Neagle, "Haiti: President Avril Asked to Step Down by Soldiers from Dessalines Barracks," April 6, 1989, https://digitalrepository.unm.edu/notisur/2959; "Presidential Guard Frees Avril," Federal Broadcast Information Service, Daily Report, Latin America, FBIS-LAT-89-062, April 2, 1989; Michael Norton, "Coup Leaders Deported from Haiti," *Washington Post*, April 5, 1989.

16. Julia Preston, "Haitian Government Announces Defeat of Mutinous Soldiers," *Washington Post*, April 9, 1989.

17. Anne Fuller and Jocelyn McCalla, *In the Army's Hands: Human Rights in Haiti on the Eve of the Elections* (New York: Human Rights Watch, 1990); Treaster, "Rebellious Troops."

18. Risa A. Brooks and Elizabeth A. Stanley, *Creating Military Power: The Sources of Military Effectiveness* (Stanford, CA: Stanford University Press, 2007), 64–65; Anthony H. Cordesman, *Iraq and the War of Sanctions: Conventional Threats and Weapons of Mass Destruction* (Westport, CT: Praeger, 1999), 78–80.

19. Ahmed Hashim, *Insurgency and Counter-Insurgency in Iraq* (Ithaca, NY: Cornell University Press, 2006), 105; Ahmed Hashim, "Saddam Husayn and Civil-Military Relations in Iraq: The Quest for Legitimacy and Power," *Middle East Journal* 57, no. 2 (2003): 32.

20. Agence France-Presse, "50 Dead in al-Ramadi Clashes; Tension High," Foreign Broadcast Information Service, Daily Report, Middle East and North Africa, FBIS-NES-95-107, June 3, 1995, 25; "U.S. Tells of Abortive Troop Mutiny against Iraq's Leader," *New York Times*, June 16, 1995.

21. Agence France-Presse, "Ba'th Party Official Notes Situation 'under Control,'" Foreign Broadcast Information Service, Daily Report, Middle East and North Africa, FBIS-NES-95-116, June 16, 1995, 35; "U.S. Tells of Abortive Troop Mutiny against Iraq's Leader."

22. Ibrahim Al-Marashi and Sammy Salama, *Iraq's Armed Forces: An Analytical History* (London: Routledge, 2008), 188; Youssef M. Ibrahim, "Iraq Reportedly Cracks Down on Clan That Tried a Coup," *New York Times*, June 20, 1995.

23. Al-Sharq al-Awsat, "Details of 'Military Rebellion' Cited," Foreign Broadcast Information Service, Daily Report, Middle East and North Africa, FBIS-NES-95-116, June 16, 1995, 34; Agence France-Presse, "Saddam's Forces Siege al-Ramadi; Supplies Cut," Foreign Broadcast Information Service, Daily Report, Middle East and North Africa, FBIS-NES-95-118, June 18, 1995, 33–34; Ibrahim, "Iraq Reportedly Cracks Down"' Sharon Otterman, "Iraq: What Is the Fedayeen Saddam?," Council on Foreign Relations Backgrounder, March 31, 2003, http://www.cfr.org/iraq/iraq-fedayeen-saddam/p7698.

24. Florence Gaub, "The Libyan Armed Forces between Coup-Proofing and Repression," *Journal of Strategic Studies* 36, no. 2 (2013): 226–229.

25. Dirk Vandewalle, *A History of Modern Libya* (Cambridge: Cambridge University Press, 2011), 149.
26. Vandewalle, *A History of Modern Libya*, 150; Luis Martinez, "Libya: The Conversion of a 'Terrorist State,'" *Mediterranean Politics* 11, no. 2 (2006): 151–165.
27. Chris Hedges, "Qaddafi Reported to Quash Army Revolt," *New York Times*, October 23, 1993; Vandewalle, *A History of Modern Libya*, 147.
28. Reuters, "Libya's Warfalla Tribe," September 1, 2011, www.reuters.com/article/us-libya-warfalla-profile-idUSTRE78028R20110901.
29. Guy Arnold, *The Maverick State: Gaddafi and the New World Order* (London: Cassell, 1996), 38; John Oakes, *Libya: The History of Gaddafi's Pariah State* (Stroud, UK: History Press, 2011), 135; Gaub, "Libyan Armed Forces," 229; Martinez, "Libya"; Alison Pargeter, *Libya: The Rise and Fall of Qaddafi* (New Haven, CT: Yale University Press, 2012).
30. Justin Leach, *War and Politics in Sudan: Cultural Identities and the Challenges of the Peace Process* (New York: I. B. Tauris, 2012), 114.
31. Bona Malwal, *Sudan and South Sudan: From One to Two* (London: Palgrave Macmillan, 2015), 122–129; Mansour Khalid, *Nimeiri and the Revolution of Dis-May* (London: KPI, 1985), 150; Leach, *War and Politics in Sudan*, 22; Charles Gurdon, *Sudan in Transition: A Political Risk Analysis*, EIU Special Report No. 226 (London: Economist Intelligence Unit, 1986), 25.
32. W. J. Berridge, *Under the Shadow of the Regime: The Contradictions of Policing in Sudan, c. 1924–1989* (PhD diss., Durham University, 2011), 176; W. J. Berridge, "Sudan's Security Agencies: Fragmentation, Visibility and Mimicry, 1908–89," *Intelligence and National Security* 28, no. 6 (2013): 845–867.
33. P. M. Holt and M. W. Daly, *A History of Sudan: From the Coming of Islam to the Present Day* (London: Routledge, 2014), 136.
34. Henry Tanner, "Nimeiry Said to Thwart Coup in Sudan," *New York Times*, July 3, 1976; Leach *War and Politics*, 22; Gurdon, *Sudan in Transition*, 25–26; Berridge, *Under the Shadow*, 176.
35. Joseph J. Wright, *The Balancing Act: A History of Modern Thailand* (Oakland, CA: Pacific Rim Press, 1991); Henry Kamm, "Thai Premier Is Slow to Consolidate His Position after Fending Off Coup," *New York Times*, May 5, 1981; Hong Lysa, "Thailand in 1981: Reformulating the Polity from Within?," *Southeast Asian Affairs* (1982): 339–361.
36. Lysa, "Thailand in 1981," 339–340; Surachai Sirikrai, "General Prem Survives on a Conservative Line," *Asian Survey* 22, no. 11 (1982): 1095–1096; Wright, *The Balancing Act*, 262–263; "Thai Generals, Citing Dictatorship Threat, Stage Coup," *New York Times*, April 1, 1981; "Thai General, Saying Coup Fails, Asserts He Has the King's Support," *New York Times*, April 2, 1981; "Revolt in Thailand Ends as Rebels Flee," *New York Times*, April 3, 1981; Paul Chambers, "Where Agency Meets Structure: Understanding Civil-Military Relations in Contemporary Thailand," *Asian Journal of Political Science* 19, no. 3 (2011): 290–304.
37. Suchit Bunbongkarn, *The Military in Thai Politics, 1981–86* (Singapore: Institute of Southeast Asian Studies, 1987), 19.
38. E.g., Eric Heginbotham, "The Fall and Rise of Navies in East Asia: Military Organizations, Domestic Politics, and Grand Strategy," *International Security* 27, no. 2 (2011): 86–125; Ulrich Pilster and Tobias Böhmelt, "Do Democracies Engage Less in Coup-Proofing? On the Relationship between Regime Type and Civil–Military Relations," *Foreign Policy Analysis* 8, no. 4 (2012): 355–372.
39. Larry A. Niksch, "Thailand in 1981: The Prem Government Feels the Heat," *Asian Survey* 22, no. 2 (1982): 193; Wright, *The Balancing Act*, 265–266; Lysa, "Thailand in 1981," 339–340.
40. "Thai Premier Promises Leniency for Rebels," *New York Times*, April 4, 1981.

Index

Page numbers in italic refer to figures and tables.

Ababou, Mohamed, 63
Acemoglu, Daron, 133
administrative control, 40, 98, 110, 112
Afghanistan, 23, 72, 148, 173n93
African Democratic Rally, 105
Ahidjos, Ahmadou, 21
Ahmad, Imam, 126
Albrecht, Holger, 20, 25
Ali Bhutto, Zulfiqar, 9
Allende, Salvador, 90
All-People's Congress (Sierra Leone), 100–102
Argentina, 23, 44
arms restrictions, 2, 111–12
Army of Defense (Yemen), 126
assassination attempts, 97–98
Atkins, G. Pope, 118
attack stage of a coup, 16, 59
authoritarian regimes: coup-prevention strategies, 1–2; coups and, 3. *See also* dictatorships; military regimes; *specific countries and leaders*
Avril, Prosper, 18, 71
Awami League, 74–75

Babangida, Ibrahim, 9
Badr, Muhammad al-, 73, 116, 125–30
Baker, James A., III, 66
Balaguer, Joaquín, 117, 122
Banda, Hastings, 21, 28
Bangladesh, 22, 36, 73–76
Bangura, John, 103
Barrientos, René, 29
Batista, Fulgencio, 108
Baynham, Simon, 98–100
Bay of Pigs invasion, 109
Bebler, Anton, 107
Belaunde Terry, Fernando, 76
Belkin, Aaron, 30–31, 87
Bhutto, Zulfiqar Ali, 9
Blake, Charles, 101
Böhmelt, Tobias, 89
Bolivarian National Militia, 137
Bolivia, 18, 29, 44

border guards, 40, 42
Bosch, Brian, 124
Bosch Gaviño, Juan, 117–25
Brache, Despradel, 122
Braun, Frank H., 64
bribery, 111–12, 136
Brigades Mixtes Mobiles (Cameroon), 21
broadcasting of coup attempts: attack phase, 16, 70–71, 131; counternarratives to coup, 24, 72
Brooks, Risa, 22, 135
Bruce, Robert, 6
Bunbongkarn, Suchit, 153
Bush, George H. W., 38, 68

Caamaño, Francisco, 121, 124
Cambodia, 44
Cameroon, 21
Canada, 44
capital cities, access to, 16, 23, 35, 42
Carmona, Pedro, 24
cascos blancos riot squad (Dominican Republic), 116, 121–25, 130
Castro, Fidel, 37, 94–95, 108–11, 114, 119, 133
Castro, Raul, 110
causal mechanisms, 131–39; linking counterbalancing to coup outcomes, 14, 19–26, *20*, 35–36 (*see also* coordination; resistance); linking counterbalancing to incidence of coup attempts, 26–32, *27*, 35–36 (*see also* coup attempts)
Center for Systemic Peace (CSP) dataset, 47, 49, 55, 80, 91
Central Reserve Police Force (India), 29, 44
Chad, 73, 148–49
chain of command, 42. *See also* military chains of command
Chávez, Hugo, 3, 24, 131, 137
Chechnya, 47
Chile, 4, 46, 90
China, 129
Civil Guard (Honduras), 29
Civil Guard (Peru), 9, 76–77

193

INDEX

civilian control, 3, 31. *See also* democracies
civilian militias, 13, 24, 95, 114, 137; in Mali, 94. *See also* militia, state-run
civil war: compared to coups d'état, 33; defined, 32; in Dominican Republic, 116–25; escalation of coups to, 2, 4, 9–10, 32–34, 37, 115–30, 134, 138; fatality threshold, 165n108; summary of case outcomes, *116*; in Yemen, 125–30
Clark, Victoria, 127
coercive institutions: defined, 155n8; regime survival and, 2, 6–10 (*see also* counterbalancing); types of, 4–6. *See also* counterweights; militarized police; Ministry of Interior troops; paramilitary forces; presidential guards; republican guards; secret police; security forces
Colamarco, Benjamin, 69
Cold War period, 39, 50, *52*; subsequent geopolitical changes, 3, 42, 46, 48, 50. *See also* Communism/anti-Communism issues
Coll, Steve, 148
Collier, Paul, 32
Colombia, 44
colonial legacies, 48, 91, 105, 133, 135
combining multiple coup-proofing strategies, 111–12
communications, 17–22, 76. *See also* broadcasting of coup attempts
Communism/anti-Communism issues: Afghanistan, 148; Bangladesh, 74; Cuba, 109; Dominican Republic, 117–24; Indonesia, 79; Mali, 105–6; Romania, 40; Russia, 71. *See also* Cold War period
conditions for successful counterbalancing: combination of strategies, 95, 111–12; summary of divergent outcomes across countries, *94*, 99, 104, 107, 110; types of forces used to counterbalance, 96, *112–13*
Congo, 96
consolidation stage of a coup, 16
Conteh, Patrick, 101
Convention People's Party (Ghana), 97–99
coordination, 14–15, 19–22, 28; evidence of, 57–58, 69–73, 78
Correlates of War dataset, 54, 82
Costa Rica, 120
cost/benefit analysis, 17–19, 22, 24; defensive advantages, 19; violent resistance, costs of, 7, 14, 18
counterbalancing: data on countries in statistical analysis, 141–47; defined, 2; hypothesis 1 (coup outcomes), 25, 35, 39;
hypothesis 1a (coordination), 25; hypothesis 1b (resistance), 25; hypothesis 2 (likelihood of coup attempts), 30, 35; hypothesis 3 (new counterweight and risk of coup attempts), 30, 35; hypothesis 4 (escalation to civil war), 34; as independent variable, 14; measuring, 39–42 (*see also* causal mechanisms; effectiveness of counterbalancing); multiple strategies in combination with, 111–12; patterns in, 43–47; policy implications, 136–38; regime survival and, 2, 6–10; risk of escalation to civil war, 2, 4, 9–10, 13–14, 32–34, 131 (*see also* civil war); theoretical implications, 133–36. *See also* conditions for successful counterbalancing; coup failure
Counter Intelligence Division (Ghana), 97
counterweights: design of, 4–6; frequency and forms of, 44; new, 79–80, 83, 86–87, 91, 93–114; types of, 40–44, 96, 111–14, 155n8; variation by country/region, 44–47, *45–46*; variation over time, 47–48, *48*. *See also* coercive institutions; militarized police; Ministry of Interior troops; paramilitary forces; presidential guards; republican guards; secret police; security forces
coup attempts: alternative arguments, 31–32, 87–92; causes of, 26–32, 81; defined, 59; as dependent variable, 80–81; evidence on causal mechanisms, *70* (*see also* causal mechanisms); incidence of, 3, 14, *27*, 35–37, 79–92, *81*; increased risk from counterbalancing, 30, 35, 79–80, 83, 86–87, 91, 93–114, 137; unfolding of, 6–10, 15–17. *See also* broadcasting of coup attempts; coordination; coup plotters; Kenya; Morocco; Panama; recruitment
coup d'état: defined, 6–7, 33, 80; fatality threshold, 165n108; "good coups," 3; ideal, 18–19, 115; preferences and perceptions of military officers during, 17–19; stages of, 15–16
coup failure, 6–10; causal mechanisms linking counterbalancing to, *20*, 38–39, 48–56 (*see also* causal mechanisms); costs of, 18–19; patterns in, 43–47; resistance and (*see* resistance). *See also* coup outcomes
coup outcomes, 13–14; alternative arguments, 25–26, 53–55; case study selection, 36, 57–58; confounding factors, 49–50; dependent variable, 48; effect of counterbalancing on, 19–26, 35–36, 132; international intervention and, 50; statistical analysis and results, 50–56. *See also* coup failure; coup success

coup plotters, 6–10, 58–59; coordination between (*see* coordination); counterweights as, 9; violence and, 115 (*see also* violence). *See also* coup attempts; military officers; nonmilitary/civilian elites, coups by

coup prevention/coup-proofing, strategies of, 1–12, 131–39. *See also* counterbalancing

coup success: belief that victory is imminent and, 15, 28, 49, 55; calculating likelihood of, 7, 17–18; costs of, 14, 23; as dependent variable, 48; future coups and, 50. *See also* coup outcomes

Cox, Thomas, 102

Crouch, Harold, 79

Cuba, 37, 94–95, *94–95*, 108–14, 118–19, 133, 137

Dahomey, 16

dataset: description of, 39–40, 43; states included in, *41*

David, Steven, 30

Davis, Arthur, 67

Dearborn, Henry, 117

Déby, Idriss, 73–74, 148

Decalo, Samuel, 21, 29

decolonization, effect of, 48. *See also* colonial legacies

democracies, 117, 120; coup outcomes, 49–54; coup-prevention strategies, 1–2; effectiveness of counterbalancing, 78–84, 88–90; norms against coups, 27; survival of, 131–39; vulnerability to coups, 3

democratization, 131–39

Desert Army (Yemen), 126

Dessalines (Haiti), 71, 135

deterrence, 13–14, 26–32, 79–92, 132–33

Dianga, James, 61

dictatorships: coups and, 3; monitoring of security forces, 21. *See also* authoritarian regimes; military regimes; *specific countries and leaders*

Dignity Battalions (Panama), 59, 67, 69, 78

Dixon-Fyle, Mac, 102–3

Doberman riot police (Panama), 67–69

Dominican Republic, 37, 72, 115–25, 129

Dominican Revolutionary Party (PRD), 117–18, 121, 123, 125

Draper, Theodore, 118

Duvalier, François, 4, 28

Duvalier, Jean-Claude, 21, 149

East Bengal Regiment (Bangladesh), 74

East Germany, 4

economic conditions, 133; coup outcomes and, 49–51; effectiveness of counterbalancing in poor vs. wealthy regimes, 82–83, 89, 92, 94; escalation to civil war, 119–20; in Kenya, 60; opportunities for intervention and, 27; in Peru, 76–77; risk of coup attempt and, 94; in Sierra Leone, 101

Ecuador, 23, 25

effectiveness of counterbalancing, 5–9, 19–32; democratic vs. military regimes, 49–51, 81–83, 89–90; during heightened coup risk, 87–90; incidence of coup attempts, *81*; incidence of coup success and failure, *48*; logit results, *52, 84*; new counterweights and risk of coup attempts, 79–80, 83, 86–87, 91, 93–114; past coups within country, 50–51, 82–83, 86–87, 89; in poor vs. wealthy regimes, 50–51, 82–83, 89; statistical analyses, 50–53, 81–86; survival of regimes, 86–87; variables, *50, 53, 83, 86*. *See also* causal mechanisms

Egypt, 3, 15, 20, 126

Eibl, Ferdinand, 20, 25

Endara, Guillermo, 67

Erdoğan, Recep Tayyip, 3

Ethiopia, 9

ethnic divisions, 1, 5, 60, 96–99, 125–30; ethnic stacking as additional coup-proofing strategy, 8, 22, 30, 60, 95–97, 100–104, 111–12, 136

ethnic wars, 33

event history analysis, 86–87

Eyadé, Gnassingbé, 28

failure. *See* coup failure

Farcau, Bruce, 23–25, 28–30, 104, 160n52

Fatton, Robert, 28

Fearon, James, 32–33

Federal Security Force (Pakistan), 9

Fiji, 24

Finer, Samuel, 31, 115

France, 135

Frantz, Erica, 21, 30, 49

Frazer, Jendayi, 62

Fyle, C. Magbaily, 104

Gabon, 16

Gall, Norman, 118–19

game theory, 28

Gandhi, Indira, 44

Geddes, Barbara, 16, 21, 30, 32, 49

gendarmerie, 4, 40

General Services Unit (Kenya), 23, 59, 61–63, 78

Gethi, Ben, 62
Ghana, 132; 1966 coup, 9, 72, 93, *94–95*, 95–100, 111–14; 1981 coup, 16; military attitudes on violence, 7, 18
Ghana Young Pioneers, 98
Gleijeses, Piero, 123
"good coups," 3
Goodspeed, Donald, 32
Gorbachev, Mikhail, 71
Greitens, Sheena, 5, 33
Grioldi Vega, Moisés, 66–69
Guaidó, Juan, 136–37
Guinea-Bissau, 4
Gulf War, 38

Haiti, 4, 18, 21, 28, 70–71, 73, 118, 135, 149–50
Halliday, Fred, 129
Harlley, John, 99
Hassan bin Hussein, 128–29
Hassan II of Morocco, 58–59, 63–66, 78
Heitzman, James, 75
Herrera, Roberto Díaz, 66
historical factors: counterbalancing and incidence of coup attempts, 82–89; recent successful coups, 50, 93; survival of regimes over time, 86–87
Hoeffler, Anke, 32
Honduras, 3, 29, 46
Horowitz, Donald, 23, 42
human rights, 3
Huntington, Samuel, 26–27

Ibañez, Enrique, 77
Ibn Saud, 6
ideal coups, 18–19, 115
Imperial Guard (Ethiopia), 9
India, 29, 44, 75, 131
indoctrination, 97, 106, 109–12
Indonesia, 6, 8, 18, 79–80
information dissemination, 2, 17–22, 42, 76. *See also* broadcasting of coup attempts
institutional interests, 92, 132; and fate of incumbent regime, 14; monopoly on use of force, 8, 23, 27, 29, 42, 132; protection of, 16. *See also* jealousies and rivalries
insurgency, 32–33, 134. *See also* civil war
intelligence agencies, 1, 40, 112, 114; frequency of use, 44. *See also* secret police
Interior Ministry. *See* Ministry of Interior troops
Internal Ministry (MININT, Cuba), 110
Internal Security Unit (ISU, Sierra Leone), 100–105, 111, 114

International Institute for Strategic Studies (IISS), 6, 39, 43
international intervention, 50
Iraq, 1, 5, 38, 72, 131, 150–51
Islamic State, 1
Ivory Coast, 4

Janowitz, Morris, 42
Japan, 44
Jatiyo Rakkhi Bahini (Bangladesh), 22, 75–76
Jawara, Fallah, 102
jealousies and rivalries, 8; key patterns, 111–14; as triggering coups, 2, 22, 29, 97–98
Johnson, Lyndon B., 123–24
Juxon-Smith, Andrew, 101

Kamara, Morlai, 101
Kanyotu, James, 62
Keita, Modibo, 36–37, 94–95, 105–7, 112, 114, 132
Kempe, Frederick, 68–69
Kennedy, John F., 120
Kenya, 23, 36, 58–63, 78, 132
Kenyatta, Jomo, 60–62
KGB (Soviet Union), 47, 71
Khan, Abdul Hasan, 76
Khan, Z. R., 75
King, Sam, 103
Kotoka, Emmanuel, 99–100

Laitin, David, 32
Lansana, David, 101–2
Laos, 17
Lenin, Vladimir, 32
Leo-Grande, William, 109
Leopards (Haiti), 71, 135
Libya, 4, 72, 151
Licona, Javier, 68
Lieven, Anatol, 47
Light Security Brigade (Morocco), 65–66, 78
Lowenthal, Abraham, 119, 121–22, 125
Luke, David, 104
Luttwak, Edward, 15, 17, 22, 115

Machos del Monte (Panama), 67, 69
Madagascar, 24
Maduro, Nicolás, 136–37
Malawi, 21, 28
Mali, 37, 94–95, *94–95*, 105–7, 111–14, 132
Maliki, Nouri al-, 1–2, 5, 131
Mann, Thomas, 123
Margai, Albert, 100, 102

INDEX

Margai, Milton, 100
Martin, John Barlow, 118–19
Mascarenhas, Anthony, 75
Matin, Abdul, 74
Matos, Hubert, 109
M'Ba, Léon, 16
McLauchlin, Theodore, 34
Medbouh, Mohammed, 63–64
Mexico, 120
Middle East, 6. *See also specific countries*
militarized police, 2, 40, 95–96, 132, 137, 155n8; frequency of use, 44; key patterns across cases, 111–14. *See also* counterweights; Ministry of Interior troops
military: institutional interest in monopoly on use of force, 8, 23, 27, 29, 42, 132; morale of soldiers, 18, 60, 98, 108, 115; new counterweights creating resentment in regular military, key patterns, 111–14; professionalism of, 5; status of, 2, 7, 14, 18, 103, 110
The Military Balance (IISS), 6, 39, 43, 159n36, 166n10
military chains of command: coup attempts and, 16; divisions within states' security sectors, 47
military officers: as coup leaders, 7–10, 15, 28, 49, 55, 159n38; preferences and perceptions of, 17–19; rotation of, 111–12
military regimes, 26, 33, 117, 120; coup outcomes, 49–54; effectiveness of counterbalancing, 78–84, 88–90; marginalization of counterweights, 78; survival of, 131–39. *See also* authoritarian regimes; dictatorships; *specific countries and leaders*
military spending, 88, 91, 94–95, 95, 103, 108; key patterns, 82–84, 111–14
military strength, 1–2, 25–26, 31–32, 39; coup outcomes and, 1–2, 53–56
militia, state-run, 40, 96, 112–14, 116, 125–30, 155n8; frequency of use, 44; key patterns across countries, 111–14. *See also* civilian militias
Miller, Judith, 38
Ministry for State Security (Stasi, East Germany), 4
Ministry of Interior troops, 40; in Chile, 90; in Cuba, 94; frequency of use, 44; key patterns across cases, 111–14; in Morocco, 59, 65–66, 78; in Peru, 77; in Russia, 71
Ministry of the Revolutionary Armed Forces (MINFAR, Cuba), 108–9
Mohammed V of Morocco, 63
Moi, Daniel Arap, 23, 58–63, 78

monitoring and surveillance, 62–63, 97, 110; effect on coup coordination, 8, 20, 21; effect on coup resistance, 23; effect on opportunity to stage coups, 28
Mora, Frank, 110
Morales, Villeda, 29
Morales Bermúdez, Francisco, 76–77
Morocco, 36, 58–59, 63–66, 78, 132, 173n93
Morsi, Mohamed, 3
motives for intervention, 26–31
Mubarak, Hosni, 15
Mugabe, Robert, 16
Mukti Bahini ("Liberation Army"), 74
Myanmar, 44

Najibullah, Mohammed, 23–24, 148
National Civic Union (UCN, Dominican Republic), 117
National Committee for the Defense of the Revolution (Mali), 106
National Gendarmerie (Ivory Coast), 4
National Guard (Nigeria), 9
National Police (Dominican Republic), 116; cascos blancos riot squad, 116, 121–25, 130
National Political Bureau (Mali), 105–6
National Reformation Council (NRC), 101
National Revolutionary Militia (Cuba), 108
National Security Police (Morocco), 65–66, 78
National Security Service (Ghana), 97
Nehru, Jawaharlal, 131
Nigeria, 4, 9
Nimeiry, Gaafar al-, 151
Nkrumah, Kwame, 9, 36–37, 72, 93, 95–100, 111, 114, 132
nonmilitary/civilian elites, coups by, 7, 15, 28, 33, 47
Nordlinger, Eric, 19, 29
Noriega, Manuel, 58–59, 66–69, 78
norms against intervention, 26–27
North Korea, 4, 44
North Yemen, 182n5. *See also* Yemen
Nuruzzaman, A. N. M., 75

O'Ballance, Edgar, 127
Odom, William, 71
operational control, 40, 98, 110, 112
opportunities for intervention, 26–28
Organization of American States, 120
Oufkir, Mohammad, 65
outcomes. *See* coup failure; coup outcomes; coup success

INDEX

Pakistan, 9, 75
Panama, 36, 58–59, 66–69, 78, 132
paramilitary forces, 2, 42. *See also* counterweights
Peña Gómez, José Francisco, 121–22
Peru, 9, 36, 73, 76–78, 135, 173n93
Philippines, 5, 44
Pilster, Ulrich, 89
Pinochet, Augusto, 4
planning stage of a coup, 15–16, 19, 59
Podesta, Don, 68
police. *See* militarized police
Police Service Act (Ghana), 98
policy implications, 136–38
political stability, *85, 88,* 91, 131; key patterns, 111–14; risk of coup attempt and, 94, *95*
poor countries. *See* economic conditions
Popular Militia (Mali), 105–7
Portugal, 44
Powell, Colin, 68
Powell, Jonathan, 22, 55, 91
Presidential Guard (Haiti), 21, 149–50
presidential guards, 8, 13, 21, 40, 42, 95–96, 125, 132, 155n8; frequency of use, 44; key patterns across cases, 111–14; resistance by, 24. *See also* counterweights
President's Own Guard Regiment (POGR, Ghana), 9, 36, 72–73, 93, 96–100, 111, 114
Preston, Julia, 149
private military companies, 40
process tracing, 2
Puerto Rico, 120
purging of opponents, 111–12, 136

Qaddafi, Muammar, 4, 72, 151
Quinlivan, James, 6, 42, 158n30, 158n34

Radio Santo Domingo, 72, 123
Rahman, Farook, 75
Rahman, Mujibur, 73–75
Rashid, Khandaker Abdur, 75
rebel organizations, 32–33. *See also* civil war
recruitment, 20–22, 36, 73
regime survival, 131–39; counterbalancing and, 2, 6–10; rates of, 86–87. *See also* coup failure; coup outcomes
regime types: counterbalancing by, *90*; coup outcomes and, 49; military strength and, 54; risk of coup attempt and, 94. *See also* authoritarian regimes; democracies; military regimes
region, variation by, 44–47, *45–46*
Reid Cabral, Donald, 120–22, 125, 130

repression, 28
republican guards, 2, 7–8, 40; in Peru, 77. *See also* counterweights
resistance, 14, 17, 20, 22–25, 57–58, 131–32; cases without, 73–78; escalation to civil war and, 34; evidence on causal mechanisms, *70*; in Kenya, 59–63; in Morocco, 63–66; in Panama, 66–69
revolution, recent, 50, 93
Revolutionary Armed Forces (FAR, Cuba), 108–9
Robinson, James, 133
robustness checks, 53–55, 87–92
Rodríguez Echavarría, Pedro, 117
Roessler, Philip, 33
Rogers, Emadu, 101
Romania, 40
Romanian Intelligence Service, 40
Rome, 2
Russia, 29, 44–47, 71–73, 173n93

Saddam Hussein, 1–2, 5, 38, 72, 150
Sallal, Abdullah al-, 127–29
Sambanis, Nicholas, 33
Saudi Arabia, 6, 128
Schatzberg, Michael, 107
Schofer, Evan, 31, 87
secret police, 7–8, 96, 112, 114, 137, 155n8; frequency of use, 44; key patterns across countries, 111–14. *See also* counterweights
Securitate (Romania), 40
security forces, 2, 7, 132; chain of command, 39; defined, 35, 40–42, 155n8; types of, 40, 44, 96, 111–14, 155n8. *See also* coercive institutions; counterweights; militarized police; Ministry of Interior troops; paramilitary forces; presidential guards; republican guards; secret police
Selassie, Haile, 9
selection effects/bias, 55–56, 72, 91–92
Siddiqi, Dina, 75
Siddiqui, Kader, 74
Sierra Leone, 37, 94–95, 100–105, 111–14, 133, 137
Sierra Leone People's Party (SLPP), 100–101
Singh, Naunihal, 7, 15, 18, 20, 49, 72
Soglo, Christophe, 16
South Korea, 5, 19, 44
Soviet Union, 2, 46, 71, 129; 1991 coup, 18; Cuba and, 108–9
Spadafora, Hugo, 66
Spanish Civil War, 4
Special Action Forces (Venezuela), 137

Special Army-Police Service (Sierra Leone), 102
Special Branch (Ghana), 98
Special Branch (Kenya), 62
Special Branch and Mobile Unit (Malawi), 28
Special Operations Troops (Cuba), 94, 110–11, 114
Stalin, Joseph, 32
State Security Department (North Korea), 4
Stevens, Siaka, 37, 94–95, 100–105, 111–14, 133
students, 61–62, 64
Sub-Saharan Africa, 29
success. *See* coup success
Sudan, 44, 137, 151–52
Sudanese Bloc, 105
Sudduth, Jun Koga, 89
Suharto, 80
Sukarno, 6, 79–80
Suleiman, Omar, 15
Supreme Council of the Armed Forces (SCAF), 20
Sûreté Nationale (Morocco), 65–66, 78
surveillance and monitoring, 62–63, 97, 110; effect on coup coordination, 8, *20,* 21; effect on coup resistance, 23; effect on opportunity to stage coups, 28
symbolic targets, capture of, 16, 59, 131
Syria, 21, 44, 126

Tactical Response Unit (TRU, Fiji), 24
Taiwan, 5
Taylor, Brian, 18
Thailand, 3, 17–18, 73–74, 152–53
theoretical implications, 133–36
Thyne, Clayton, 55, 91
time: regime survival over, 86–87; variation over, *47,* 47–48
Tjakrabirawa Special Regiment (Indonesia), 79
Togo, 28
Tonton Macoutes (Haiti), 4, 28
Torrijos, Omar, 66
torture, 61, 66, 106
Traoré, Moussa, 107

tribal militias, 116, 125–30
Trujillo, Rafael, 116–18, 121, 124
Trujillo, Ramfis, 117–18
Tsiranana, Philibert, 24
Turkey, 3

Ukraine, 44
United Arab States, 126
United Kingdom, 26, 129
United States: coup prevention policies, 138; in Cuba, 109–10; in Dominican Republic, 117–24; norms against intervention, 26; in Panama, 66–68; in Venezuela, 136–37

Valdés Menéndez, Ramiro, 110
Van de Ven, Wynand, 55
Van Praag, Bernard, 55
Velasco Alvarado, Juan, 9, 71, 76–78
Venezuela, 2–3, 24, 120, 131, 136–37
violence: avoidance of, 18–19, 115; costs of, 7–8, 14, 18–19, 135; threat of, 6–7. *See also* civil war

Walker, Phyllis, 109
Waterbury, John, 63, 65
Wedge, Bryant, 121
Weinstein, Jeremy, 34
Wessin y Wessin, Elías, 118–20, 122–24
Wilson, Larman, 118
Worden, Robert, 75
Workers' Brigade (Ghana), 98
Wright, Joseph, 21, 30, 49

Yahya, Imam, 126
Yates, Lawrence, 68–69
Yeltsin, Boris, 47, 72
Yemen, 12, 37, 44, 73, 116, 125–30, 133, 182n5
Young Pioneers (Malawi), 21

Zaydi tribal militias, 126. *See also* tribal militias
Zimbabwe, 16